EIGHT
LIVES DOWN

www.**rbooks**.co.uk

EIGHT LIVES DOWN

The story of a counter-terrorist bomb-disposal operator's tour in Iraq

CHRIS HUNTER

CORGI BOOKS

TRANSWORLD PUBLISHERS
61–63 Uxbridge Road, London W5 5SA
A Random House Group Company
www.rbooks.co.uk

EIGHT LIVES DOWN
A CORGI BOOK: 9780552155717

First published in Great Britain in 2007 by Bantam Press
a division of Transworld Publishers
Corgi edition published 2008

Addresses for Random House Group Ltd companies outside the UK
can be found at: www.randomhouse.co.uk
The Random House Group Ltd Reg. No. 954009

The Random House Group Limited supports The Forest Stewardship
Council (FSC), the leading international forest-certification organization.
All our titles that are printed on Greenpeace-approved FSC-certified paper carry
the FSC logo. Our paper procurement policy can be found at
www.rbooks.co.uk/environment

Typeset in 11.75/16.25 Electra by
Falcon Oast Graphic Art Ltd.

Printed in the UK by CPI Cox & Wyman, Reading, RG1 8EX

6 8 10 9 7 5

This book is dedicated to the memory of
those who made the long walk
and never returned.

The people of England have been led, in Mesopotamia, into a trap from which it will be hard to escape with dignity and honour. They have been tricked into it by a steady withholding of information. The Baghdad communiqués are belated, insincere, incomplete. Things have been far worse than we have been told, our administration more bloody and inefficient than the public knows. It is a disgrace to our imperial record, and may soon be too inflamed for any ordinary cure. We are today not far from a disaster.

T. E. Lawrence
'A Report on Mesopotamia'
Sunday Times, 22 August 1920

Acknowledgements

I am indebted to my editor, Bill Scott-Kerr, for his matchless vision, amity and stoic perseverance, and to all the staff at Transworld without whom this book would not have been possible. There are so many of you across the sales, marketing and publication disciplines to whom I owe a huge debt of gratitude, but I would like to thank the following for their unstinting support: Katrina Whone, Rebecca Jones, Stephen Mulcahey, Phil Lord, Stina Smemo, Laura Sherlock, Dan Balado, Sophie Holmes, Janine Giovanni, Larry Finlay and Zoe Howes. Your encouragement and enthusiasm has made writing this book a thoroughly rewarding and edifying experience and I am grateful to you all.

My special thanks go to Mark Lucas, my friend, mentor and literary agent. Your patience has been truly saint-like and you have shown me the perfect blend of encouragement and pressure necessary to allow me to get the book finished. For the hundreds of hours you spent working with me on *Eight Lives Down*, for your guidance and wisdom and for the email exchanges at three o'clock in the morning, I am hugely grateful. I am also indebted to your colleagues at LAW and in particular to Alice Saunders for her characteristic efficiency and her perpetually infectious enthusiasm. Working with you both has been an inimitably enjoyable experience.

I must also thank the Ministry of Defence for its invaluable advice and assistance, particularly those at the Directorate of Defence Public Relations (Army) and my former colleagues at the Defence Intelligence Staff and across the Ammunition Technical Officer community, who offered invaluable advice and provided the necessary checks and balances to ensure I didn't inadvertently write something that could compromise the safety of our servicemen and women.

Additionally I must thank my team, especially Mick and Dan for allowing me to tell their stories, as well as those who cannot be named for obvious reasons. You know who you are, and for your stoic professionalism and devotion to duty I have nothing but admiration for you all. Serving with you was the single most enjoyable experience of my career.

I will for ever be indebted to my mother. You started the race, and you were there to greet me at the finish line. Thanks for your constant encouragement, for always being prepared to drop everything when Lucy and I have needed your help and for sharing your constructive thoughts with me on the initial drafts of the manuscript.

And finally my very special loving thanks are to my wife, Lucy. In spite of the loneliness and uncertainty, the disappointments and the stream of broken promises, you never lost your faith in me and you never gave up on me. Now it's your time . . . the love that I have of the life that I have is yours.

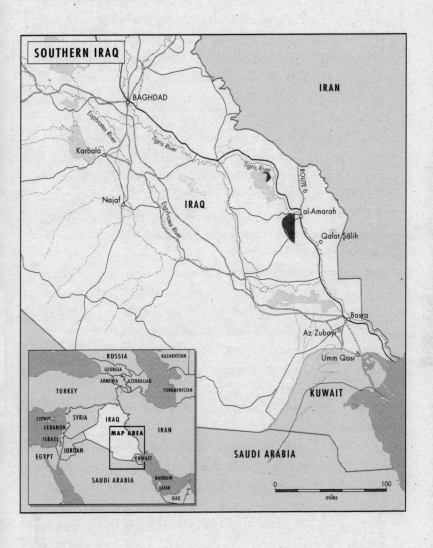

SOUTHERN IRAQ

IRAN

BAGHDAD

Euphrates River

Tigris River

Karbala

Tigris River

ROUTE 6

Najaf

IRAQ

al-Amarah

Qalat Şālih

Euphrates River

Basra

Az Zubayr

Umm Qasr

KUWAIT

SAUDI ARABIA

0   100
miles

RUSSIA

GEORGIA

KAZAKHSTAN

ARMENIA AZERBAIJAN

TURKEY

TURKMENISTAN

CYPRUS   SYRIA   IRAQ

LEBANON

IRAN

ISRAEL

MAP AREA

JORDAN

EGYPT

KUWAIT

SAUDI ARABIA

BAHRAIN

QATAR

UAE

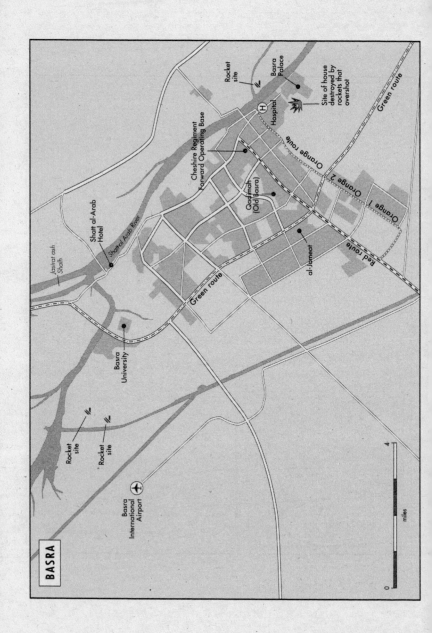

BASRA

Rocket site

Rocket site

Basra International Airport

Basra University

Jazirat ash Shaikh

Shatt al-Arab River

Shatt al-Arab Hotel

Cheshire Regiment Forward Operating Base

Qadimah (Old Basra)

al-Jameat

Green route

Green route

Red route

Orange 1

Orange 2

Orange route

Hospital

Rocket site

Basra Palace

Site of house destroyed by rockets that overshot

0   miles   4

Prologue

February 2004

Now I am in my other world. Outside sounds become muted and I am aware only of the sound of my own breathing and the drumming of my heart. This is the moment when I leave everything else behind. The moment when the drawbridge closes behind me and I am truly alone.

The long walk to the target seems to take for ever. I'm carrying 90lb of equipment and wearing a bomb suit that weighs another 80lb. Sweat drips into my eyes and my visor is beginning to mist up in the fearsome tropical heat. The Colombian Jungle Commandos have taken up fire positions in the rainforests and mountains that tower above the ICP. Their job is to stand between me and a sniper's bullet.

I try not to hold my breath as I take each step, but it isn't easy. Only 75 metres to go; I'm halfway to the target vehicle. The twin-flex firing cable snakes out of my carrying case as I go.

I'm struggling to see. My visor has completely steamed up now. I wipe away the condensation with a cloth. Twenty seconds later it's steamed up again. The humidity in this place is outrageous.

I go over the threat assessment again in my mind. There are three options. There's the timed IED, which could go off at any moment. There's the command initiated device, usually detonated by wire or radio control; it requires an observer, and this terrain offers thousands of potential firing points. I hope to God it's not RC: the Colombians don't have any radio jammers, and as I'm here working with them, nor do I. Finally there's the VO, the booby trap. The Colombian police officers have walked all around the car, so there's unlikely to be anything buried in the ground, but there's still every chance of a VO inside it.

So, what is the terrorist trying to achieve? Does he want to get me? Trying to confuse as to intent is a classic Provisional IRA tactic, and I know they've been here teaching the FARC boys some new tricks. That's why I've been sent here.

The sweat is pouring off me and my heart's beating like a drum as I finally reach the target vehicle, one of those 1950s grocery vans you only see in Tintin books. It's still; eerily silent. There are no tripwires and there's no disturbed earth, but I can see the improvised mortar through the windscreen. It's pretty much identical to the last PIRA mortar I saw in Northern Ireland, the barrack buster, a huge projectile which contains as much explosive as your average car bomb. This one's in a highly volatile state because it's a misfire – which means it could go live any second. And it's pointing directly at the village of Espinal.

If it launches now I'll be engulfed by the blast. As it lands moments later, the fuse will kick into life and the 120kg of ammonium nitrate and sugar explosive will detonate, fragmenting the bomb into hundreds of super-sonic pieces of molten metal. All windows within 200 metres will implode, wreaking havoc and causing massive casualties. Hundreds of pieces of shrapnel will smash through unprotected vehicles and structures. Shards of glass will sever limbs, and what little remains of the shredded bodies will almost certainly be destroyed by the napalm fireball that follows.

In May two years ago, three hundred people crowded into a small church in Bojaya, whispering prayers as they hunkered down on the cement floor, seeking sanctuary from the FARC gunfire outside. They thought they would be safe there. They were wrong. A PIRA-designed improvised mortar exploded on the church roof, which collapsed, killing 119. At least forty-five of the victims were children.

I've been an operator for seven years and completed three tours in Northern Ireland. I've studied the IRA obsessively and I know their tactics inside out. There could be any number of surprises lying in wait. I have to render this device safe. *Now*.

I begin clearing a safe area around the vehicle. Even if there is no secondary device this time, the bomber will still be watching me. Tracking my procedures and trying to second-guess me the next time we meet. This is only one battle in a very long war.

My body is starting to shake.

I check inside the van for alarm sensors, but there are none. Good. I carry a couple of pieces of ceramic with me – I've taken them from a broken spark plug. I throw one at the bottom left-hand corner of the side window and the glass shatters instantly. It's amazing what tricks you can pick up at school.

I ease my head inside the cab and check out the bomb's timing and power unit. My most obvious target is its battery pack. If the TPU is the brain of the bomb, the power source is its heart. I edge my EOD disruptor towards it, to get a better shot.

The disruptor is finally good to go. But as I'm about to pull off target and head back to the ICP to take the shot, I notice something else. A length of fishing wire stretches between the underside of the driver's seat and the door panel. Bastards. They've put a victim-operated IED in there too. A secondary. If I'd opened the door instead of leaning through the window it would have been Goodnight Vienna. The FARC boys have listened carefully to everything our Northern Irish friends have taught them.

I have to shatter both circuits. I can't do them one at a time: if there's a hidden collapsing circuit, disrupting one device could initiate the other.

I wipe the sweat from my eyes again. I'm going to neutralize them simultaneously.

1

Only those who will risk going too far can possibly find out how far one can go.

T. S. Eliot

Autumn 1981

It's not who our parents are that counts; it's the things we remember about them.

My dad's pulled me out of school as a special treat. We've spent the day in the arcade on Brighton pier, playing the fruit machines, and now we're back at the Old Ship Hotel. This is where we come to have some father and son time when he's taking a break from the pub he and Mum run in Hertfordshire.

The oak-panelled bedroom is warm and inviting. Its damask-covered sofas and chairs have a familiar smell; a musty, comforting smell. Flower-patterned curtains hang over the casement. Outside, the rain drums against the window and the waves crash on to the pebbled beach. I sit, spellbound, and stare out across the angry, beguiling ocean. This is my favourite place in the whole world.

I love spending time here with Dad. I'm eight years old and I'll never get to know him properly, but I already know he's a wonderful man. He's blessed with a mix of compassion and acceptance that makes everybody love him.

Everybody, that is, except Mum. I don't think she loves him any more. She used to, but now he makes her sad. Not because he's nasty to her; he adores her. It's just that he's always gambling and it makes her cry.

So for now it's just the two of us, father and son, sitting on the edge of the bed in our hotel room, pitched together like two volumes of the same book.

He looks down at me with a warm smile and puts his arm around my shoulders. I feel safe. I wish every day could be like this.

But as I look up at him, I see that something strange is happening. Beads of sweat are beginning to form on Dad's forehead. He looks desperate and pained. Tension and fear are etched on his face. His eyes are fixed on the images unfolding on the TV screen in front of him.

Smoke is billowing from bombed-out houses. ARP wardens run down the street, shouting at the mothers, screaming at them to take their children to the shelter, and quickly. At the foot of St Paul's Cathedral, a man in khaki fatigues is lying in a freezing puddle at the bottom of a shaft. He's hugging a massive bomb, lying face to face with a monster. The young officer runs his hands cautiously beneath the beast – a thousand kilograms of steel and TNT. He finds a fuse and slowly, carefully, he begins to unscrew it.

But there's something else. A second fuse. He hesitates . . .

Dad is squeezing my shoulder. I look up at him. His eyes are filled with torment. He's in agony. 'Don't touch it,' he pleads. 'Don't touch the second fuse. It's rigged.'

He's no longer sitting with me in this faded Georgian hotel room. He's back in 1944. He's somewhere else, a long way from here. His hands are shaking. His breathing is shallow and fast. He's become part of another world. Another life. His former life.

We're watching *Danger UXB*. Only, he's not just watching it, he's living it.

Later that night, I can hear Dad praying. 'Dear God,' he says, 'make me the kind of man my son wants me to be.' Before I go to sleep, I pray that one day I'll be the kind of man my father is.

2

Life is a storm, my young friend. You will bask in the sunlight one moment and be shattered on the rocks the next. What makes you a man is what you do when that storm comes.

Alexandre Dumas, *The Count of Monte Cristo*

March 2004

As I step off the plane I want to kiss the ground. The cold winter air is crisp and clean – a million miles away from the bug-infested humidity of Colombia. I've never been so happy to see the green fields and grey skies of England.

I'm a thirty-one-year-old captain and once again I've been pitted against our unremitting adversary, the IRA. The Provisional IRA's 'Colombia Three', at least two of whom are known to us as expert bomb-makers, have gone on the gallop. Niall Connolly, James Monaghan and Martin McCauley have been charged by the

Colombian authorities with training FARC rebels in the construction of IEDs but have fled the country. I'd been deployed there as part of a defence diplomacy mission to teach the Colombian EOD operators how to outmanoeuvre them. The task has gone like clockwork and now, finally, I can go on leave and spend some time with my family. I need to be with them. Things haven't been too good lately.

I walk into the arrivals lounge at Gatwick and I'm greeted by Lucy and our two little blonde bombshells. They've grown so much in the two months I've been away. Sophie runs across the terminal screaming 'Daaaaaadddy!' at the top of her voice. She jumps into my arms and I swing her upside down and blow a massive raspberry on her tummy. There are a few disapproving looks from other passengers, but I can't help myself: hearing her giggle makes my heart melt. Lucy cradles the baby, Ella. She looks more stunning than ever, almost regal, in her long navy overcoat and pink pashmina. She's still the most beautiful woman I know.

I remember the night we met like it was yesterday. I was on my bomb disposal course and she was at uni. She didn't wear make-up; she was what my mother would call a natural beauty. I found her totally enchanting, not just because she was so pretty, but because she was warm and vital and clearly didn't change her style for anybody. It took me about two minutes to realize she was the loveliest person I'd ever met, the sort of girl you instantly fall in love with.

We talked for hours. We talked about everything – about our dreams, our desires, and our disasters. She spoke with such passion; I hung on to her every word. I was smitten, locked in the mesmerizing gaze of her piercing blue eyes.

That was seven years ago. A chance encounter in a hallway. A moment in our lives when we didn't have a care in the world. And two years later we were married.

How have I let things get so out of control?

The journey back to Oxfordshire is a congenial one, but I don't know how long it's going to last. As usual, we crawl around the M25, the world's biggest car park. We swap small talk and catch up on the gossip from the camp. As we head west on the M4 Lucy's now doing most of the talking. In fact she's on permanent send; she's got a lot of stuff to get off her chest. I try to keep the conversation light and neutral. I've only just got back. I don't want to pile straight into another argument.

We cross the Downs and drop towards the Didcot cooling towers. There's a build-up of storm-clouds on the horizon.

The moment we pull into the gates of our house in

Vauxhall Barracks, Lucy's mood changes. We've lived in this camp, opposite Didcot Power Station, for almost a year but only now do I realize that she isn't just unhappy, she actually hates being here. Living in this place is eating away at her.

Or maybe it's living with me.

She manages to keep it together at first, but when the kids are in bed, she turns and looks at me solemnly.

'We need to talk.'

I know she hasn't packed her bags, but I think I know what's coming next.

For a moment, her face appears to soften. But it doesn't last.

'Chris, I need more than this. You've been away pretty much the whole time we've been together. You've spent more nights out of our bed than in it.'

It's a fair one. I've been on near constant ops for the past six years.

'I've tried,' she says, 'I really have, but I don't think I can take any more. It's not easy being married to you, Chris – the risks, the uncertainty, not knowing where you're going or for how long. And then there's the everyday stuff . . .'

I wish there was something I could say, something to reassure her, but I'm defenceless. I try to tell her I know it's hard for her, that I understand how difficult it is for

25

her, moving home every two years and dealing with the day-to-day dramas: the burst pipes, the broken washing machines, the kids being sick . . .

But it's not enough.

'Without you around, everything's got to be done by me. And I hate it. I don't want to have to cope on my own.'

Perhaps for the first time, I appreciate what she's trying to tell me. She's lonely. And I've been too wrapped up in my soldiering to see it coming. All I ever wanted to do was make her proud, get my hands dirty one last time, then settle down to a more sedentary life. I try to reassure her that everything will be OK, that we're finally going to have a normal life. I've been promised a staff officer's posting any day now and we're going to enjoy some quality time, like a normal family. She's just got to hang in there a bit longer.

But she's having none of it.

For the last seven years I've been serving as an ATO – an ammunition technical officer – in the British Army. The term 'ATO' is given to the military's ammunition and explosives specialists, although our primary role is actually Counter-Terrorist Bomb Disposal. The majority of ATOs serve at 11 EOD (Explosive Ordnance Disposal) Regiment Royal Logistics Corps in Didcot, and for the past two years I've been commanding Alpha Troop, the regiment's specialist bomb disposal team, responsible for supporting airborne and seaborne assault forces as well as police tactical firearms units. It's easily the most interesting posting I've had, but the constant time away from home on exercises and operations has placed a significant strain on our marriage.

'You need to hear this, Chris,' Lucy continues. 'I want you to understand how *I* feel. You promised me you wouldn't be going anywhere for at least another year, and all of a sudden you tell me you're going to be deployed to the South Atlantic for six months.'

'That was months ago. And I managed to get it changed, didn't I?'

I'm becoming defensive. I need to cool it.

'Yes, you did get it changed – to six weeks in Colombia. Don't you get it, Chris? Six months, six weeks, it's still time away from me and the girls. Have you any idea how it feels?' She stares at me, her eyes red with tears. 'I know it sounds pathetic, but I've lost count of the visits and family gatherings we've had to cancel at the last moment. And what about the girls? The missed birthdays. The broken promises. Do you have any idea what effect your job is having on them? They need a father, Chris.'

She's getting more and more wound up, but I know she's right. I've been a part-time dad at best. It's a miracle I managed to make it to the births of either of our girls.

Six hours after Ella was born, I deployed on an al-Qaeda arrest operation. I had to leave Sophie with friends overnight.

Lucy sits next to me. Dejected and silent. I turn to face her.

'It's not just the missed birthdays, is it?' I say quietly.

She shakes her head. 'Every single time you leave the house to go to work . . . every time you close the door behind you . . . do you have any idea how it feels for me to know that we could have kissed goodbye for the last time?'

She shifts in her seat, turns and offers me a forlorn look. I know where this is going. I resign myself to the inevitable. She's going to tell me she wants a divorce.

She takes my hand.

'I love you to bits,' she says, 'but I can't live like this.'

My stomach lurches.

'Promise me you're not going away again.'

I can't believe it. I'm in shock. She's giving me another chance. Right now I'll tell her whatever she wants to hear.

I take a deep breath and mentally cross my fingers.

'I promise.'

3

Sacrifice is the law of life. It runs through and governs every walk of life. We can do nothing or get nothing without paying a price for it.

Mahatma Gandhi

4 May 2004: Day 1

The pilot descends into Basra Palace at full speed, and within seconds we're on the ground. The Chinook's ramp lowers and we spill out. As we run, we're hit by the scorching blast of the rotor engines. The heat is fearsome. As the last man leaves the chopper, the pilot is already beginning his ascent. I shield my eyes, and close my mouth to ensure I don't get a lungful of burning sand as the Chinook roars over us and beats its way up over the Shatt al-Arab.

Within seconds it has disappeared from view.

I'm met at the HLS by Phil, one of my staff sergeants from 11 EOD. He began working for me several years

29

ago during my first troop command; for several weeks he's been standing in for me while I've been in Colombia. Phil's in his mid-thirties and is a hard man. He has a shaved head and looks like a younger version of Bruce Willis. Originally from Cheshire, he's fiercely loyal and very funny, and one of the best operators and most dependable senior NCOs I have ever worked with. He's also a good mucker.

'Welcome to Basra, the most fucked-up place on earth. How's Didcot? And how are things with you and Lucy?'

Phil has never been one to beat around the bush.

'Oh, you know, pretty shitty,' I reply. 'I got back from Colombia two months ago and promised her I wouldn't be going away again. But instead of going straight on leave, I made the schoolboy error of nipping into the squadron to drop off some kit, and ended up getting collared by the OC to come out here. So here I am, banging out a four-monther in Iraq. I'm not exactly top of her Christmas card list right now.'

'And they wonder why EOD stands for "everyone's divorced",' he remarks bitterly. He and his wife split up last year.

We make the short walk from the HLS to the Det, and inside it's buzzing. The Chemical Brothers are blasting out along the corridors. Raucous laughter spills out of the two crew rooms. I can sense the undercurrent of tension, but it's a vibrant place, a place with real energy. I've always felt happiest when I'm in the heart of the crew out on operations, and I already know I'm going to enjoy it here.

Phil shows me around and introduces me to the blokes, then we get straight down to the handover brief.

'First things first,' he says. 'You're supposed to do a two-week acclimatization package at Shai'ba Log Base before you go on duty. Unfortunately there isn't scope for you to do it, because I have to fly back in two days and there's nobody else to cover in the meantime. So you're just going to have to acclimatize on the job, I'm afraid.'

Outside, it's fifty degrees in the midday sun. But hey, shit happens.

'Secondly, young Nick here, from the brigade's intelligence section, has put together a PowerPoint presentation for you on the current intelligence situation in Basra.'

It's standard operating procedure to get an up-to-date int brief whenever any new members join the team. A couple of the lads sit down and listen in too as Nick flashes up a detailed map and gets straight into the meat of it.

'Basra is the capital city of the al-Basra Governorate. It's located on the western banks of the Shatt al-Arab waterway in the south-east, and is the country's second city, with a population of approximately one point four million inhabitants . . .'

He's given this part of the brief so many times he's on autopilot.

He goes on to explain each part of the city in detail.

'Moving north-west, this is Old Basra, Qadimah, home of the thieves' market, where just about anything is on sale, from baby powder to RPG rounds. The souk is a tight-knit community, so the arms dealers rarely end up getting caught. It's also more densely packed than Del Trotter's lock-up, so surge operations are no picnic. 'The Five Mile Market is not much better. It's a major choke-point in the mornings and after about sixteen hundred hours . . .'

I hoover up every detail as Nick flicks his laser dot from location to location.

Eventually he gets to the part I've been waiting for – the insurgent threat. He tells us about the four separate groupings. The first consists of the disaffected, criminal and tribal elements. The second, the Shia Militants, are the bad-boy lunatics who run Basra and, crucially, the Iraqi Police Service. Then there are the Sunni Former Regime Elements – Saddam's mates – and finally the international Jihadists, foreign fighters aligned closely with al-Qaeda's Zarqawi network.

He goes on to describe the various types of attack.

Rocket and mortar attacks are pretty much daily affairs, but small-arms and RPG attacks are even more common. For sheer devastation, though, improvised explosive devices (IEDs) win out every time.

An hour passes, and Nick fires up the final questions slide.

'So, gentlemen, in a nutshell, that is Basra.'

Rob Powell, one of the newer members of the team, nudges me. 'So, gentlemen, in a nutshell, we're all fucked,' he whispers.

He has a point. I can't see me bringing the family here on an all-inclusive any time soon.

Phil and I resume the handover and moments later a double-tasking comes in: the team has been tasked to an explosion, and a company commander from the Cheshires has requested ATO support for an imminent surge operation. Normally we'd prioritize the taskings, but as there's two of us it makes sense to split. We agree that I'll cover the Cheshires' task.

I've been travelling for thirty hours and in the Det for a matter of minutes. Now I'm about to deploy straight out on task. It doesn't get much better than this. This is the business. It's what I love about our job: we get to enjoy the best of both worlds. We may be technical officers, but we're soldiers first and foremost and we're frequently called to support the infantry on jobs like this when there's a chance that ammunition or explosives may be found.

'Fuck me, you're in for some fun,' Phil says.

He's not wrong.

An hour later I'm standing in a fortified coalition base near the Qadimah souk. The team whisked me across the city on their way to the explosion and now I'm stood dwarfed by the 20-foot-high sand barriers and concrete blast walls shielding us from the outside world. At the end of each stretch of the wall, an austere watchtower, dark and brooding, looms over us like a sentinel waiting for war. Outside, the warm desert air is heavily perfumed with the stench of shit and decaying rubbish.

The camp is bustling with activity. Worn-out soldiers are busy preparing for the next mission. Their tanned faces and weather-beaten combats tell me all I need to know about their operational tempo.

I think ruefully of my promise to Lucy, but the truth is, I feel exhilarated. I should have been able to suppress my adolescent desire for danger and uncertainty by now, but it's no good. All I want to do is get out there and see some action.

I'm met by the company commander, a stocky, grey-haired major.

'So, you're the bomb disposal chap. Royal Engineers?'

This isn't a good start. Apart from the fact that I don't really like his condescending manner, he's requested ATO support without appearing to have a clue what it is. I've lost count of the number of times infantry officers have asked me if I'm a Royal Engineer. I take a deep breath and try to mask my irritation.

'I'm an ATO, an ammunition technical officer. All counter-terrorist bomb disposal is carried out by ATOs. We're Royal Logistic Corps.'

I'm not normally anal enough for something like this to bother me, but the alarm bells are ringing. Most infantry officers cut their teeth in Northern Ireland, where they work closely with ATOs. If this guy doesn't know who we are, it means he's not served in NI, which means he's got fuck all experience when it comes to counter-insurgency. And I don't want to go out on the ground with some numpty who talks a good battle but has actually spent his whole career behind a desk.

'Of course, I've heard of you guys. You're the ones they used to call Felix in Northern Ireland – the boys with nine lives.'

Fuck me. It's astonishing. I take it all back.

We exchange a bit of polite small talk then the major briefs me on the weapons market operation. He runs through his plan as if we're just two regular blokes chatting over a pint.

'I'll cut to the chase,' he says. 'The IEDs we're being hit with are put together from components sold at the souk. The brigade commander wants something done about it, and sharpish. So we're going to disrupt the distribution of IEDs in southern Iraq by conducting an aggressive raid on the thieves' market.'

I've completely misjudged this character. He really does know his onions.

We talk tactics and procedures and he fires a stream of questions at me about IEDs. I explain how, after the war, Iraqi insurgents began arming themselves. There were more than a hundred major arsenals and literally thousands of ammunition dumps dotted around the country, all of which contained vast quantities of high-grade explosives. Somehow these were left unsecured by the coalition forces after the war.

The insurgents thought all their Christmases had come at once. In just twelve months they'd surpassed the level of bomb-making ability achieved by the IRA in thirty years. In Iraq there were over two thousand IED attacks a month, using every type of electronic gizmo imaginable, including car alarms, wireless door bells, cell phones, pagers and encrypted GMRS radios. Global Jihadists from Chechnya, Afghanistan, the Balkans and the Middle East were sharing technologies, tactics and procedures at a lightning-fast pace, via the internet, terrorist training camps and CD-ROM. The IED became one of the most dangerous and effective weapon systems we'd ever faced, and the insurgents' weapon of choice.

Blokes are running around like maniacs doing their last-minute checks and tests. The lads are stuffing magazines and grenades into every available inch of their webbing, leaving behind bayonets, night vision goggles and any other crap they're not going to need for a daylight arrest op. The company sergeant major has told everybody to mark their zap numbers (a soldier's personal identification number) on the front of their body armour and carry their morphine in their right map pocket. That way, everyone knows where it is if things go tits up.

We're going to be hitting the market from three different directions, blocking off any escape routes in the process and arresting all the city's arms traders in a oner. It's a bold plan. I'm just a new kid on this particular block, but even with my limited time in-country I have doubts about our ability to pull it off. We'll be going in with about twenty vehicles so the moment we leave the camp, Haji is bound to be straight on his mobile, telling the terrorist head-sheds that an op is about to go down. For a moment I picture us having a *Black Hawk Down* moment – our lightly armoured vehicles weaving through a warren of narrow, dusty streets, being hammered from the rooftops by insurgents bristling with RPGs and automatic weapons.

But it doesn't happen like that.

We scream down stone-vaulted streets and into Basra's stolen goods emporium without a shot being fired. The tight mass of shop fronts are crammed up against the road, bustling with shoppers. The souk is a kaleidoscope of colour, noise and chaos. Salesmen sit cross-legged next to piles of household tat, office furniture and stacks of copper chiselled from downed electricity pylons. Further along, we pass stalls selling vegetables, meat, bread, you name it. As we debus, my senses are assaulted by a myriad of different odours: the sweet smell of incense and spice, the stench of fly-infested fish and meat, sewerage, and donkey shit.

The dark, bearded traders gaze at us impassively.

Minutes later I'm stood with my back up against a wall, attached to an infantry section. Our weapons cover every arc – forwards, backwards and out to the flanks. I'm the last man in the team, so I'm covering the rear; the guy in front of me covers the windows above us. We patrol forwards, hugging the walls. If anybody decides to have a pop, they're going to have to lean out to take the shot; and if they do that, they're going to get a good brassing up.

At thirty-one, I feel like the old man in the patrol. I

joined up when I was sixteen, but I still love the buzz of live operations. The rest of the lads are all in their late teens or early twenties. There's a blatant look of terror in their young faces, and to a man they are all breathing out of their arses. They're not unfit; their panting is the product of stress and fear.

We push through a series of narrow passageways and a dark tunnel right into the heart of the teeming souk. It's a frenetic place, chocker with people. It sells everything the black market has to offer. If you have the greenbacks, you can buy pretty much whatever you want. But something's not right. There are empty pitches in the market, and it's obvious they've only just been vacated. We'd expected to see piles of bullets, handguns and Kalashnikovs, all laid out carefully next to grenades and machine guns. But there's nothing.

The fuckers have been tipped off. They've managed to pack up and sod off, all in the space of the ten-minute window between us driving out of camp and arriving here. This isn't quite the way I'd expected things to pan out. I'd hoped we were going to go in with speed, aggression and surprise. Perhaps have a covert surveillance capability on the ground to cue us on to any targets, and an outer cordon to stop any runners. These boys are pros. This is a slick operation. We've been seen off.

One of our interpreters is busy interrogating a local

when out of the blue he turns and points to a man running across the roof of one of the houses behind us. He's going bananas, waving his arms like a madman. His eyes widen and he begins yelling furiously at us to capture the bad guy. 'He's Basra's main arms dealer!' he shouts. 'Don't let him escape!'

The arms dealer turns on the spot, cradling his AK-47, and jumps from one roof to the next. Unbelievable. He's like fucking Spiderman.

And with that the place goes kinetic. People shout, troops take up fire positions, everything suddenly becomes serious. The shooting will start any second. The trouble is, the place is full of civvies – women, children, the whole shebang.

The section I'm with stacks up in a line, and on the section commander's 'Go!' we charge through an archway and into a labyrinth of near identical passageways. We're chasing the terrorist, one after the other, without a plan and not having a clue where we're going. We're running through people's houses and yards, through living rooms and up and down flights of stairs. It's like something out of *The Benny Hill Show*. It's outrageous. But I've never experienced a rush like it. The hairs on the back of my neck are standing on end. This is it. We're in one of the most hostile areas in Basra and things are about to go noisy. It feels good. I feel alive.

We pile through dozens of two-storey shacks, to a chorus of screams from the families whose homes we're invading. And then we come to an enclosed courtyard.

We are at a dead end.

After a moment's impasse, two of us scale the wall and there in front of us, at the top of another set of stairs, is our quarry. We order him to stay where he is, but he takes off again. We split, and I chase the terrorist up the stairs. In the few seconds it takes me to get to the top, he vanishes. He has to be somewhere close, but I'm damned if I can see him.

Just then, two other troops appear on the top of an adjacent building. It's good to see some friendly forces. I give them the nod and walk slowly forwards, my pistol in the aim.

I reach the edge of the roof. There's a 6-foot gap and a 20-foot drop between me and the next house. Under normal circumstances it might not be a drama – if you ever contemplate jumping from one roof to another under normal circumstances – but I'm wearing a Bergen brimming with heavy EOD kit.

Fuck it. The adrenalin is coursing through my veins. I take a Buster Keaton-style run and jump and somehow make it across the gap.

What am I thinking?

Then, from the middle of nowhere, he appears again.

He can't be more than 10 feet away from me. I draw my Sig back into the aim and fix him in my sights. This is surreal. I've been in the country fewer than six hours and here I am about to top a terrorist. I go into tunnel vision mode; the two troopers do the same. We bark orders at him in unison. He's not happy. He looks like a fox that's just run slap bang into a whole lot of hounds.

Then I have a worrying, irrational thought: what if he's a suicide bomber? Ten per cent of all suicide bombings kick off because the bomber's been cornered or compromised. But this maniac isn't wearing the intense, fanatical expression I'd expect to see on a suicide bomber who's about to throw the switch. He's shitting himself. He definitely isn't planning on meeting up with seventy-two virgins today.

His expression suddenly changes. He starts to relax. He's going to make a move . . . but what's he going to do? If he raises his AK, we'll give him the good news there and then. And he knows it. He'd have to be insane to try to take us on.

He looks me straight in the eye and grins. And then he steps back and drops through an open skylight into the house below.

We've lost him.

4

A pint of sweat saves a gallon of blood.

General George Smith Patton

7 May 2004: Day 4

I sit outside the Det, basking in the heat of the fierce desert sun, drinking iced tea and thinking about home. Fishermen idle away the morning, casting their rods into the Shatt al-Arab from its palm-fringed banks. An impassioned call to prayer rings out from the tower of a nearby mosque. Its cadences are mystical and hypnotic.

The fragile tranquillity is elbowed aside by a flurry of activity. We've received a tasking message. This is my fourth task in as many days. The atmosphere is thick with anticipation. Dan, my number two, shouts over to me, 'Boss, it's an IED shout. I'll brief you on the way.'

I grab my kit and head for the team vehicles. There are people everywhere, shrugging on their CBA and Kevlar helmets. Weapons are being loaded, radios checked,

ECM switched on, goggles fitted, engines fired. Everyone is running through their last-minute mental lists, triple-checking weapons, rehearsing actions-on. We mount our vehicles, adrenalin pumping, and embrace the uncertainty that lies ahead.

Rob Powell, one of our infantry escorts, runs through the route. Every time we leave the safety of our base here in Saddam's palace we take a different one. Every routine is logged by hostiles. There's always someone watching, waiting for us to drop our guard. This is a highly sophisticated, state-sponsored guerrilla war. Our enemies have people on the ground, and instant comms. If we set patterns they'll be noted, and a roadside bomb will be lying in wait next time.

Ten minutes later, blues and twos flashing, our convoy pulls out of the gates and into the bustling city. Our mood changes as soon as we leave the shelter of the camp. We flick the switch from full-off to full-on. Alert . . . weapons in the aim and ready to react.

The first thing you notice about the city is its stomach-turning smell. Rubbish and excrement fester on every corner. The city's sewers have been blocked for months. We drive fast through the sprawling mass of flat, sand-coloured homes, public monuments and seventies-style concrete apartment blocks. Soon we're weaving our way through the back streets. The place is teeming with donkey carts, trucks, taxis, pedestrians, market stalls. We take in every feature we pass. Everything simmers with unease.

Twenty minutes later we finally break out into the desert. I see the airport – the home of our Divisional HQ – on the horizon.

As we race towards the incident, my mind flashes back to my ATO course at the Felix Centre – the UK Counter-Terrorist Bomb Disposal School. I loved my time there. It's considered to be the foremost authority on IEDD in the world. We learned about every type of terrorist device imaginable; we were taught, in meticulous detail, all the phases of an IED task from arrival through to completion; and most importantly, we learned how to defeat devices using remote, semi-remote and manual IED techniques.

I run through the day one, week one basics: the need for caution and vigilance when approaching the area; the risk of gunmen lying in wait to ambush the vehicles; what type of device I'm going to be facing when I get there. Where it is, what time it was laid, how long the area's been secured, what else was seen and heard. I also think about our greatest enemy of all: concealed secondary devices, hidden bombs specifically designed to kill us at any stage during the task. They might be on the cordon position, on the route to the device, or in its immediate vicinity. Whether a bomber places a secondary or not, the risk of it is always there, preying on your mind.

I try never to think about failure, whether or not I'll come away with life and limbs intact. As far as I'm concerned, survival is a given.

I allow myself a brief moment to picture my family, safely back at home in Oxfordshire, far away from the ruthless men who have become my adversaries. And I remember the phone call with Lucy last night. Not a good one. She seemed irritable and uninterested, as though my getting in touch had in some way inconvenienced her. It seems to have become the norm, these days . . .

We are at the cordon. Now there is only the task in hand.

We locate the ICP, park the two Duros to form a protected V and drop the blast skirts to prevent explosive debris shooting underneath the vehicle. The Snatch pulls in across the back of us to close the triangle.

The heat is intense, and the desert is almost bare. We can see, and be seen, for miles. Any movement in the open can be observed by the enemy. It's every sniper's dream – a gift of a shot.

A crowd has formed at the edge of the cordon. Setting up a cordon is a simple affair. You start by tying a piece of white plastic mine tape – similar to police tape – across the road. The real difficulty lies in controlling it. A few young soldiers facing an angry crowd with nothing more than a piece of 2-inch-thick plastic tape to separate them can be an intimidating experience. And the Iraqi collapse has flooded the region with unemployed young men, most of them angry, jobless and humiliated. One of them shouts at me, 'When? When go? Why no dead yet? Your luck – no last for ever.' There is hatred in his eyes.

I locate the cordon commander, a young RAF flight lieutenant, and fire a barrage of questions at him. The IED is 250 metres away and consists of an unfired salvo of Iranian 107mm rockets on an improvised timer circuit. Nobody has approached closer than 50 metres, and the ground between us and the IED is impassable to vehicles. I'm going to have to make the approach on foot, in the suffocating heat of the midday sun.

I get on the radio and request a high-risk search team from the Royal Engineers to carry out a perimeter search for additional devices. The last thing I want to do is neutralize the main device then be blown to bits by a hidden command-wire IED. I'm told by Brigade HQ that no search teams are available. I ask for a heli to provide aerial top cover. I'm fobbed off. There's a shortage of airframes and it's too hot to fly. This op is beginning to get up my nose.

To top it all, the ditches and mounds of earth that surround the device won't allow me to send in my wheelbarrow robot. The barrow is a 3-foot-high, 300kg tracked vehicle that travels at a speed of up to 6 mph, and has an extendable robotic arm mounted on the chassis which can be fitted with a wide selection of disruptor weapons. It's saved hundreds and thousands of lives.

Instead of inspecting the device remotely – diagnosing its type, size and construction – and then attacking it from a safe distance, I'm going to have to go in myself. Things have not got off to a good start.

I fight back feelings of futility. I'm going to have to do what I can. Lives depend on me – in this case, the thousand or so people living and working at Basra Air Station, where this deadly salvo is headed. I want to let the device soak, to leave it well alone until I am certain the timer has completely run down, but I can't. I can't risk the rockets launching. The results would be catastrophic. Each one of the 4-foot-long projectiles would scream towards its predetermined target at twice the speed of sound. Those on the receiving end wouldn't know they were being attacked until the second before the strike. As each rocket landed, the high-explosive warhead would detonate on impact and fragment into 1,200 supersonic shards of molten metal. The glass windows in every structure within 200 metres would implode in an instant, turning any exposed personnel into human colanders.

I have no choice.

I brief the team and prepare to face the task ahead. My pulse is racing, every sense on full alert. I have to keep my wits about me. I have to maintain a healthy measure of paranoia. No matter how much faith I have in my equipment and skills, at some stage my time, and luck, is going to run out. Right now, it looks like both are slipping away.

I say a quick prayer to myself. The one every bomb tech says before he goes forward. *If fate is against me and I'm killed, so be it, but make it quick and painless. If I'm wounded, don't let me be crippled. But above all, don't let me fuck up the task.*

The team has sprung into action around me. Rob is organizing the infantry escorts, placing them in fire positions and barking commands. He's in his element. A redoubtable Welshman, he looks like a stockier version of Jack Dee, and has the same dry sense of humour. Rob's a part-time soldier who spent fifteen years in the regulars and now owns his own close protection company. He's been called up for service in Iraq and is losing a fortune by being here, but he loves the job and is worth ten regulars.

Scotty, my electronic counter-measures operator – affectionately known as a 'bleep' – sits in his wagon carrying out an electronic sweep of the area. At thirty-eight he's the oldest member of the team, but despite his greying hair, he is, irritatingly, a Brad Pitt lookalike, and has the physique of one of those gits in the Diet Coke ad. Although he's only attached to us for a couple of weeks the lads love having him on the team because there's a constant stream of women flowing past the Det whenever he's around.

Dan gathers the working equipment I'm going to need: my ECM set, a mini disruptor (designed to destroy the timing and firing mechanism of the device before it can launch the rockets), my personal role radio (through which I'm going to give a commentary to my team), and a bagful of hand-held tools, including some search kit and a hook-and-line set.

Despite the fact that he's the number two, and thus the de facto second-in-command, Dan doesn't say much. But he is, as ever, smiling and cheerful. He seems to derive a huge amount of satisfaction from predicting exactly what kit I'll require for each task. So far he's been bang on every time. He's the essence of unquestioning dependability. He's already a superb number two, and as soon as he's promoted to sergeant he'll be eligible to train as a Number 1 IEDD operator. He'll be outstanding.

I decide I'm not going to wear the protective bomb suit. The cumbersome armour is made up of layers of

Kevlar and weighs 80lb. It's 40°C in the shade today and if I wear it I'll probably die from heat exhaustion before I get anywhere near the bomb. And besides, if the device explodes when I'm on top of it, the shockwave will tear the limbs from my torso and kill me instantly whatever I've got on. I choose the lighter, general-issue combat body armour and Kevlar helmet instead, but frankly, I might as well be wearing a T-shirt and shorts.

Dan hands over my equipment and I prepare to take the long walk. Two hundred and fifty metres. It doesn't sound far, but I am carrying 90lb of equipment, the sun is already starting to fry my brain, and the ground is difficult and uneven underfoot. Each footstep is laboured. Sweat pours off me as I shuffle under the fearsome midday sun. It feels like 250 miles.

RAF Regiment troops have taken up fire positions at each end of this barren wasteland, ready to retaliate should a sniper be lying in wait. Apart from the village behind me and Divisional Headquarters on the horizon to my front, there is nothing but featureless terrain as far as the eye can see.

I try to regulate my breathing. To get my pulse down. I inhale deeply through my nose and exhale slowly through my mouth. But my heart is racing. This is taking for ever. I've only travelled 100 metres and I am physically drained; and however much I try to convince myself that I am not in danger, I know I can't take anything for granted. I'm saturated with sweat and mentally fried, and I'm not even halfway to the device.

I feel a sharp tug. The twin-flex firing cable snaking out of my carrying case has snagged on a rock. It's a pain having to trail it all the way to the device, but it's a necessary evil – I need it to fire off my EOD weapon. Dan is already jinking it free. He gives me the thumbs up and I move on.

The heat is brutal.

I go over the threat assessment repeatedly in my mind. I wonder which of the three types of IED it will be: time, command or victim operated. Perhaps it will be all three.

Twenty metres short, I carefully set down my equipment, get down on my stomach and prepare to search for tripwires and buried pressure IEDs. Even the smallest device can be powerful enough to blow a man's leg into his stomach and blind him with the shrapnel of his own bone fragments.

I'm halfway there. I'm crawling on my belt-buckle, scanning the ground for any hint of disturbed earth, the tip of a plastic box, a piece of fishing line . . . I remember the life-saving phrase from training – *look for absence of the normal and presence of the abnormal*. In this job, Murphy's Law rules. Always expect the unexpected.

I slide my tripwire-feeler gingerly forwards. I move the

foot-long telescopic rod close to the earth, but not touching it. I focus on its tip. Everything else becomes a blur. I raise it an inch, then two, until eventually I am standing. I am totally oblivious to outside sounds now. I move the feeler left . . . slowly . . . then right . . .

No tripwires. I lay the rod down and begin searching the ground beneath this virtual 3D box. I use a small metal detector to locate pressure-plate devices. It's painfully slow, laborious work. I am up against the clock, but I have to clear this safe route first. Even if there is no secondary, I have to assume the bomber is watching me. Tracking my procedures. If he sees me run straight up to the device, the next time he'll place a secondary for sure.

Sweat is pouring off me, running into my eyes, stinging them. My pulse is racing. I search with my fingertips, stone by stone, inch by inch, before crawling forward half a metre and then repeating the whole process.

The crowd behind the cordon is getting more and more hostile; their low murmurs have turned to shouts. The insurgents will almost certainly be preparing an attack. We've got to get off the ground. My mouth is dry. My movements are becoming slower and slower. I feel like I've been drugged, like I'm in a trance. It takes a deliberate effort to clear my head, to refocus on the task in hand.

I'm finally at the objective.

My eyes are drawn to the crude TPU, the timing and

power unit: a 14-volt motorcycle battery with a mechanical timer on top, attached to the four rockets by a series of interconnecting red and white wires. Beads of sweat crawl across the back of my neck. I swallow hard. The timer is on its final graticule. There is one minute left.

But it's stuck fast.

Fate may be on my side today, but I know it could start again at any moment. The slightest movement could still free it. I anticipate the blinding flash as the four rockets engulf me in the white-hot back-blast of their launch.

I have to break the circuit. But I can't cut into it by hand, because I can't see everything I need to see. Normally, I'd cut the wire to the power supply – job jobbed. But if there's a hidden collapsing circuit, cutting the power will activate the relay. I'll be killed instantly.

I'm going to go with the lesser of the two evils. I'll place a scalpel weapon and fire it from the safety of the ICP.

I study what I can see of the circuit and choose my precise target. I edge the weapon up to the wire leading to the battery's positive terminal. My hand is trembling. My stomach lurches. I tell myself to keep going . . . And then the scalpel is in place. I wipe the sweat from my eyes and make my way, light-headed, back to the ICP.

I strain to look at my watch. I've been on the ground

for thirty minutes. The midday sun has now got me by the throat. I am dizzy, nauseous. One hundred metres to go . . . 50 . . . 20 . . . Dan sees me stumble and runs out of the ICP to help. He brings me cold water. I gulp it down. I want to stop myself from puking, but I'm power-less. My stomach begins to cramp up, I feel the bile rising in my throat and I begin to vomit, uncontrollably. I stagger back to the ICP, stopping every few steps to throw up, my legs giving way below me. Dan somehow keeps me on my feet.

For the first time in fifteen years of service, I regret ditching a promising career as a restaurateur in favour of something that would make my heart pump a little faster. I am in a shit state. This is positively taking the piss. Exhausted.

I order everybody to get under hard cover, including the thousand or so occupants of the airport, and when I'm satisfied, I tell Dan to fire off the scalpel.

Dan takes control of the Shrike firing device. 'Stand by . . . firing!' His thumbs come down simultaneously on the circuit and fire buttons. There is a whip-crack as the mini disruptor unleashes the scalpel blades into the bomb's circuitry, ripping through its nerve centre. Then a moment of nervous anticipation as each of us waits for the earthshaking launch of the rockets that will tell us we've failed.

But there's nothing. We're in business.

I wait for a few moments, trying to throw as much water down my neck as I can. But time is still against me. I've got to get back to the device. I *think* I know it's been disrupted, but there's every chance something has gone wrong. The EOD weapon might have blown over in the wind and completely missed, or it might have only partially fired. The scalpels might have done nothing more than nudge the device, freeing the stuck-fast timer and making an already angry bomb even angrier. I take another weapon with me, just in case, and make another approach.

I force myself forwards, step by step. Only halfway there and I'm exhausted again. When I eventually do reach it, I examine the circuitry, following the bird's-nest loop of wires obsessively with my eyes, like re-reading the same sentence in a book again and again until it makes sense.

I'm slowing down.

I finally find the cut in the wire made by the scalpel blades. I pull out my reel of insulating tape, tear off a strip and wrap it around the bare end. Then I do the same to the other wire. The rockets are now harmless – to the people in the airport at least. It isn't yet over for me. There might be an anti-handling device to prevent the rockets being moved. The desert heat might have made the explosive unstable. There might even be a secondary booby trap device, triggered by the disruption of the first. This isn't paranoia. I've seen it before in other high-risk theatres.

I clear my mind and press on. I pull out the line from my kit bag and loop it around the TPU. Then I slide plasti-ties around every rocket and attach another line to each of them.

I am drained; my head is thumping like a hammer drill. But I am so close. Just a few more minutes . . .

I make it back to the ICP, but the heat exhaustion has fully kicked in now. I seem to be able to keep it under control when I am at the device, but as soon as I am out of the danger zone my body allows the sickness to take over. I am vomiting and slurring my words. I've gulped down about 8 litres of water, but I keep throwing it up. My head is pounding. My brain has slowed down completely.

I feel drunk. I'm hallucinating. I feel like I'm going to croak it any second.

I've got to dig deep now. I grip the line and pull it with all my strength. I drag the rockets and the TPU backwards down the mound of earth, and everything remains silent. Thank fuck for that. I'm on my chinstrap here.

I let the device soak for a while. An excruciating cramp

begins in my stomach and works its way through my entire body.

Still no explosion. Fantastic.

I use the portable X-ray generator to take a series of radiographs of the device, then I bag up the forensic evidence and place a series of plastic explosive charges along the length of the rockets. Rob gets everybody under hard cover, and when I give the word Dan fires off the charges. There's a blinding flash, followed by a deafening crack. Oxygen is sucked out of the air. A pillar of smoke rises hundreds of feet into the sky.

Task complete. We've done it. Now I can collapse in peace.

I lie in the confined space of the back of the Duro, gulping down lungfuls of cool air, and close my eyes in a moment of ecstatic relief.

It's been a tough day.

5

We think too small. Like the frog at the bottom of the well. He thinks the sky is only as big as the top of the well. If he surfaced, he would have an entirely different view.

Mao Tse-tung

8 May 2004: Day 5

I love the cathartic release of tension that comes after neutralizing a device.

Dan and I are sitting on the edge of the pontoon in companionable silence. We're drinking freshly brewed coffee. This is how I come down after a task. This is how I unwind and forget the tensions of the job: I sit quietly and reflect. I don't have to be alone, just somewhere where I can shut out all the noise and the daily grind. Somewhere I can think.

I'm pleased for the company. Dan is proving to be the perfect number two. He's witty, savvy and smart as a whip. Although we're the same age, he didn't fancy the idea of being a commissioned officer, so he joined up as an enlisted soldier instead. He's quiet and calm; in fact, he's probably the most laid-back NCO I've ever met, so unflappable you'd think he was on beta-blockers. But he's sharp, and has lightning reflexes. He's also got a fearsome sense of humour. I think we're going to get on like a house on fire.

Right now, life is good. But it will only be a matter of time before the days start to merge into the nights and the weeks drift into the months. Pretty soon the groundhog routine will take a hold and before we know it we'll all need reminding of what day of the week it is. For now, though, I'm embracing it.

Dan breaks the silence. 'Can you imagine what would happen if we actually did go on strike?'

My mind wanders back to a conversation we had in the Det last night. One of the translators described us as fire-fighters because he didn't know the Arabic for bomb disposal. Some of the team got very tetchy about it. There's a lot of bad feeling within the military towards Fireman Sam at the moment. Most of us have returned from operations at some stage and been ordered to go and man the Green Goddesses because the fire crews have downed tools.

Dan hands me an article he's dug out.

In the face of industrial action by members of the armed forces, the government has announced that the Fire Service will, as an interim measure, carry out military operations in Iraq. The army, who have demanded a 40% pay increase on the basis that their job has become rather more technical since 1945, will begin strike action next Thursday unless a compromise pay deal can be agreed in the meantime. It is understood that they will spend their time standing around little bonfires, rubbing their hands together and waving at passing vehicles who honk their horns at them. Crack Fire Service personnel, highly trained in playing darts, brewing tea and sliding down poles, are understood to be on standby to take up front-line operations.

It says it all really. If EOD is the military's equivalent of fire-fighting, we're doing it in a city full of arsonists. During the seventy-two hours of my handover with Phil, we were out on task every day. It was relentless. He flew back yesterday, but somehow I don't think things are going to get any quieter.

Right on cue, the bat-phone rings. It's another task. To more rockets. Here we go again.

*

Thirty minutes later we're back in the desert. In virtually the same spot we were yesterday. The sun is still insanely hot and the billiard-table terrain again offers the would-be sniper a dazzling array of opportunities. He can see for miles. This is a definite case of déjà vu. And it makes me uneasy.

And something else isn't right. Something is different. I can't figure it out at first, but then the penny drops. There's nobody around. Yesterday there was a huge reception committee. There were loads of them. Today there's nobody.

Why? Have they been told to stay away?

After we rendered safe the rockets yesterday, the cheeky bastards must have come straight back and placed these new ones. This time, though, they're configured differently. They aren't set up in a salvo ready to launch. They're in a pile off to a flank.

Is it a come-on? We've been tasked here as the result of another tip-off. And I know that the Taliban have booby-trapped rockets like these in Afghanistan. Maybe the insurgents have done the same with these. We already know the bombers are using particularly sophisticated devices and there's a huge amount of IED information-sharing between insurgents in Iraq and Afghanistan. The technique could easily have migrated here.

I don't like it. The hairs on the back of my neck are standing firmly on end. I tell myself to get a grip. I'm going to have to carry out another series of manual approaches.

One by one, I make sure the rockets are all safe. This time I don't destroy them. I neutralize them by hand and then place them in a forensic bag ready to send back through the evidential chain. The terrorist's mantra is 'We only have to be lucky once, you have to be lucky always.' But there's a flip side to that message: it's only a matter of time before we'll have enough forensic information to identify the bombers and their suppliers. And when we do, they'll need all the luck they can get.

We've been on task for hours and now we've got to get the rockets to the Joint EOD HQ at Shai'ba. Quite often we'll destroy bulk ordnance, but if we come across a rocket or an armament of particular interest, we'll make it safe to move and transfer it for further examination.

The routes leading from the rocket site are lined with landmines and unexploded ordnance. And the roads themselves are in a terrible state. To make things worse, if you travel in convoy, the dust churned up by the vehicles in front of you means you're effectively driving blind. What could possibly go wrong?

We arrive at Shai'ba and drop off the rockets with the movements staff. So far so good.

Next we head over to the REME section and it all starts to go tits up. The place is like a ghost town, a mechanics' graveyard. There are broken-down vehicles all over the place but not a human being in sight. We check all the corridors and rooms then hang around for an hour or so. Finally a sergeant shows up.

'Where is everybody?' I ask.

'Playing football,' he replies.

Of course. Why didn't I think of that? I try to mask my impatience.

'We've got some EOD kit that's been damaged on ops. Any chance you can fix it for us?'

He starts sucking his teeth and testiculating – waving his arms about and talking bollocks. 'And anyway,' he concludes, 'it's my day off today.'

There are clearly two types of support troops at Shai'ba, those who work and those who shirk, and the shirkers are about as rear echelon as they get. I'm beginning to see why the front-line troops have nicknamed the place Sh'Ibiza. What depresses me most is that this guy is a REME NCO, and they're normally mega-diligent when it comes to operations. This maniac is definitely an exception to the rule.

He's not in my chain of command, so I can't order him to pull his finger out. I try appealing to his better nature.

He looks at me blankly.

I feel my blood pressure rising and start to lose it. I go into a diatribe about how my team are working day and night in the most extreme conditions imaginable while tossers like him are busy monging it in the rear with the gear.

It washes over him. He treats me to a look of utter contempt, mutters 'Yeah, whatever' under his breath, then turns to walk away.

We've been on the ground all day and the boys are on their chinstraps, yet this prick thinks he's going to take the piss. I'm just not in the mood. I realize I'm going to have to change tack so I flick the switch.

6

People sleep peaceably in their beds at night only because rough men stand ready to do violence on their behalf.

George Orwell

Day 5

Several hours have passed and the kit is repaired. A swift bollocking and a few threats of ultra-violence was all it took for the REME NCO to become a born-again good bloke.

We head back to Basra Palace.

I'm dog tired. We've been on the ground all day and the fatigue is hitting us hard. We cross the bridge into the southern part of the city. The moonlight cuts through the desert night and glimmers on the canal beneath us. The roads are empty, except for two Iraqis who've broken down on the bridge. I don't envy them. Basra is no place to be waiting for the AA man at this time of night. This is the Wild West.

We turn into the barren marshlands of the Shia Flats. The smell is nauseating. Another twenty minutes and we'll be back at camp. We pass a series of three-storey whitewashed houses with flat roofs, surrounded by blocks of muddy stone huts. Thousands of Shias live in this maze of darkened streets, yet it is eerily calm. I can't put my finger on it, but something's up. The streetlights are out, even the dogs are silent. This is what they call combat intuition, when a soldier senses an enemy before he sees him. I don't know exactly how it works – probably in much the same way as the brain draws on memory mass from the central cortex during periods of high stress – but I know it accumulates through experience.

A kilometre later we turn north into the heart of the town. Maybe I was just being paranoid, because the street has a little more life in it now. Arabs in *dish-dashas* huddle in the doorways, watching us with a mixture of curiosity and suspicion. Nothing new there. Others sit at tables, drinking tea, smoking *shisha* pipes, playing cards and talking. Nothing *looks* out of place, but I still feel uneasy. Perhaps *this* is what they mean by combat intuition.

A little further on we come across a group of young Arab men standing in the middle of the road. Taff slows down the Snatch vehicle in front of us almost to a halt to allow them to clear out of the way. Ollie and Vince are riding top cover, their heads and upper bodies exposed above the cabin as they watch for snipers and roadside bombs.

And then it dawns on me. The Iraqis in the broken-down vehicle, were they scouts, a lookout party? Is there something nasty lurking around the corner?

Seconds later two men in crisp white *dish-dashas* jump up from their card game and run into the building behind them. This isn't right at all. I shout into my radio: 'Stand by, stand by.'

The air pulsates, and almost immediately Dan, Rob and I feel the jolt of a grenade detonating next to Taff's Snatch vehicle. Then all hell breaks loose. The sky fills with gunfire – first a few loud pops and cracks, then a roaring barrage. The place is now alive with noise and movement as black-uniformed Shia fighters swarm all over us.

Fuck me, this is a planned ambush. We're in trouble. The rooftops are crawling with gunmen. Tracer is streaming past us like hot razors, slashing open the air above our heads. The distinctive sound of Kalashnikov fire – I remember it from Bosnia.

Then the boom of an RPG launch. The rocket, with its flaming orange dragon-trail, speeds towards our vehicle. It hits about a metre or two short of our right wheel and explodes; the blast sends up waves of dust and sparks all around us. I can hear machine-gun fire from the rooftops to my right and the whoosh of another RPG overhead. It detonates against a wall opposite with a brilliant flash and a gut-wrenching blast.

This is a fucking mare. What have we got ourselves into? Bullets are flying everywhere, ricocheting off the ground and the surrounding buildings. This is it. We're lambs to the bloody slaughter.

I scream a contact report into my radio: 'Zero, this is Lima One One, contact wait out!'

Seconds later: 'Zero, this is Lima One One . . . contact at Orange Two . . . RPGs and small-arms fire . . . am engaging, over!'

There's no reply.

I try again on VHF, HF, sat-phone and even mobile. I'm starting to wish I'd brought a fucking carrier pigeon. We are either in a comms blackspot or we're being jammed. We could be killed or captured and nobody would know a damn thing about it.

The sense of isolation is indescribable. The adrenalin and tension in my stomach make me feel trapped and sick with dread. I can't think straight; my brain seems to go into meltdown.

This is crisis point.

Apocalyptic.

I freeze. The lining of my stomach forces its way up

into my mouth. Terror and anxiety are threatening to squeeze the very life out of me. I'm not just scared for myself but for the men I'm responsible for.

The volume of fire is awesome. The air is filled with dust and smoke, orange tracer and the eye-searing flashes of yet more exploding rockets.

This is the first time I've experienced complete and total dread, and it locks me in its grip. Fear. Deep, base, raw fear. It's that simple. It has never been much of a problem for me in the past, but this is something else. A chill sweat breaks out on my forehead. We are inches away from death. It's staring us in the face, taunting us. I am shitting myself. In a moment we're all going to be massacred, torn to shreds in this storm of fire and lead.

The logical part of me knows what I should be doing: making a plan, giving orders, looking for targets and killing them. But the emotional side doesn't want to play. It says, 'Fuck that! Close your eyes. Ignore the problem. It'll all go away.'

But I know it's not going to. I'm going to get shot. I'm about to die.

At that moment I realize that all the stuff about your life flashing before your eyes is complete and utter bollocks. The only thing I can think about is my family. I think about my beautiful wife Lucy and our troubled marriage. I think about my oldest daughter Sophie and her sister Ella, the five-month-old baby girl I've hardly seen and now won't see again. And I think about dying here, in this Godforsaken shit-hole in the middle of nowhere, thousands of miles from home.

But I'm not ready to die. I have to survive this. I want to see Lucy and my girls. I don't want everything I love and value on this earth to be taken away from me. I can't leave them without a husband and father.

And I can't let down my team. My men. I'm their commander. They're looking to me for direction. I have to lead them out of this mess.

And then, in that moment of maximum terror, I stop being scared. It is a Jekyll and Hyde moment. My men, whom I've known for only a few days, are now more important to me than life itself. So far, we've survived a well-laid ambush through luck alone. But luck doesn't, cannot, last.

My fear turns to anger. After those few seconds of helplessness, the adrenalin kicks in. We are here protecting innocent Iraqis from indiscriminate bombers, and in return they are intent on killing us for the sheer hell of it. Fuck them. I'm not going to lose a soldier on this filthy street for anybody. Not today.

It's crunch time.

In a matter of nanoseconds, a series of adrenalin-fuelled thoughts race through my mind – instinctively, and simultaneously – as I battle to find a way out of this mess.

The only way we are going to survive is to defy logic and face fire with fire. It seems so unnatural and so far removed from what any of us wants to do, but we are going to have to fight back, with complete and total aggression. We are a three-vehicle convoy, so stopping and reversing is totally out of the question. Forcing every vehicle through is our only option. If we can get enough rounds down and kill some of them, maybe they'll slacken off just enough for us to drive straight out of the killing zone.

It's time to initiate the fight-back, to repel the ambush with concentrated, accurate fire. It's about to become one of the defining moments of our lives. It'll mean the difference between living and dying. My heart fills with a cold black fury.

I scream a set of QBOs into my radio. 'Ambush – enemy right! All callsigns engage enemy at will! Drive, drive, drive!'

Then I have a terrible thought. Are the lads going to follow my orders, or will they panic? Will I be left to fight on my own? And when I glance to my front, I feel a dreadful sinking feeling. The two top cover men, Ollie and Vince, are nowhere to be seen. Have they been killed? Have they just frozen? Where the hell are they? We're in serious shit.

Then I look again and see them firing like men possessed from the back doors of the Snatch. Good lads. We're in business. Maybe, just maybe, we can survive this after all.

I look across to Corporal Harris. 'Dan, it's time we gave these pricks some payback. Time for a bit of two-way traffic. You drive, I'll shoot.'

I get out of my seat, half perch on the dashboard so I can get a better shot at the enemy, and wedge open my door with my left foot. I lift the butt of the SA80 into my shoulder and begin seeking out targets. The hail of enemy bullets continues to zing past my face. A man in dark fatigues comes running out of an alley no more than 10 metres away, firing his AK Beirut-style. I disengage the safety catch, take aim and squeeze the trigger. He clutches his stomach, bent double, and stares at me in disbelief. Then he slumps forward.

Retribution. It feels good. I'd read all sorts of stuff about what goes through a man's mind before he takes another man's life. It doesn't happen for me. There isn't much time for reflection right now anyway. Every second counts.

More explosions; frag, dust and debris scatter in every direction. This is surreal. There are civilians running around all over the place. The streets are bustling with screaming Iraqis, even women and children. What the fuck? How did the street fill up so fast? People are scrambling in all directions. Some run towards the fight, others run away from it. Chaos reigns. Some Iraqis are tending to the wounded, others are yelling for help, yelling for people to get out of the way, yelling for Allah. I see a civilian lying on his back in a pool of blood. The air is filled with AK fire and the thunderous explosions of RPGs.

A mother stands in the middle of the road, caught in the crossfire, clutching her child. Numb, confused. Caught like animals in a trap. The panic's sweeping over them both in waves. Fear has frozen her to the spot. A burst of gunfire spits along the street beside them. Then the earth shudders beneath her feet. The explosion shakes her from her trance. She looks left and right and lifts the boy into her arms.

She's moving now, the terrified boy clasped tightly to her side. She's tucked low and running. The scarf around her head is coming loose. She's mumbling . . . no, she's praying. Her legs are pumping like pistons but there's nowhere to go. Her eyes widen – the Snatch is heading straight towards her like an express train. In a final act of desperation she drops the child and tries to shield him from the oncoming vehicle. Taff swerves, missing them by inches, and nearly ends up in a drainage ditch.

The adrenalin is really flowing now. I level my weapon

and position the leaf of my sight on the middle of a group of five Shia gunmen standing under some palm trees. I aim where their concentration of muzzle flashes is greatest and start firing. I hit the gunman at the centre of the group and he crumples to the ground.

A scrawny-looking man in a grey *dish-dasha* appears from nowhere and pulls his RPG on to his shoulder. Deep red blotches appear all over him as he pulls the trigger and launches the unaimed round. Then his head and chest explode as he is hit with small-arms fire – chunks literally fall off him. I follow the grenade's trajectory across the front of our vehicle and on to its unintended target on the far side of the road. A lone teenage girl is standing outside her house. There is a sudden flash of light to one side of her. The blast rips away most of her clothing, yet miraculously she is otherwise unscathed. She stands by the wall, trembling and paralysed with fear.

I look back and see two other gunmen crash into the street. Ollie and Vince engage them from the back of their Snatch. Then Ollie puts more rounds down a side street, annihilating a third. Jesus, this boy is the Angel of Death. Aim, shoot, next. The insurgent's head cracks open like an egg.

Rounds continue to clip the tarmac around us and we can hear them puncturing the thin metal and fibreglass body of our Duro. The fire-fight rages on and the ferocity of the enemy's attack is incredible. It feels like we're receiving incoming fire from every direction now. And if life isn't difficult enough, the gunmen are positioning themselves among civilian bystanders.

A militiaman shoots at us from a doorway, firing wildly from the hip, bright flashes flaring from the muzzle of his Kalashnikov. I put two rounds into him, punching him backwards, legs and arms flailing. He is young, perhaps in his late teens, early twenties. But outnumbered and outgunned and with rounds still screaming past us, now is not the time to be sentimental. Bollocks to him. I hope the murderous little fucker burns in hell.

An RPG man breaks cover, only to shield himself among yet more civilians. We're travelling too fast and I can't take the risk of missing him and shooting one of them by accident. He launches his grenade straight at us. Fuck. Dan swerves and brakes. The RPG whooshes past us with inches to spare.

Another maniac comes running at our almost stationary vehicle and empties his AK-47 mag straight at us. I can almost hear the shell cases hitting the pavement. He's right alongside the door and the volley of machine-gun fire slams into the cab all around us. Amazingly, not a single one of his bullets hits us. What is he on? How can anybody be such a shit shot? A round passes through the edge of my boot and trousers and another skims my helmet. Tens of rounds pass within inches of our bodies. Dan accelerates. I lower my rifle and take a shot. His skull explodes and his lifeless body collapses on to the ground.

Behind us, Scotty and Tom's vehicle is getting a good malleting as well. Two grenades have detonated next to their Duro and they are now taking some serious incoming small-arms fire. Their vehicle is finding it difficult to keep pace with the rest of us, and just as they start gathering speed an RPG piles towards them. They brake, and it misses the cab by just a few metres.

In an astonishing act of bravery, an RPG gunner runs straight up to their vehicle and fires from fewer than 10 metres. It is a ballsy move, but a foolish one. The back-blast hits two enemy gunmen square-on, and flings them screaming on to their arses. The rocket hits the Duro, but instead of destroying it, simply bounces off and trails away into the distance. It's been fired too close to arm – lucky, lucky bastards!

Rounds are still coming in thick and fast. Two Shias are firing a PKC from one of the rooftops about 30 metres away. The belt-fed machine gun is unleashing a savage storm of lead into the killing area. One feeds the snake of bullets into the chamber, the other pans the gun and squeezes the trigger. They are joined by a larger group of insurgents firing AKs. Destruction rains down on us and I can't get a shot at any of them – we're travelling too fast. It's unbelievably hard to hit a target from a moving vehicle at that distance. Especially at night.

I feel a sharp pain in my left shin. It feels like someone has taken a knife and driven it in with a sledgehammer. I don't believe it, I've been hit. This should not be happening. The wound burns like hell.

Then I feel nothing. It must be the adrenalin anaesthetizing the pain.

Dan seems dazed and confused. He's driving with his left hand and holding his shoulder with his right. He doesn't seem quite himself, which is pretty understandable under the circumstances. I ask him if he's been hit. He tells me he's fine. I tell him I think I've been hit. I look down at my leg. Nothing. Christ, I'm imagining things. 'Obviously I'm just being a wuss,' I say.

A lad in his early teens comes running out of a shop and lobs a grenade at our vehicle. I could shoot him easily but he's already done what he was going to do, and I realize I definitely can't bring myself to kill a child. There's a shuddering explosion next to the vehicle and we are knocked sideways by the blast.

Then silence.

Not a single noise. Nothing. Just a strange, unnatural silence.

I realize I've gone deaf. My left eardrum is shot to bits. It's actually kind of peaceful. Surreal, but tranquil.

It doesn't last for long. Another burst of gunfire and tracer crackles past my face. I duck down into my body armour once again. RPGs scream through the smoke-laden air; tracer rounds stream across the road from the Shia ambush cut-off groups.

And then, gradually, finally, the firing seems to subside.

Just at the point when my hearing starts to return we appear to have driven out of the killing zone and into relative safety. We've fought our way along this kilometre-long stretch of road-from-hell, under constant fire from RPGs, grenades, small arms and machine guns, and we've actually made it. I can't believe it. Everyone seems to be alive. How the fuck did we survive that? It's too good to be true.

We go firm in a rally point to get our shit together and try to establish comms with one another. It's also an opportunity for a breather. Complete bedlam still rages behind us, and there is always the threat of a follow-up ambush. But right now we're safe.

Dan reaches for a cigarette. His left shoulder is bleeding from a round which has fragmented after ricocheting off his door frame. The burning sensation in my leg has come back. I look down again and pull up my trouser leg. I *have* been shot. Struck in the shin by a high-velocity bullet from an AK-47. It's left a small red hole the size of a penny. Luckily for me it must have been near the end of its trajectory, because it hasn't gone in too far. It's hit with enough force to hurt, but not enough to penetrate the bone. I've always wondered what it would be like to be wounded, and now I know.

I light up too, instinctively winding down my window, then realizing that there's no glass in the frame. I look down. It's all over my lap and in the footwell. The cocktail of tension and elation becomes too much and we piss ourselves laughing.

I get on the radio and ask the team for a sitrep. The Snatch vehicle has gone firm to our front and Rob tells me everyone in it is visibly shaken but OK. Dan and I have both been hit, but not seriously. Our vehicle has been shot to pieces, but it's still drivable. It's now just down to Scotty and Tom to let us know their status.

They were only 20 feet behind us the last time I looked, but for some reason they don't respond to my radio call. I call them again. Nothing. I keep calling, maybe ten or twenty times, but there is no response.

I ask Vince if he can see them behind us from his top cover position and he tells me that he has visual for at least 300 metres and they definitely aren't behind us. This is bad, very bad; the most sickening, gut-wrenching feeling I have ever experienced. We've lost two men and the second EOD vehicle. Everything's suddenly gone to ratshit again.

A thousand thoughts race through my mind. Scotty and Tom are on their own. They're probably dead, but if they aren't, they're almost certainly going to end up in orange boiler suits, begging for their lives on grainy homemade videos, waiting for the inevitable beheading.

We've no comms with the outside world, which means we have no support. If Scotty and Tom stand any chance of being rescued – supposing they *are* still alive – then it's going to have to be by us. And that means going back.

Nobody ever survives an ambush, yet three quarters of the team have somehow just made it out alive. That in itself is a miracle. Is it really worth risking their lives for two blokes who are probably dead anyway? It would be sheer suicide.

We've got fuck all in the way of firepower. There must be at least fifty insurgents back there, compared to only six of us who have made it back to the rally point. We are only armed with SA80s. I have a back-up AK and an RPG22 behind my seat which Phil left me, just in case. The 22 is only a single-shot weapon, but I guess it will send the right message. If we do go back in, I'm going to put it to good use. If that car comes anywhere near us, it's going to get the message. Bollocks to the rules of engagement. Better to be tried by twelve than carried by six.

Fuck me. This has got to be the hardest decision I've ever had to make. I'm balancing the lives of my remaining team against those of two men who are probably already dead. I can't order them to go back in. Doing so would be downright fucking stupid. But I can't sit here and do nothing either. I know I'll spend the rest of my life regretting it. I don't want to face their families, or my own, and be asked, what if?

I make up my mind – *never let adversity stand in the way of the right decision*. I look at Rob and Dan, then Vince and Ollie. The boys know what's coming. I can read the look of dread on their faces, but deep down I know that at this moment every single one of them is prepared to go back and fight with their bare hands if it means saving the lives of their oppos. These qualities – loyalty, courage and selfless commitment – are precisely what give the British soldier the edge.

There are six of us. We'll go in stealthily, on foot. Two of the team will need to stay with the vehicles. That leaves four to mount the rescue. When we are as close as we can possibly get, we'll go noisy. Speed, aggression, surprise. And pity the fucker who tries to corner us.

I am about to give the order to execute the mother of all suicide missions when I see Vince jumping up and down like a screaming madman. Before I get the chance to ask him what planet he's on, he yells, 'Boss, boss, you'll never fucking believe it! They've fucking made it!'

He's right, I can't believe it. It can't be true, but it is. Like a phoenix rising out of the ashes, the wagon emerges from the smoke and Scotty and Tom pull up alongside. Terrified, but alive.

7

War is a game that is played with a smile. If you can't smile, grin. If you can't grin, keep out of the way till you can.

Winston Churchill

Day 5

I don't know whether it's the adrenalin or the cold air that's made the hairs on the back of my arms stand on end. Dan hasn't said a word since we left the rally point – I think he's either exhausted or in shock. Basra is a dangerous enough place as it is, but what's happened to us tonight has taken the conflict to the next level. I think this is going to affect us all for some time yet.

At last we turn into the palace approach road and the armoured personnel carrier blocking the front gate kicks into life, reversing back and letting us through the huge marble arch. Dan drops me at HQ and he and the team go back to the Det.

It's past midnight and the ops room is virtually empty, but Will is still hunched over his desk as usual, studying reports and taking caffeine and tobacco intravenously. We've been good muckers for years. Like me, he joined the Army as an enlisted soldier and then went to Sandhurst after a couple of years as a junior NCO. I was best man at his wedding. The two of us were on the same ATO course and served at 11 Regiment as EOD troop commanders.

Most of us found the job more fulfilling than we could ever have dared hope; it was a vocation, a way of life. But not Will. The buzz appealed to him at first, but he quickly realized he needed something more. He craved a different kind of challenge, so he jacked it all in and transferred to the Intelligence Corps. He probably made the right choice. He's a natural. But as I look at him now I can see that, despite the banter, the years of smoke and mirrors are starting to wear him down. The worries of the world are etched around his eyes, and he lives on a diet of black coffee and Marlboro Reds. It's a miracle he's not had a heart attack yet.

He doesn't notice me standing in the doorway.

'Jock, I've just been fucking shot.'

They say action is like a drug. Right now I'm as high as a kite.

'You should know bloody better, shouldn't you, you wanker,' Will says.

'Don't tell me, if I'm looking for sympathy, I'll find it in the dictionary between shit and syphilis.'

He grins. 'At least the brain still works . . .'

Just then, Will's wife Emma phones.

'Hang on a minute, love, Chris reckons he's just been shot. Can I call you back?'

What sort of lunatic tells his wife something like that? Poor girl, what must she be thinking? *Another busy day at the office?*

'Do you fancy coming out for a ciggie, mate?' I ask him.

'So you've finally succumbed. I wondered how long it would take. I suppose you'll be wanting one of mine?' He eases himself upright. 'You'll be glad to know that while you've been out mincing around Basra, we've been working like bastards here.'

'What happened, did you run out of Tippex?'

We trade a few more insults as we walk outside to the bank of the Shatt al-Arab. The sky is jet black.

'I'm not kidding, actually,' Will says. 'It's been fucking outrageous. We were malleted by rockets today.'

I realize he's being serious. I'm paying attention now.

'Any casualties?'

'Fortunately not,' he says. 'But three landed inside the wire and a couple of vehicles were fragged.'

'Fuck me, they're sharpening up.' They've had a few cracks at us in the past, but never managed to lob anything inside the compound.

'The brigadier has labelled today Crazy Saturday. It's been absolutely barking. Muqtada al-Sadr's boys have been running riot. So far we've had reports of three of our guys injured and twenty Mahdi Army killed in Basra alone.'

That figure must be way out. We've not reported our stats yet.

'We knew fuck all about it until the first volley of rockets dropped into the palace. When Salamanca Company deployed they got hammered too. They said there were literally gunmen on every corner. The city has gone bananas.'

I nodded. 'We were hit at Orange Two by the world's supply of RPGs and AKs. I kid you not, Will, I thought we were history. The bastards were everywhere.'

'Did you really get shot? I thought you were taking the piss.'

'Yeah, mate, I did.'

'Did it hurt?'

'Not really, just burned a bit.'

'Nice. You're still a wanker though.'

As we walk back into the Det the lads are wide awake but sitting in silence, each of them deep in their own private world. Tom and Ollie are watching *Black Hawk Down*. Vince is writing a letter to his girlfriend, and Taff is staring blankly at the map on the wall. It's like a scene from *One Flew Over the Cuckoo's Nest*. Dan and Rob seem pretty unaffected, but Scotty still looks fairly shaken up by the whole episode. It's hardly surprising.

In time, each of us will have his own thoughts and memories about the ambush, and we'll be able to laugh about it and take the piss. But right now it's still too fresh in our minds. Still too raw.

Dan catches my eye and gestures towards the secure cabinet. I give him the nod and he pulls out the emergency vodka bottle. We're on a two-can rule, but rules are for the guidance of wise men and the blind obedience of fools. What's the worst that can happen? We're disciplined and sent back to the UK? I won't be going anywhere; there's nobody available to replace me. And I can think of worse punishments for the lads right now.

Dan hands out the mugs and passes around a bottle of Coke from the fridge. The team regains the power of speech, but they're exhausted and still in shock.

I reckon it's time for a team talk. I tell them our mission is to protect the innocents, to help those in need, whatever side of the fence they find themselves on. Most importantly, we're impartial. But tonight, all that was thrown back in our faces. I tell them the fact that we all survived is nothing short of a miracle. I can see how dull their eyes still are. I know they're as amazed as I am that we came out of it alive. I tell them our success was almost entirely down to the way they responded. They were fucking brilliant out there. 'No matter what each of you achieves on this tour, and whatever you do from this point onwards, you'll always be able to remember tonight and hold your heads high. Every single one of you cut the mustard out there. They say that it's only when you risk going too far that you find out how far you can actually go. Well, tonight you pulled it out of the bag when it counted, and you did it in style. What more can I say? I am truly proud of you.'

I want them to have a drink, and to talk. To talk to each other, to me, to Will, to the padre, to their families. Talk to the fucking dog if they think it'll help. They need to start getting it out of their system. What we do – on immediate notice to move twenty-four seven, never knowing what's around the corner – puts a formidable strain on us. The pressure is fearsome, it's not sustainable, and everybody needs to decompress.

I raise my glass. 'OK, that's enough chat from me. Here's to you, and the guardian angel that watched over us tonight. May we all live in interesting times.'

We throw back the vodka.

I need to speak to Lucy. But before I do I need to get

my leg checked out. The wound is throbbing again. I'd actually forgotten about it until a couple of moments ago. I ask Will to stay and chat with the team, and to provide a bit of top cover in case an over-zealous duty officer decides to try to stamp out what little morale the boys have left.

I step out into the cool night air.

The Med Centre is buzzing. The medics themselves look completely shagged. They've been treating patients all day, and the corridors are heaving with people wrapped in bandages.

One of the staff sergeants approaches me. These guys are awesome. They are the real deal, the unsung heroes of the armed forces. He takes off his specs and gives me a broad grin.

'Hello, boss, how are you?'

Andy Parker and I served together in Bosnia and then again in a specialist unit a couple of years ago. We catch up on who's been doing what to whom, then get down to business. He asks me what I'm in for.

'As it happens,' I reply, 'I've been shot.'

His expression changes, and before I know it there are medics everywhere and I'm flat out on an operating table.

'Don't worry,' I tell him, 'it's only just pierced the skin. I just need you to clean it up and give me the all-clear.'

I give them a quick rundown on the ambush. One of the young female medics asks if I killed anybody. I tell her I did. She asks how it felt.

I hesitate.

Sensing that this is neither the time nor the place, Andy pipes up. 'Did any of you see that CNN Afghanistan piece yesterday? A reporter was interviewing a load of US Marines. He turns to a sniper and asks, "What do you feel when you shoot a terrorist?" The guy just shrugs and says, "Recoil." Fucking priceless.'

I give him a smile. He knows there's a whole lot more to it than that, and I'm grateful to him for deflecting her question.

Andy undoes my laces and slowly pulls back the tongue of my boot. The bullet comes out with it, leaving a perfect round hole in the front of my shin.

'Sir, if I may say so, you are one lucky, lucky bastard,' he says.

The younger, less experienced medics edge forward to get a better view. I feel like a one-man freak show.

'The heat from the round has cauterized the wound,' Andy continues, talking them through it. 'And there's no damage whatsoever to the bone. I can't believe it. You'll have a nice scar to show the grandchildren, but no lasting damage. Good drills, boss.'

A couple of his mates clean and dress it and I'm back

in business. If I have to get shot again, this is definitely the way to do it.

I take a couple of deep breaths and stroll back over to the Det. I'm not a religious man, but I'm pretty certain that right now somebody up there *is* watching over me. I've only been on the job for five days and already gone down with heat exhaustion, been shot, killed a bunch of enemy militiamen and dealt with a fistful of lethal IEDs. If I'd turned up a couple of days earlier, I'd have had to deal with a suicide bomber too. This is definitely going to be a tour like no other. I don't often reflect on my own mortality, but the more I think about it, the more I'm convinced we go when we're meant to go.

In the meantime, we need all the luck we can get. For every insurgent removed from the food-chain there are five more prepared to take his place. They believe that every single shot fired has Allah's blessing, and a seventy-two-virgin welcome awaits them in the afterlife. That has to give them an edge. Thank fuck they can't hit a horse's arse with a banjo when it comes to firing a rifle.

I walk back into our crew room and the lads are bouncing off the walls. The combination of vodka and adrenalin is working a treat. They've got their second wind and they're now on permanent send, vying for airtime to broadcast their version of events.

Will's in his element, swigging vodka with the boys

and geeing them on. He's a soldier's soldier, a great officer and an even better listener. But then he should be. He's been trained in the dark art of source handling, so when it comes to playing Jedi mind games, he's up there with Yoda. That's obviously how he got Emma to agree to marry him. You definitely wouldn't want to buy a used car off him, but it's good to have a guy like him around.

I sit at the back of the room trading banter and grinning like an idiot. I'm really proud of these guys. I've only known them for a few days, but they really are the business. They come from all sorts of places, but share the same hunger. Some are overachievers in search of a new challenge. Others are on a different kind of journey. Maybe they took a wrong turning after leaving school, or found themselves on the wrong side of the law. Some are from broken homes, and the Army has given them the family they never knew. They've taken it up on its challenge to be the best, and whatever their personal goals once were, each man has a single focus now: keeping his mates alive. It's already forming a bond between us. We can never hope to replicate it when the tour is over, but while we're here, it will be the foundation stone of our existence. That, and killing bombs.

Vince is an easy-going, happy-go-lucky kind of guy, but when riled, he has a fearsome temper. He may look like the Milky Bar Kid, but appearances can be deceiving – he's hard as nails. He did a stretch at Colchester for insubordination and going AWOL, and has earned a reputation as his battalion's bad boy. But when all's said and done, he's a storming bloke.

Unusually, he chose to soldier on when he was released from Collie, though it was too late to do a complete re-gain; his company commander had it in for him big time, and nothing he could do was going to change that. His sergeant major didn't want the responsibility of looking after him either, so he's been seconded from the Cheshires as my infantry escort. He's proved himself from day one, both during the ambush and out on task. He hasn't let us down, and I know he won't. The team is his family now. He's at home here; he's treated with respect. I see something of myself in Vince, and we get on like a house on fire.

Taff is a big man, a lance bombardier seconded from the Royal Horse Artillery. He's a quiet and popular soldier, originally from the South Wales valleys, and he's played rugby for his country at schoolboy and under-twenty-one level. His arms and legs are like railway sleepers and he has a formidable reputation. He also happens to have the world's biggest arse, and the lads never lose an opportunity to remind him of it.

Ollie is a brilliant career soldier; he's also one of the

most determined and resolute men I've ever met. He's a trained sniper and one of my infantry escorts, seconded from the Royal Welch Fusiliers. Unlike some of the others, he's been seconded because he's considered to be one of his battalion's superstars. He's a superb NCO and a natural warrior who I'm certain will make RSM one day.

He's tall, athletic and handsome, clever, articulate and witty – basically, everything any normal bloke would hate in another bloke, though Ollie is saved by the fact that he is crap at pulling women. He just doesn't have a clue how to talk to them. And he's crap at telling jokes: he always starts giggling too early, and by the time he gets to the punchline it's no longer funny.

At twenty, Tom is one of the youngest members of the team. He's the archetypal grey man: he can sit in a crowded room and go unnoticed for days. At first sight you could be forgiven for thinking he's nervous: he's painfully quiet and often struggles to find the phrase he's looking for. But he has one of the sharpest minds I've ever come across, and the heart of a lion. He's also completely unflappable. It's not that he doesn't care about what happens to him or his mates; he just doesn't allow himself to get excited – about anything. He's a good man to have on the team and a calming influence for all of us. Tom is the benchmark when it comes to judging the blokes' morale. If I see he's pissed off, then I know I need to pull my finger out.

The night resonates with the sound of gunfire. Tracer fizzes sporadically across the sky. After tonight, I wonder if I'll ever be fazed by anything again. Until now, I've planned, prepared and mapped out every aspect of my life – a typical Capricorn, my mother would say. But the experiences of the last five days have taught me one huge lesson: life is just too short. There are far too many things over which I have no control. From now on, I go with my gut instinct.

I'm completely hyper. I've been prowling around the palace all night and I just can't seem to relax. I must have covered five miles, just walking around the perimeter walls, trying to get my thoughts in some kind of order.

I'm concerned about the team. There's no EOD policy for soldier welfare after an ambush, but I suspect tonight's shenanigans could have a lasting psychological impact on the boys. If I leave it unchecked, I could end up with a bunch of fruit-loops. I'm probably ten years too late, but time with the trick cyclist should definitely help.

In Northern Ireland we all had to see the shrink at the end of each tour, even if it was a so-called 'ceasefire tour', where there were no tasks. It provided a release. Just spending six months on immediate notice to move can be a highly stressful experience.

I phone the theatre psychiatric nurse. Phil Emerson is a major in the RAMC and obviously a good bloke. You can tell that because I've just woken him in the middle of the night and he's still enthusiastic about talking with me.

I explain my predicament, and he agrees that by ordering each of the team to see him, rather than giving them the choice, there won't be any stigma. The last thing we want is for somebody to feel he's being singled out. Post-traumatic stress is a serious problem and in an EOD team it can surface at any time. I need to do everything I can to ensure that the blokes don't turn into fully fledged nutters.

We hatch a plan. In a couple of days we'll sit around a table with Phil doing the group hug thing, then each of us will have a private fifteen-minute consultation. If anybody needs extra time, they can blame it on him 'taking a phone call' during the consultation.

As I step inside the Det, I know all too well that I've been wandering around sorting out everyone else's problems, yet failing to deal with my own. No wonder my marriage is in a shit state. What sort of a crap husband am I?

But it's the middle of the night. If I phone Lucy now I'll wake the baby and it will only cause another argument. I'll send her an email instead.

8

The mark of your ignorance is the depth of your belief in injustice and tragedy. What the caterpillar calls the end of the world, the Master calls the butterfly.

Richard Bach

9 May 2004: Day 6

I've been awake all night. The call to prayer echoes across the city. '*Allahu Akbar*' rings out four times, then '*La Allah il-la Allah . . .*'

Rob rocks up. He's usually the first one about in the mornings.

'Hello, boss. Fancy a brew?'

'I'd kill for another coffee.'

'Julie Andrews?'

'Madness not to.'

We grab our mugs and go and inspect the vehicles. A couple of the lads have already beaten us to it. The expression on their faces tells its own story. There's a bullet hole in my fuel tank, bullet holes in the wheels, bullet holes in the body and a shit-load more in the cab. The windscreen looks like a spider's web, my door like a colander. My window was shot out completely and I can see daylight through the punctures on Dan's side where the rounds exited. More slugs have gathered like gleaming pebbles in his footwell. One has lodged in the door frame, inches from his head. Another would have taken his foot off, if he hadn't floored the gas pedal. The whole side of the vehicle is riddled with grenade fragments, but the biggest miracle of all is the round that missed the red phosphorus grenade I keep in the door. A centimetre closer to that little rascal and Dan and I would have been toast.

The rest of the lads come over in dribs and drabs and we give every vehicle a thorough going over. Some of the kit has been damaged by small-arms fire but the majority of our equipment is pretty much good to go. We all sit round and relive what happened last night. The big question, of course, is why.

Right on cue, Will comes over to put the meat on the bones.

'Want a brew, Jock?' I ask.

'Yes please, mate. Put me down for a Julie.'

Tom's brow furrows. 'Boss, sorry for asking, like, but

this has been bugging me for days. What the fuck is a Julie Andrews?'

For the rest of the team, this is an open invitation to hurl abuse at the new boy. I let the piss-take run its course before putting him out of his misery. 'White, nun,' I say.

Will begins enlightening us about just how close we came to pushing up the daisies.

'The city went berserk last night, as you don't need me to tell you. Muqtada's boys clashed with British troops right across the city, and with a ferocity we haven't seen for some time. I expect most of you are wondering why. Well, this is what we know so far.

'Two days ago, Piers Morgan, the editor of the *Daily Mirror*, published photographs of alleged Iraqi prisoner abuse at the hands of members of the First Battalion, the Royal Regiment of Fusiliers. We're certain they're forged, but in the aftermath of Abu Ghraib, they're dynamite.

'At Friday prayers in the al-Hawi Mosque, Sheik Abdul- Sattar al-Behadli told three thousand worshippers that a three-hundred-and-fifty-dollar reward would be given for the capture of every British soldier, and one fifty for each one killed. Anyone capturing a female British soldier could keep her as a slave. He also called on them to launch jihad against us here.'

I look around the room. The lads are hanging on Will's every word. The atmosphere is electric.

'He also offered a suitcase full of readies to anyone capturing or killing a member of the Governing Council, the interim administration appointed by our American friends ten months ago.

'Al-Behadli is Muqtada al-Sadr's main man in southern Iraq. This is the first time an anti-occupation activist has publicly offered a reward for the killing or capturing of coalition troops. He kept an AK-47 beside him as he spoke, and was holding what he said were documents and photographs of three Iraqi women being raped at British-run prisons in Iraq. The crowd loved it, as you can imagine. Hundreds of them went on the rampage last night. The Mahdi Army hit the governor's offices and hosed us down with rockets and RPGs here at Brigade HQ.

'It's not much consolation, but you guys weren't the only ones to get nailed; and although it probably doesn't seem like it, you were pretty lucky to have diverted from Red Route. Our reports suggest that there were at least a hundred militiamen waiting for you there, compared to the sixty or so you bumped into on Orange.'

There's a stunned silence.

I still can't believe how close we came to checking out last night. None of us can. Piers Morgan has now accelerated past Muqtada al-Sadr, right to the top of my shit list. There's a rumour that his brother is a serving officer, yet even that didn't dissuade him from putting the lives of our guys at risk. What sort of a man would do that?

9

I think it is well also for the man in the street to realize that there is no power on earth that can protect him from being bombed. Whatever people may tell him, the bomber will always get through. The only defence is in offence, which means that you have to kill more women and children more quickly than the enemy if you want to save yourselves.

Stanley Baldwin, House of Commons, 10 November 1932

Day 6

After Will's little talk, the team is visibly shaken. Each man is lost in his own private thoughts. Then somebody cracks a gag and the place is echoing with laughter again. The sense of camaraderie has returned. It feels as though we've been together for years, rather than just six days.

But beneath the joviality, we all know that the rules have changed. The insurgents have crossed the line. Soldiering is about fighting. It's about killing people before they kill you. But until last night, we weren't here to kill. We were fighting to keep the peace.

Maybe we've been a bit naive. Maybe fighting for peace is as witless as fucking for virginity. Soldiering is dirty, dangerous, ugly work. And if the insurgents want to take the piss, then so be it. Bring it on. From now on, there won't be any pleasantries. They're not getting it both ways.

We begin squaring our kit away. Packing, modifying and re-packing. I thought I was a clued-up operator but I now realize my assault vest is full of very Gucci but totally useless crap that I'm never going to use in a million years. Everything from the designer balaclava to the foot powder gets replaced by ammo, grenades, comms kit, rations, water, a spare pistol and a big fighting knife. All of us have stripped our kit of all pictures and reminders of loved ones too.

I track down a couple of old acquaintances on camp and manage to blag some flash-bangs for our vehicles. If we're stuck in a public order situation, if our vehicles are boxed in by unarmed civilians, they'll be just the job for dispersing the crowd non-lethally.

I arrive back at the Det feeling a bit pleased with myself, only to find I've been massively upstaged by Vince. He's brandishing a Minimi squad assault weapon, and the lads are stood around him marvelling at his new trophy.

'How the fuck did you manage to get hold of one of those?' I ask. 'They're rarer than rocking-horse shit.'

'You're not wrong,' he says proudly. 'And they pack a fuck of a lot more punch. Those little cunts try to take us on now and I'll saw the fuckers in half.'

Bill, an old friend from a former posting, comes over to the Det to run through a bit of skills training. He's a natural warrior and a twenty-year veteran of some of the most extreme combat ever experienced by British forces.

'Now, I don't want to teach you fellas how to suck eggs,' he begins, 'but I'll run through a few drills and skills just so we're all singing from the same hymn sheet.'

He spends the next two hours beasting us, going through every conceivable scenario and the best way to react to it. He sounds like one of the Kray twins; you wouldn't want to turn your back on him. The lads are immediately in awe of him. They stare at him googly-eyed and hang on to his every word.

One of the lads wants a steer on firing the SA80, our assault rifle, from the cab of a vehicle. The weapon is quite long, which means you can't put it into the shoulder and fire through the windscreen. There simply isn't room, and besides, the screen is protected by a metal grate. 'None of us wanted to fire through the windscreen last night in case a bullet ricocheted back at us. So we had to shoot out of the doors instead.'

Bill turns the weapon on its side and rests the butt on top of his shoulder. 'Hold it like this, find your target, and bam, bam, bam.' He grits his teeth and there's an uncomfortable gleam in his eye. 'The first round will go through the mesh and the rest will engage the target.' He puts the weapon down and smiles. 'The only downside is you'll be as deaf as a fucking post afterwards.'

After Bill's lesson I take a stroll across to Brigade HQ. It's time for the CO's morning prayers. The palace ballroom is a noisy, manic place, the nerve centre of British operations in Iraq. Radio traffic booms out of the speakers and live video feeds are playing constantly on plasma screens. The chief of staff and his team are planning ops; his engineers are discussing the reconstruction strategy for southern Iraq; and the press information staff are brainstorming their next media campaign. Everything's done at a furious pace; everyone's shouting; the phones are constantly ringing. It's like the floor of the Stock Exchange, but without the seven-figure bonuses.

Lieutenant Colonel Sanderson is the CO of the Brigade's Engineer Regiment, the unit to which the two counter-terrorist bomb disposal teams have been attached. Because of the tempo of operations, we've still not been formally introduced; this morning is the first opportunity we've had to actually get some face time.

The colonel is the archetypal old-school officer and gentleman. He has the physique of a marathon runner, and looks like he's just run a couple. His slightly pocked face is unshaven and his eyes are blood red. PJ, his adjutant, tells me he's had a virus for the last three days but refuses to go sick. That figures. He exudes the thoughtful self-assurance of a man who's been there and done it all. He's not the type to go sick.

The briefing begins with an intelligence update from the regimental intelligence officer. She talks about last night's events, but her focus is very much geared towards reconstruction, and which parts of the critical infrastructure were hammered by the insurgents. A shed-load of power cables and electricity pylons were destroyed.

The operations officer gives an update on the field squadrons' activities. They're mostly engaged in road-building, water purification and, now, the repairing of power lines. They're also trying desperately to fortify the British Coalition Force bases, which are coming under increasingly sustained mortar and rocket attacks.

Next, the colonel asks for an IED update. The adjutant uses this as an opportunity to introduce me. After the formalities, I brief the group on our recent shenanigans.

I explain that we've been deployed to a number of explosions, rockets and devices over the past four days, and that we've managed to recover some quality forensics linking Shia militants to the rockets and Sunni insurgents to the radio-controlled IEDs. He seems pleased. I talk a little about where I think the threat is heading and what we need to do about it, and it's all going swimmingly until the ops officer decides to try to win me some brownie points.

'You should probably be aware, Colonel, that Chris and his team were ambushed in the Shia Flats area of the city last night. They managed to fight their way out and back to the palace with all three vehicles and only minor injuries.'

The colonel gives me a strange, quizzical look that makes me feel like I've just got caught staying out late. I can feel the rush of blood to my cheeks.

'Three vehicles?' His eyes narrow dangerously. 'How many escort vehicles did you take with you?'

'Er, one, Colonel.'

'Haven't you read the divisional standing orders? All road movements are to be supported by two escort vehicles.'

He gives me an earbashing for putting other people's lives unnecessarily in danger. It pisses me off. I'm being made to look a prize prick in front of a load of strangers for something that's not my fault.

'Sorry, Colonel,' I say. 'I've just arrived in theatre, and tracking down a copy of divisional standing orders hasn't been at the top of my list of priorities. As far as I'm aware, though, IEDD teams have always consisted of three vehicles: an EOD vehicle, an ECM vehicle and a Snatch escort vehicle. That's what I was briefed on when I arrived in theatre, that's the way it is in Northern Ireland, and that's the way it's been here since the ground offensive began. What's more, we're only an eight-man team, which means we don't have the numbers for a second escort vehicle. If you give me more manpower, I'll gladly deploy with another escort vehicle.'

The ball is in his court. But he doesn't see it that way.

After the CO's prayers, PJ takes me to one side.

'That's quite a first impression you made in there, Chris,' he says.

I detect a note of sarcasm.

'Is he always that miserable?' I ask.

'No, he's actually a top bloke. Like any head-shed, he has his moments, but actually he's a cracking guy and a first-class CO. He's just under a phenomenal amount of pressure right now, and the virus has knocked the wind out of his sails a bit. Give it time. By the end of the week you'll like and respect him as much as the rest of us do.'

10

It is foolish to fear what you cannot avoid.

Publilius Syrus

10 May 2004: Day 7

A distant explosion echoes around the palace walls. I check my watch: 0900. Bang on cue. The insurgents have been hitting the logistic resupplies on pretty much a daily basis. Every day between 0800 and 1000 the convoys take the water, rations, ammunition and fuel from Sh'Ibetha to the British bases around the city. The timings never change, and, surprise, surprise, the bad guys have cottoned on to it.

I head back over to the Det and await the tasking message. On average it takes about twenty minutes from the point of explosion to us receiving the 'go'. For a second or two the blokes are all stood around, staring at one another in anticipation. They don't know whether to be apprehensive or excited.

People often ask me why any intelligent human being would willingly go into combat. In truth, the vast majority of British soldiers never experience it. Most soldiers spend their lives training for operations, year in, year out, constantly wondering what it would be like to do it for real. As I said, very few ever get to experience it, but everyone craves it. A soldier not wanting to go into combat would be like a surgeon never wanting to set foot in an operating theatre.

Half an hour passes and the lads are beginning to look really anxious. We need to get out on the ground. Hanging around in the palace is doing nothing for their morale. Too much reflection can be a bad thing. The longer the fear has to take control, the harder it is to overcome.

Thankfully, the call comes in: a patrol has been hit by an IED – another Sunni keyless entry system RCIED. This is exactly what we need; it's like falling off a bike and getting straight back on again. Four blokes from the Royal Engineers rock up to provide the second escort team. This is good news. The extra firepower might come in handy.

Rob pulls me to one side while the lads are throwing on their kit. 'Boss,' he says, 'the target grid is at the inter-section of the Red and Orange Routes. We're going to have to drive straight back through the ambush site.'

Fuck.

British soldiers trust their leaders not to risk their lives unnecessarily. Yet here I am about to lead them straight back into the most dangerous part of the city. I can't help but wonder, is it really worth it? I mean, it's not as if there's a device to dismantle. It's *only* an explosion. There might be a secondary device, but I doubt it. On the other hand, we might just find the evidence – the smoking gun – that leads us to the bomb-maker. We can't just sack it. We owe it to the poor bastards who've just been blown up to get out there and find out who did it.

It's time for a team talk.

'Fellas, there's no easy way of breaking this to you: to get to the bomb scene we're going to have to drive through last night's ambush area. For those of you who have just joined us, welcome to the team, and forgive us if we're a bit jumpy. You've no doubt been briefed on what happened to us last night.'

I turn to the new guys.

'Out of interest, how many of you have been in a fire-fight?'

None.

'Bearing that in mind, and at the risk of stating the obvious, I want you to be aware that being a part of this team means you're now a high-value target. The chances are we're going to get hit, and if we are hit, for the first few minutes or so you're going to be scared shitless. After that, you'll feel really pissed off that they're shooting at you, and then you'll just want to blow their fucking heads off. Your instinct for self-preservation and your natural common sense will tell you that your best chances of surviving are to stay as calm as possible and go with your drills and skills.

'As for the rest of you, you know the score. Personally, all I want to do right now is go back in and hand out some retribution, but as gratifying as it might be to crack a few skulls, it will achieve fuck all. So I want to make it clear that unjustifiable retaliation is not an option.

'But be under no illusions, last night everything changed. Behadli and his crew have upped the ante. They've made their intentions perfectly clear. As far as I'm concerned hearts and minds went out of the window right about the time they fired the first RPG at us. So, no more smiles and waves to the locals; those fuckers can't be trusted. From now on, everybody is to be treated as hostile. From now on, it's big boys' rules. I want to see weapons in the aim and cold, aggressive, hard targeting. If there's a shit-storm out there I want each and every one of you to be in the best possible position to respond. We wanted to show them that there's no greater friend than a British squaddie. Now they need to know there's no worse enemy.'

*

We move a few hundred yards along the Shatt al-Arab before turning west past the hospital and then south on to Orange Route. Life among the shop fronts appears normal, but millimetres below the surface the place is bristling with anger and tension. We're taking no chances: our safety catches are off and our windows and doors are all open, ready to lay down fire the moment things kick off. We scrutinize every single person we pass, and scan houses, donkey carts, piles of rubbish and parked cars for IEDs and shooters. Rob gives us a blow-by-blow commentary on the radio. He's covering the likely threats as well as alerting us to any other potential dramas, including the kamikaze Iraqi drivers screaming towards us on the wrong side of the road.

Now we're driving through a residential area. The smell of shit and rotting garbage lingers in the back of my throat. It makes me want to gag. And as we pass through the ambush area I feel a mixture of intense unease and extreme excitement. The adrenalin is kicking in again.

Children are playing in iridescent green puddles. They smile and wave. We respond with frosty, impassive glares. I feel bad looking at the locals through such cold eyes; it's no wonder we're perceived as arrogant westerners who don't give a shit about their country. But at times like this, we're left with no choice. Only two days ago a British patrol boat was hit on the Shatt al-Arab as it passed under a bridge lined with waving kids. As it slowed, an insurgent moved the kids to one side and dropped a grenade on to the deck. Two young sappers were hit by the blast. In my heart I want to reach out and connect with the Iraqis, but now is not the time. We drop our guard, we die.

Ten minutes later we arrive at the explosion site. The scene is horrific. Body parts are strewn among the crumbled buildings, splintered trees and blast-damaged cars. One man, an Iraqi, has died; virtually all that remains of him is a pool of crimson blood. The troops have taped off the street, but scared and angry locals are massing on the cordon. Some are tending to the wounded, most are screaming. This is chaos.

I find the incident commander, a young Royal Artillery subaltern. He briefs me on the scene, and says that a lone bomber was seen driving away in a car, having detonated the device by remote control. The poor guy looks deeply traumatized, and concerned that he's missed something vital. But he's done a good job. He's established a tight cordon, is treating the casualties and has cleared the area to make sure no one's still in the danger zone. I offer him a cigarette and tell him I'll take over from here. A wave of relief washes over his face.

The team kicks straight into life. Rob is barking commands to the escorts. Tom, Ollie, Taff and Vince check the ICP for secondaries. Scotty's doing his electronic sweep and Dan is prepping the kit in the back of the wagon.

'Clear, boss!' Ollie shouts.

No secondaries. We're good to go.

I enter the zone. I'm leaving the team to do their work while I begin the process of building the situational picture. Every terrorist attack has a tactical design. Every attack is planned with a certain objective in mind. I have to get inside the head of the terrorist and discover what that is. Only then will I be able to determine exactly how and why he planned and carried out this attack.

I stand perfectly still, taking in the scene, while I allow my heart rate those vital few minutes to come back down.

First I identify the seat of the blast. It's 70 metres to my front. The IED was buried beneath a kerb-stone and was detonated as the second vehicle passed. The detonation ripped through the Land Rover and the truck, shattering the windscreens and scattering shrapnel and concrete for hundreds of metres in every direction. The canvas roof covering the soft-skinned Land Rover has been shredded, along with most of the occupants. One of the Brits is critical. Another is probably going to lose an arm. He's eighteen years old. Technically they should both have been killed outright by a blast of this size. It's a miracle they're alive at all.

I need to identify if there are any secondary devices around the seat of the blast. This is a lesson we've learned the hard way. The initial explosion pulls in the first responders and the second device takes care of them too. In August 1979 six members of the Parachute Regiment were killed at Warrenpoint in Northern Ireland when a 500kg bomb hidden under a lorry-load of hay was detonated as the army convoy drove past. Twenty minutes later a second device exploded on a cordon position close to the gate lodge on the opposite side of the road, killing a further twelve soldiers. The IRA had been analysing how the British Army responded to bombing incidents and correctly assessed that the soldiers would set up an incident control point in the nearby gatehouse.

A similar attack occurred in 1996 when scores of civilians were killed by an IRA device in Omagh; they were evacuated to the exact spot where the secondary device was placed. It was the single greatest terrorist atrocity in the history of the Troubles. It's a tactic I have since seen replicated all over the world. It's become a particular favourite with Iraqi insurgents.

I edge my way to the target area. Ollie and Vince have taken up fire positions out to the flanks. I'm searching for secondaries as I take each tentative step.

Absence of the normal. Presence of the abnormal.

I notice shell fragments embedded in the surrounding

houses, blast-damaged windows, and dark blood spattered across the walls.

I reach the seat of the explosion. There are no secondaries. Not this time.

Several minutes have passed. I've identified the terrorist's firing position, his aiming markers and his escape route. I take a closer look at the damaged vehicles and take swabs to determine the explosive used. It's TNT, which figures. He's used three high-explosive artillery shells. Jesus, that's enough to destroy a small town. This guy's obviously not concerned about slotting innocent Iraqis. Or maybe it's the Shias he's not bothered about. Yes, that's it. This is a Sunni bomber. Somebody who's equally happy killing Shias as he is British soldiers.

I continue my search. There's some litter at the firing point. Good, I should be able to gather some forensics from it. Then the real nugget: a fragment of circuit board with electrical wires protruding from it – the remains of the bomb's improvised firing circuit. I also find a small piece of plastic moulding, part of the case for the radio-controlled keyless car entry system.

As I make my way back to the ICP I stop and take in the mayhem around me. I wonder how many more British soldiers are going to be killed before we find the bastards who did this. The clock is ticking.

11

What lies behind us and what lies before us are small matters compared to what lies within us.

Ralph Waldo Emerson

Day 7

Later, when we're back at the palace, I call Lucy. We've not spoken for a couple of days and I'm desperate to hear her voice. She's distant, I can tell that immediately. But it's not until we end the call that the full magnitude of what she's told me actually starts to sink in.

Something's died in her. Hope. Hope that I'm going to return safely to her and the girls.

Lucy hadn't seen the email I sent her last night before news of the ambush reached 11 EOD HQ. Rules are rules, and if you're injured, whether it's a scratch or a sucking chest wound, your unit is informed immediately. She saw the silhouettes of my OC and his wife at the back door. They'd come to tell her I'd been shot – that's all they knew. The bell rang but she didn't want to speak to anyone.

She immediately assumed the worst and became completely hysterical. There was nothing more to say, as far as she was concerned. She'd been crying for hours, clutching our wedding photo, but her tears have long since run dry. She feels as if someone has ripped her heart out and torn it into a million pieces. Nothing she's ever experienced comes close to the crushing fear she's being made to endure right now. Her life has been stolen from her. She has never felt so vulnerable and powerless.

If only I'd phoned her and explained everything last night, instead of trying to write it in some cryptic email she didn't even know I'd sent, I'd have saved her from this. What was I thinking?

She can't go on like this any more. She can't go on having no control over the events that are shaping her life. The only way to survive is to work on the assumption that I'm not coming home this time. She's already planning a life without me.

I go for a stroll around the lake. I want to be distracted, to think about anything but Lucy, but all I can think about is the conversation we've just had. It's crucifying me. The thought that there might come a day when she is no longer at my side is too painful to bear. But I won't give up on her. I'm going to return to Lucy and the girls in one piece, and I'm going to make them proud.

As I make my way back over the dusty roads towards the Det, I notice Scotty standing alone, staring out over the Shatt al-Arab. It's not that he looks unhappy, but his reaction to my approach troubles me. I've known him over ten years, yet when I ask him if everything's OK, he responds as if I'm a complete stranger.

The rest of the lads are a bit shaky after our return trip to the ambush area, but on the whole they're pretty philosophical. Different people react in different ways to extreme circumstances.

The first time I had my head read was during the psychiatric evaluation phase of my ATO course. According to the chief shrink, the head of Army Psychiatry,

Candidates have to be of at least bright intelligence, satisfied with their careers, wholly identified with ammunition work, free from serious personal worries, in good physical and mental health, methodical and courageous, fairly adventuresome, thoughtful and decisive and free from group dependency. The ideal operator would also be socially at ease, have good impulse control and not suffer from nervousness or hypochondria, self-doubt, delinquent traits or perfectionism. Furthermore, an operator has to have an analytical mind. He has to be able to receive, digest and analyse information, then produce a response at the sweep of a finger.

I remember thinking at the time, that's me fucked then. I won't even get through the door.

I'd read somewhere that I should treat my first interview with the trick cyclist as if I was dealing with a bomb: I was going to be placed in an unfamiliar situation, I wouldn't have a clue what to expect, and I'd have to be extremely guarded because if I fucked it up it was going to be the end of my career.

The tactic worked.

But it's only now that I'm in Iraq, six years later, that I've come to truly appreciate the importance of the military shrink. I've been here less than a week and already I can see cracks appearing in the team. Whatever happens, I can't afford to let those cracks get any bigger.

Fortunately for us, Phil Emerson, the theatre psychiatrist I woke up yesterday morning, has come to speak to us today.

'At some point,' he says, 'everyone experiences difficult or stressful events in their lives. Sometimes these can be difficult to come to terms with, or at the very least highly distressing. All of us think we can cope, and some of you probably can, but you won't know for sure until you're back home. That's when it really kicks in – the moment you try to pick up where you left off. That's when you'll realize you're fucked. But by then, of course, it's too late.

'The reaction of the person to the event, whatever it may be, is dependent upon many things, such as the nature of the event, the person's state of mind and the support they receive from their family, friends and unit. 'Everybody has his own way of responding to difficult or traumatic events, and different people react to the same event in many different ways. There's no right or wrong way to feel. But, it may help you to know how others have reacted in similar situations.'

As agreed, Phil then sets the scene with a brief on the psychological responses of soldiers during combat in WW2, Vietnam and the Falklands. It works a treat. Every case history strikes a chord with the blokes. Every man in the room can totally identify with what's being said. Phil talks about the thoughts and emotions that have gone through the minds of the generations of soldiers who have fought before us: confusion, shock, fear, dread, family, exhilaration, anger, lucidity, aggression, gratification. It's kind of ironic really. These guys might be the Playstation generation, but psychologically they're just the same as the guys who were getting shellshock in the trenches on the Somme.

After the big group therapy session, which went swimmingly, each of the blokes has a private fifteen-minute interview. Each man gives his own account of what happened; some struggle to open up, others are able to express their feelings with disarming honesty. Later, we'll all be able to go away and mull over the events privately, and over time the wounds will start to heal. Scotty in particular looks as if the weight of the world has been lifted from his shoulders.

But the euphoria is short-lived. The palace is rocked by a large explosion. It's close. Outside the wire, but still close. I run outside and check the sky for clouds. Sometimes, when the cloud base is low, the blast wave can bounce off it and thus travel further, but the sky is awesomely clear. That means the explosion is really close – within half a mile of camp. The target is almost certainly another British patrol.

We start rolling out of the gates the instant the tasking message comes through. The cordon is only 300 metres from camp. At least we're not going to find any nasty surprises in our ICP: it's over-watched by the front sangar, the large fortified watchtower in front of the palace that looks north along the riverside cornice. Because the sentries are watching the area constantly, I know there aren't going to be any hidden secondary devices.

This is going to be a quick and dirty job.

We head out of camp, sirens wailing, and skirt along the riverside promenade towards the target area. We pass a huge children's playground on our left and then the Accident and Emergency Hospital. As the road splits, we come to rest and set up the ICP just before a bridge about 50 metres away.

It's complete chaos.

I grab the incident commander, a young corporal involved in the attack, and ask him to fill me in. He tells me the Cheshires' mobile patrol had been travelling north out of Basra Palace, along the same route we've just taken, and as the rear Snatch vehicle passed over the bridge, the device detonated. 'The Snatch vehicle was hit by a massive wave of blast and fragmentation from the artillery shell. Three of the lads were seriously injured. One of the poor bastards had his bollocks blown clean off.'

The casualties have been casevaced to Shai'ba Military Hospital, and with no threat of secondaries, we can afford to crack straight on.

We race through the area and begin investigating the scene. We manage to identify some quality intelligence, including fragments of a keyless car entry system and a witness who tells us two Iraqi males were seen running away immediately after the explosion.

They threw the transmitter into the Shatt al-Arab and escaped by boat, along with one of their mates, to the opposite bank.

When we return from the task I sit outside with Will and go through the chronology of the incident. The adrenalin is still pulsing through me; I'm on permanent send. He selects his first cigarette of the conversation and begins puffing away as though his life depends upon it.

'Any Iraqis injured?' he asks.

He's thinking what I'm thinking. The Sunnis carried out an attack yesterday in a Shia enclave and didn't give a shit about how many Shias they killed, because they hate them just as much as they hate us. And today, there's an attack in a Sunni area without a single Iraqi victim. Why? Because they were warned to stay away. What's more, all the eyewitnesses have suddenly developed amnesia.

I nod. 'This must be the work of Basra's northern Sunni bomber team.'

'What about tech-int? Did you recover much?'

I give him a grin. 'Shit-loads. We've got some key IED components: the circuit board and parts of the keyless entry system casing. We also managed to get a swab from a gorse bush near the seat of the blast. One of the Bravos must have nicked himself on a thorn while he was placing the IED. Couldn't have happened to a nicer guy.'

'What about the transmitter?'

'A couple of divers from a Royal Engineers search team are trawling the Shatt al-Arab right now.'

'Nice work, mate,' he says, still puffing away. 'But I'll tell you something, it wasn't this busy before you arrived. I think you're fucking jinxed.'

I think he's right. Over the next few days the pace of operations goes off the scale. We're being run ragged by the bombers and there's fierce fighting on the streets. The Shias seem to be having a competition with the Sunnis to see who can kill the most people. It's like the Wild West. We're being tasked to incident after incident and we're gathering shed-loads of forensics, but as each day passes there are more and more civilian casualties. And they're not alone. Our troops are getting hit every day too. It's only ever a matter of time before another British soldier is killed.

One of the networks we've been concentrating on is Behadli's. Up until recently we didn't have a great deal on them, but that all changed a few days ago when one of our snouts tipped us off about the location of a Shia weapons cache – in the back of a known Mahdi Army member's garden. We hit the house in the middle of the night and went to town on it, inside and out. We recovered mortars, shells, explosives, detonators, even a perfectly preserved anti-tank guided missile. Since then, we've been tasked to several other Mahdi Army caches including heavy weapons and 107mm rockets.

We're piecing together the network. It's painstaking stuff, but the bombers' days are definitely numbered. It's only a matter of time before they get the knock on the door.

12

You have to protect yourself from the sadness. Sadness is very close to hate. Let me tell you this. This is the thing I learned. If you take in someone else's poison – thinking you can cure them by sharing it – you will instead store it within you.

Michael Ondaatje, *The English Patient*

17 May 2004: Day 14

Everybody is doing his best to look alert, but most of us aren't making a very good job of it. There's a brilliant sunrise this morning and it has the makings of an achingly beautiful day. But the team's exhausted.

The tempo of operations has been fearsome. We're getting at least one task a day, and at all times of day and night. Basra Province is some 7,500 square miles, with over two and a half million inhabitants, and Basra itself is Iraq's second largest city. We're the only IEDD team operating here.

I think we're all starting to feel the strain.

Last night I slept on the roof of the Det, staring up at the crescent moon, thinking about my family. The homesickness is kicking in big time now. I pulled out my folded black and white photo of Lucy. I'd removed it from my kit after the ambush, but replaced it the next day. I'm not giving it up. It's the one treasure I still have. Her beautiful smiling face seemed so remote. I know things will never be the same again. How could they be?

I called her the moment I thought she and the girls might be awake. I wanted to hear her voice; I wanted to picture the light in her eyes; I wanted her to know that I love her and that everything is going to be OK. But when she answered, it was like a signal from a distant planet. Then I realized what's been missing from our exchanges for so long: she doesn't laugh any more. I could hear the sadness in her, and it broke my heart.

I endured the long silences at the other end of the line for a few minutes more, then decided to end her ordeal.

'I love you,' I told her. 'Please give the girls a kiss from me.'

As I hung up I thought I heard her tell me she loves me too. My heart missed a beat. I put the receiver back to my ear.

'Lucy? Are you there?'

She'd gone.

Now I'm sitting with the lads, conscious that my mood might be rubbing off on them. But whatever self-pity I'm feeling is brought to an abrupt halt. A call comes in to a command-wire IED on a bridge about 10 miles north of Basra. A Danish EOD team had originally been tasked to the incident, but it seems the operator drove away when he realized it was going to be complicated. I can't believe it. The Danes are good soldiers and even better operators.

And right now I need 'complicated' like a hole in the head.

'This'll be one to tell your grandchildren,' a staff officer says as he waves us off.

'The boss won't have any grandchildren if he's dead,' one of the lads quips from the back of the Land Rover.

Where would we be without a bit of good old-fashioned black humour at a time like this?

The gates swing open and we hammer our way through the city. Basra is hot and angry today. The tension is so thick I can taste it. There are groups of agitated Iraqis on every street corner. A thousand eyes follow our every move through a veil of *shisha* pipe smoke and steam from hot, sweet *chai*. We head north, across the river and into a wasteland of dried mud banks and deserted Marsh villages. We're fully focused now, both hands on our weapons, ready to respond to whatever comes our way.

'Two hundred metres, boss,' Rob shouts over the radio.

Here we go. We're approaching the objective. Saddam's contempt for the Marsh people still hangs over the village like a shadow. The buildings that haven't been reduced to rubble are pocked with bullet scars. Splintered telegraph poles lean at ominous angles, their severed wires long since stripped for sale. The air is heavy with the smell of shit and rotting detritus.

We pull into the ICP. The incident commander, a Household Cavalry second lieutenant, tells us that two devices were emplaced this morning by black-clad Shia insurgents. They put a demolition charge under each of the bridge's support beams and then ran command wire from each of them to a single firing point. On the plus side, the maniacs dropped one of the charges in the river in the process. One down, one to go.

'Where's the firing point?' I ask.

'There.' He gestures towards a raised bank about 500 metres downstream. 'We've obviously not been anywhere near it, but I checked it out through my binos. They've used waterproofed command wire and run it down one of the pillars and along the river bed.'

I see a hint of admiration in his eyes. I'm not surprised. I don't know whether to hate these bastards or be in awe of their ingenuity.

'And where's the charge?'

'Underneath that panel.' This time he points to a section of the bridge immediately in front of us. 'Are we a bit close? This is all rather new to me . . .'

The young subaltern has sited us about 20 metres away from one of the bombs. We're completely exposed and overlooked. There could be a hidden secondary anywhere in the surrounding debris and the first we'd know about it would be the flash of white light. Something icy crawls down my sweaty spine.

'IED, boss!' Vince yells. He's found the device under the bridge.

'Roger that. Stand by. We're going to pull back.'

Rob and I quickly scan the map.

'We'll go for those buildings at the crossroads,' I say. 'They'll be able to see diddly squat if we set up there.'

The team kicks into life. Once we're established, I grab the young officer and get to the bottom of the Danish EOD caper. The operator said he wouldn't be able to reach the device without climbing equipment, and because they don't hold any, he thought there would be no point in hanging around.

'That's fine,' I say. 'Except for one tiny detail: we don't hold any either.'

This is taking the piss. The Dane should at least have had the decency to give me a handover brief. I've got no idea what he's already cleared or where he's been. Maybe he's already identified tripwires or an RCIED. I don't have a clue, and nor does the poor subaltern. But at least *he* had the decency to hang around.

I'm going to have to go in blind.

I get on the radio to Brigade and request a high-risk search team to locate and isolate any command wires. The Royal Engineers search teams have shot to the top of my Christmas card list over the past week, but today they're otherwise engaged. There's a huge riot going on in Basra and Brigade's called a lockdown.

'What about a heli?' I can hear the tone in my voice; it sounds suspiciously like pleading. 'Can I at least have a heli? I need climbing equipment to get to the device. And aerial top cover.'

'We don't hold any climbing equipment in theatre. And besides, even if we did, we wouldn't be able to get it to you. There's a shortage of airframes and it's too hot to fly.'

I try to fight back familiar feelings of futility. A lack of assets . . . There are plenty of bloody assets in Northern Ireland, where there is currently a ceasefire and no bombs, but none here in Iraq. What would happen if one of us got injured here today? Would they send assets then? I suspect not. One of us would almost certainly have to end up dead before support arrived. Fucking politicians. What's the point of being here if we don't have the tools for the job?

We're on our own. We're just going to have to do the best we can.

I leave the device to soak for a while and make my way towards the bridge under the fierce gaze of the desert sun. I need to get some eyes on. It's time for a manual approach.

The stench from the river makes me gag. The sewage from the village empties into it and only washes down into the Shatt al-Arab when the rains come. We're now well into the hot season. And I'm going to have to wade through it.

I glance across at Dan. Needless to say, he's thinking pretty much what I'm thinking. This is the mother of all shit creeks. And we're not alone. I take one last look along the deserted street behind me. Back at the ICP my team are bent double, pissing themselves with laughter over what I'm about to do.

I don't get paid enough for this.

I'm in the river and I've found a wire. I make two careful cuts. By breaking it at a safe distance from the main explosive charge, I should be removing the firing switch and taking control of the device. I only wish I could be a hundred per cent certain that this is the command wire. There might be hundreds of them along this river bed.

As I look back towards the bridge, I spot the main charge on one of the crossbeams. I swear it's been placed there to taunt me. It's in a bastard of a position, virtually impossible to get to without the right gear.

My combats are drenched in shit and I've reached an impasse. But I have an idea.

The Household Cavalry are the cream of the cream. They're recruited as much for their charm as for their leadership skills. And I'm desperate here. I ask the sub-altern to find me a boat. Amazingly, he conjures up something and comes paddling along the river in it about five minutes later. It's more a hollowed-out tree than a canoe; it's like something out of *The Last of the Mohicans*. Training can teach you to cope with stress, but it can't teach you improvisation. As far as I'm concerned, this guy is the dog's bollocks.

I need somebody to steady the canoe while I climb under the bridge, but bomb disposal is supposed to be a single-man risk. I ask the subaltern if he'd be up for it. Basically, I'm asking him to take me directly below the bomb so that I can take it apart by hand. He'd be no more than a few metres away from it.

'Delighted,' he says. 'I'm going to be dining out on this for years.'

I give him a grin. Whatever else he picked up behind the Eton bicycle sheds, you can't fault this boy's style.

I take a long, slow, deep breath as we slide beneath the shadow of the bridge.

Symmetry wasn't uppermost in the mind of whoever designed this thing. It looks as if the builder was given a job lot of RSJs, 2-ton steel plates and hand rails, and told to get on with it. It's only about 15 feet high, but that's plenty high enough to make my life difficult. The heat is fearsome and the stanchions are covered in a thick coating of grease. This is the proverbial slippery slope. No wonder the bastards dropped one of the devices into the Oggin.

The canoe provides just enough of a platform for me to reach up and heave myself on to the nearest girder. I take another deep breath, swing my legs up and twist my body so that I'm lying on top of it.

Now I'm up close, I can see that the grease is almost all that's holding the bridge together. I wonder whether my greatest threat is the bomb or the entire structure collapsing in a cloud of rust. Either way, this is definitely not the time to hang around.

Sweat stings my eyes. I take a moment to rub it away. At first glance, the conventional demolition charge looks like a church bell. It's only a metre away, staring at me. I shimmy along the girder, trying to ignore the rasp of the rivets against my skin, until I'm hunched over it.

The top end of the foot-long cylinder – the business

end – is sealed by a concave copper disc, beneath which the explosive is packed. It's been modified with the command wire, which trails down into the river from the detonator at the base of the device. When it's triggered, the explosive transforms the disc into a fist-sized projectile of molten copper, travelling at well over a kilometre a second. It'll smack straight through the metal panels that form the road surface and into the underbelly of the patrol vehicle passing above it.

Keeping a firm grip on the girder, I reach down to my thigh pocket, unbutton it and slide out my hand-entry kit. I remove my snips and edge the jaws slowly towards the exposed wire. The only way I can be certain it's the right one is if I can see where it joins the bomb's circuit. No joy there: the circuit is inside the cylinder. If I cut the wrong wire and it turns out to be a collapsing circuit, I'll be vaporized. The shockwave will crush my entire cardiovascular system. Milliseconds later, the skin will be torn from my body by the blast wave and my bones will shatter and fragment. Then, before what's left of me hits the water, it will be engulfed in a ball of flame. It won't be good news for the subaltern either. Best I don't fuck it up then.

I breathe out, rub the sweat from my eyes one more time, and ease the tip of the cutters forward until they're touching the wire. Focusing hard, aware only of the steady beat of my heart, I open my palm and gently squeeze the jaws shut.

I feel rather than hear it snap. Then nothing. It's one of my favourite sensations in the world.

The bomb is dead.

I climb back down into the boat and remove my helmet. A faint breeze dries the sweat on my skin. I step on to the bank and make my way to the firing point.

As we're packing up, preparing to head home, a woman emerges from her house to hang out some washing. She grapples with the line and her *burqa* slips, revealing a delicate heart-shaped face and striking almond eyes. We find ourselves gawking, more out of curiosity than anything else. It's rare to see an Iraqi woman's face, and there's something intensely moving about her demure beauty in this devastated landscape.

She's hurriedly trying to cover herself up when her husband appears. He sees the team staring at her and goes ballistic. He rushes towards her, grabs her long, dark hair with one hand and punches her square in the mouth with the other. She recoils, stumbles back into the gate and slips to the ground, trembling, pleading. He's having none of it. This is a matter of honour. He stands over her, his fists clenched, and begins the most frenzied attack I have ever seen on a human being. He rains down blow after blow. When he finally tires, he steps back and runs his blood-stained hands through his dark, sweaty hair and allows himself a look of satisfaction. I'm not sure whether it's for his benefit or ours.

But he's not finished yet. In fact he's hardly begun. He begins kicking her repeatedly in the head and stomach. I can feel my own stomach clenching, as hers must be, and bile gathers in the back of my throat. And just when I think things can't possibly get any worse, her robe slips further, revealing a bump.

Fucking hell, she's pregnant.

I look at the team and their expressions carry the same message: *Boss, do something.* I feel the weight of this barbaric world on my shoulders. I'm not seeing her tear- and blood-stained face any more; I'm seeing Lucy's, then Sophie's and Ella's. I want nothing more than to wade in and give this fucker the beating of his life.

But I know what will happen if I do. It just isn't an option. I'm powerless.

Dan and I don't exchange a single word for the entire journey back to the palace. Instead, I find myself replaying those brutal images in my mind, over and over again. I'm racked with guilt. I've never felt such a coward in my life.

Back in the Det, the team sit around, sullen and silent. I've got some explaining to do.

'Fellas, I know we're all reeling from what we witnessed out there today. I want you to know why I didn't lift a finger.

'Last year, shortly after the ground offensive, two squaddies patrolling the streets of Basra stopped to chat with an eleven-year-old girl. There was nothing improper or unusual about their conversation; they were just passing the time of day. Unfortunately her dad didn't see it that way.

'The soldiers could hear the kid screaming as they stood helplessly outside the house. The following day they saw her again. She'd been beaten black and blue. They decided to dish out a bit of justice of their own. They waited for the father to appear and gave him a seriously good kicking.

'After today, I'm sure we all know just how they felt. But I'm pretty certain they wouldn't have laid a finger on the little bastard if they could have predicted what he was going to do next. The dad grabbed his daughter and cut her throat.'

I pause.

'He said he did it to save his honour.'

No one's moving a muscle, but their eyes are still burning with anger and distress.

'The team is not here to play judge and jury,' I add quietly. 'We've got a job to do. Nothing more, nothing less.'

13

There are only two ways to live your life. One is as though nothing is a miracle. The other is as though everything is a miracle.

Albert Einstein

19 May 2004: Day 16

It's only eight thirty, but the air is already hot enough to strip paint off a door frame. My face feels like somebody's holding a hairdryer to it. We're belting down IED Alley on blues and twos, weaving our way past a succession of kamikaze drivers and the world's biggest collection of donkey carts. Herds of sheep are being coaxed between them by cadaverous old farmers. Stallholders line the road, staring at us through cold eyes.

Whoever designed the Basra traffic system must have been banged off their heads. Junctions appear randomly, out of nowhere, and every few seconds a car travelling in the opposite direction suddenly veers straight into our path. It's as if they're goading us, challenging us to a game of chicken. Back home, anyone with a flat tyre tends to pull over to a place of safety. Here, they just grind to a halt in the middle of the fast lane and crack on with the wheel change regardless.

I'm on top cover for this task – just for a change of scenery. Vince and I are in the front vehicle, driven by Taff. I'm facing backwards and Vince is covering the arcs to our front, our heads and upper bodies exposed above the Snatch's parapet. We scan the flat-roofed buildings like hawks for snipers and roadside bombs.

There's a burst of fire to our right flank. Here we go again. But this time I'm ready for it. There's no panic, no crippling fear, just a wave of adrenalin as I pan my weapon round and mentally prepare myself to unleash hell.

'Small-arms fire!' Rob yells into his radio. 'Two hundred mikes quarter right!'

I swivel instantly to the source of the shooting, but instead of black-clad insurgents I see a bride and groom stepping out of a tent followed by scores of men in *dish-dashas* and *shemaghs*. The wedding party fires another long celebratory burst into the air to honour the matrimonial union of the two families.

'Stand down, stand down. It's a wedding party.'

Jesus. I take a deep breath.

It's not long before we encounter our next challenge. We need to cross the intersection but the traffic is full-on, and it's moving at high speed. Trucks and cars are screaming past us, and nobody's letting us out. The drivers leer at us as they charge past, their version of the one-fingered salute. It's soon getting beyond funny. We need to get to the bomb scene. These maniacs are taking the piss. They have developed a longstanding immunity to sirens and flashing blue lights. The majority of them seem to have little respect for anybody or anything. Their deference is reserved for tribe, religion and country. As members of the coalition, we're way down the food-chain, alongside the maggots and floating turds.

Suddenly, and without warning, the deadlock is broken as Taff decides to pull out. It's not one of his sharpest moves, I have to say. The volume of traffic is still outrageous and he only manages to make it a few feet before coming to an involuntary halt. We're half on and half off the main drag. It's the world's lousiest parking space. Scores of cars and trucks are dodging and weaving, fists pressed to their horns as they dart around us. It's a miracle we've managed to avoid a collision so far.

Just when I think things can't get any worse, one of the kamikazes decides he's going to take the game to the next

Right: March 2004. Teaching Colombian EOD operators how to defeat improvised explosive devices (IEDs) allegedly provided to Colombian terrorists by the Provisional IRA (PIRA).

Left: Me (*centre*) with my syndicate of Colombian EOD operators. The two operators on the front row were later murdered by Revolutionary Armed Forces of Colombia (FARC) terrorists in separate IED attacks.

Below: Having 'disrupted' the device using the robot, one of the Colombian EOD operators prepares to make the 'long walk' to the IED.

Right: The team's vehicles parked outside the Det in Basra Palace. The 'Snatch' Land Rover is parked next to the two six-wheel-drive EOD vehicles.

Left: The team. Our motto: 'Damned if you do, damned if you don't.'

The view of Basra Palace – Brigade HQ – from the eastern bank of the Shatt al-Arab waterway. I spent many long hours here, sitting on the edge of the bank, drinking brews with Will.

DAY 4 (7 May 2004). The view as I approached a bank of 107mm rockets aimed at Divisional HQ. The rockets were wired into a timed circuit, but the timer had stuck fast. If they had launched at this point, I would have been fried alive by the back-blast.

Me neutralizing the 107mm rockets aimed at Divisional HQ. The high-explosive warheads are designed to detonate on impact, causing the rocket casing to fragment into over 1,200 deadly pieces, each travelling at twice the speed of sound.

Above: DAY 5: The Hayy al-Shuhda area of South Basra, where the team was ambushed on 8 May 2004. The white dots represent the two men in *dish-dashas* whose sudden movement alerted us to an impending attack, the red dots represent the Mahdi Army ambush positions, and the black bars signify our team's vehicles. Dan and I were in the middle vehicle.

Below and right: Fighting erupted all around us; bullets were flying everywhere, ricocheting off the ground and the surrounding buildings. It was only because we'd received similar training to these soldiers (*below and right*) that we survived the ambush that night.

Above: An armoured Bucher Duro 6x6 similar to our EOD vehicle. Before the ambush I used to keep a smoke grenade and a red phosphorus grenade in my door shelf. That all changed after one of the bullets came straight through the door within inches of the phosphorus grenade. Had the bullet hit it, we'd have been toast.

Below: Going through vehicle anti-ambush drills with members of my troop in Britain before I deployed. When it happened for real, the adrenalin and tension in my stomach made me feel momentarily trapped and sick with dread.

Left: DAY 18: Feeling exposed and vulnerable. Behadli and his Mahdi Militia have just tried to target me for the first time with a radio-controlled IED in North Basra.

Right: An image of the radio-controlled IED taken with the wheelbarrow's on-board camera immediately before we shot it with a disruptor.

Above: The device the Mahdi Army used to target me the first time. The soldier who found the device told me the container was made of cardboard. It was only when I came face to face with it that I realized it wasn't.

Left: The container held over ten kilograms of high explosive.

The bridge command-wire IED task north of Basra. The insurgents tried to plant devices on two bridges but dropped the first one in the river while they tried to emplace it. Location (*top and above*) and detail (*left*) of the main explosive charge under the bridge.

Left: The wheelbarrow robot remotely neutralizing an IED. The 'barrow' is a three-foot-high, 300kg tracked vehicle with an extendable robotic arm mounted on the chassis which can be fitted with a wide selection of disruptor weapons. It's saved thousands of lives.

Above: Dan and I collecting evidence from a bomb scene in Basra. The majority of explosions in the city were caused by radio-controlled keyless car-entry system IEDs.

Above: DAY 15: This young trooper from the Household Cavalry came within a whisper of losing his life. While he was on top-cover his vehicle was hit by a roadside IED. A razor-sharp chunk of bomb casing embedded itself in the butt of his rifle. It knocked him off his feet, and destroyed the weapon completely. Had he not been holding his rifle properly, the fragment would probably have taken his head clean off.

Below: The 107mm rockets and fuses we found on the bank of the Shatt al-Arab.

level. With a look of cold defiance, he heads straight towards us. He can't be more than 50 metres away. I hold up my hand, gesturing for him to stop, but it's no use. This guy's on a mission – he's probably doing about 60 mph now.

'He's going to write off the Rover,' Vince says.

'Fuck the Rover,' I reply.

I'm not at my most eloquent right now, but the damage he'll cause to our Snatch is the least of my worries. If he connects, we'll all be killed.

He's almost on top of us.

Fuck it. This is serious. We need to do something. *Now*.

I lower my rifle, deliberately enough to leave him in no doubt about what's going to happen next, then bring it back into my shoulder and aim it straight at his face. I scream at him to stop.

'Whatever happens, Vince,' I say, 'don't shoot this maniac until I tell you to.'

Twenty metres.

I disengage the safety. 'Stand by . . .'

Fifteen.

I place my finger on the trigger.

'FUCKING STOP!' I yell in one last desperate attempt to make him come to his senses.

He does. Just as I'm about to apply second pressure, he slams on his brakes and pulls hard right, sending his car into a flat spin. He rebounds off another vehicle, darts into the adjacent lane and screeches to a standstill.

Vince and I look at each other, amazed. How the hell did he miss us?

We get ready to go and check him out, but as we're about to step down from the Rover a huge truck comes screaming down the carriageway and piles straight into the back of him. There's a huge bang and a screech of tortured metal. Dust and smoke fill the air. The kamikaze's car is catapulted into a ditch.

I think I've had bad days, but Jesus, this guy has redefined the term. I find myself praying for the poor bastard under my breath. What's left of his vehicle is well and truly mangled.

'Let's fuck off out of here!' one of the lads shouts. 'Come on, go, go, go!'

'We're not going anywhere,' I say. 'That guy's going to need stitching back together.'

But once again, the lads are right and I'm wrong. As the dust settles, the Iraqi climbs unsteadily out and lights a cigarette. There's not a scratch on him.

Having screamed through the city with pedals planted firmly to the metal, we finally make it to the scene of the explosion, an area known by its designation on our military maps, Blue 19. It's just on the edge of Qadimah, where the thieves' market sells IED components at bargain prices.

I'm met by a female officer from the RMP. Her petite manicured hands are still trembling and her warm blue eyes are fighting to shut out the images that are replaying over and over in her mind.

She and her team were on their way back from Shai'ba in an eight-vehicle convoy. As they headed through the urban wasteland of northern Basra towards Blue 19, the seventh vehicle – her vehicle – was engulfed by the blast and hit by hundreds of fragments from a high-explosive artillery shell detonated in a drain beside the road. The truck was sent careering across the road and was a complete write-off, but both she and her driver emerged unscathed.

This is the latest in a line of astonishing things I've witnessed over the past two days. The Sunni bomber teams have been hitting us like men possessed with their keyless car entry system RCIEDs, and the Shias have been doing their best to keep up. Yet not one of our troops has been killed or seriously injured.

Yesterday a young trooper from the Household Cavalry came within a whisper of losing his life. He'd been pulled up by the sergeant major of B Squadron that morning for monging it – being shoddy out on the ground – and was given the rifting of his life. 'When you go out of those gates, you'd better fucking start switching on, Macintyre,' he told him. 'And when you're on top cover, I want to see both hands on the rifle and your weapon in the shoulder. Otherwise there'll be more fucking dramas than the Second World War.'

Macintyre's ears must still have been ringing later in the day when he was providing top cover in the lead vehicle of a four-vehicle convoy travelling along Route Topeka, just south of Basra. They had just been waved through a police checkpoint when one of the patrol noticed the Iraqi coppers flashing their lights at the civilian cars behind them, aiming to stop them entering the road. Instead of having his weapon resting on the roof of his vehicle, as he had done every day previously, Trooper Macintyre had pulled it firmly into his shoulder. As his vehicle passed a lone palm tree in the central reservation, there was a blinding flash and shards of white-hot shrapnel shot past his head at warp speed. A fraction of a second later, a razor-sharp chunk of bomb casing embedded itself in the butt of his rifle. It knocked him off his feet, and destroyed the weapon completely. But if he hadn't taken his RSM's threats seriously that morning, it would have taken his head clean off.

14

Human nature will be the last part of Nature to surrender to man.

C. S. Lewis

Day 16

It's late evening but the sun's still blazing. I'm sitting on the edge of the pontoon, watching the bee-eaters and kingfishers dart through the date plantations, captivated by their mesmerizing choreography. For a moment I'm somewhere else. Somewhere far away from here.

But not for long. I feel the thunderous roar before I hear it. The molecules of air around me have ganged up and decided to use me as a punch bag. Seconds later there's a deafening explosion and a flash of white light. The blast wave hammers the air out of my lungs and makes me gasp for breath. There's another ear-splitting whoosh, followed by a second thunderous explosion. I'm momentarily blinded. Bright, kaleidoscopic shapes run riot on the back of my eyelids.

It's time I was somewhere else.

I start running towards the Det. I run hard, low and fast across the waste ground, using the ranks of ISO shipping containers as cover. I'm running faster than I've ever run before. I'm running for my life.

One hundred metres.

For a couple of seconds, there's nothing but silence. And then there's a whoosh and another massive quake. A wave of heat, sound and light tears past me like a juggernaut, and continues on its destructive path.

Fifty metres. The blood is rushing in my ears.

I see the fourth rocket scorching out of the launch site on the opposite bank of the Shatt al-Arab, screaming towards the palace at twice the speed of sound. But this monster is on a different trajectory to the others. This one's higher. Its shadow careers across the palace grounds. Moments later there's another massive explosion, intense and angry, followed by another deep, rumbling boom.

I hear smashing glass, and feel a tremor as part of a building collapses. There's a gut-wrenching scream. The rocket has overshot the palace and hit someone's home. I hear more agonizing wails. Smoke is billowing from one of the buildings.

*

A troop from Salamanca Company – the brigade's force protection company – has been on the ground for the past half an hour. They deployed as soon as the last rocket was fired. They're gutted. Their usual businesslike expressions have been replaced by looks of solemn desperation.

The entire street beneath the seat of the explosion is a mass of twisted metal, shattered glass and debris. A thick layer of rubble and dust coats the cars, and battered and bloodied faces have begun to appear at bedroom windows.

A man sits in a corner, quietly weeping. He's covered from head to toe in thick black soot. A fireman hands him a tiny parcel. It's his dead son. He lets out a gut-curdling howl, a sound that I know will follow me to the grave. Tears stream down his face. He rocks backwards and forwards, mumbling to himself.

I ask the Iraqi translator what he's saying.

'Nothing,' he replies coldly. 'Just incoherent nonsense.'

'Ask him if we can help him. Ask him if there's anything we can do.'

The translator looks at me quizzically. *Why on earth would I consider showing compassion to a Sunni?*

'Just do it.'

The translator spends the next five minutes shouting at

him, trying to bully him into a response, but he's a broken man. He doesn't care any more. Everything he loves and cares about has been torn away from him. His reddened eyes stare into the distance.

I sit next to him and touch my right hand to my heart. There are no words powerful enough to bridge the gap between us. He turns slowly and looks deep into my eyes. All I can see in his are the echoing depths of his despair.

'Where is the justice, Englishman? My peace-loving wife and children, they are dead. But you and your soldiers? You bring war and bloodshed to my country, and yet Allah allows you to live.'

For the first time, I feel a crushing sense of guilt about my presence here. If there were no coalition forces, the rocket would never have been fired. His family would still be alive.

'I'm sorry.'

I know it's completely inadequate, but I mean it sincerely, from the bottom of my heart.

'No, Englishman. It is I who should be asking for Allah's forgiveness.' The tears glisten on his blackened face as he speaks. 'I should have been with them. I should have protected them. I was gambling. My wife, my children, they had so much to live for. I should have given my life for them. Instead, they gave their lives for me. What sort of a Muslim am I?' He looks up towards the heavens. 'I should lie in hell for what I have done.'

I touch his shoulder. I know there's nothing I can say to ease the despair that has etched itself on to his soul.

I head into the house. In the children's bedroom lie two charred corpses, mother and daughter, locked in a final embrace.

The rocket struck the corner of the house, blowing out the windows and flooding the rooms with broken glass and acrid black smoke. I picture the explosion throwing the mother from her bed, knocking the wind out of her. She's gasping for breath, surrounded by a wall of flame. The air is becoming hotter with each passing second. For a moment she has no idea where she is, or what has happened. She screams out for her babies. But there is no reply. She stumbles through to the children's room and calls out for them again. She steps on something soft. She reaches down, praying for a miracle, but this is God's will. She touches her little boy's lifeless face.

Outside, people are screaming up to her, pleading with her to drop the children out of the window. But their pleas are futile. She can't hear them. Her eardrums have been shattered by the explosion.

And then she sees movement, a tiny blackened face. Thank you, God. Her daughter is lying on the floor, trembling, paralysed with fear but alive. The mother tries to drag her towards the window but part of the floor has already collapsed. There's no other way out. They are trapped in this terrible inferno.

She wants so desperately to live. She wants her daughter to live, but neither of them can breathe. The two wretched creatures embrace for one last time.

I know I shouldn't be doing this. I should be concentrating on gathering the forensics, tracing a path back to the bastards who did this. Instead, I'm allowing the anguish of these events to take hold. I'm thinking of Lucy, Sophie and Ella again. As my eyes redden and the lump forms in the front of my throat, I look skywards and silently question what sort of God allows such things to happen.

15

All that is necessary for the triumph of evil is for good men to do nothing.

Edmund Burke

20 May 2004: Day 17

A deep, corrosive misery has engulfed the Det. A little part of all of us died in that burning house last night. We need something to take our minds off it. We need to get out on the ground.

When the bat-phone eventually rings, it feels like we've been thrown a lifeline.

Dan takes the call.

'It's for you, boss.' I can hear his disappointment. 'It's the Yanks.'

A social call, then. We're not going anywhere.

'Christoph,' a voice booms at the other end of the line. I recognize it immediately, not least because Chuck Russell is the only person in the world who calls me

Christoph. He's a gladiator of a man, one of the US ambassador's close protection detail. I met him at a conference in Washington DC last year when I was invited to speak about countering suicide bombers. We both ended up getting pissed in the bar afterwards. Then, when he heard I was the ATO here, he asked me to give an IED lecture to the protection detail about a week ago. It works well: I keep him updated with the latest threats and he keeps us stocked with beers.

'We've just had a walk-in. A guy called Ali; says he's the father of the kids killed in the rocket attack last night. He wants to speak to you.'

I grab a Land Rover and drive over to the CPA building on the other side of the palace. I don't know what he wants, but I think it's best if I go and speak with him alone.

'Englishman.'

I can barely hear him.

'I have lost my wife. I have lost my children. There is nothing left for me in this life.'

He's a broken man. He looks as though he's on the brink of collapse. The weight of his emotional turmoil is too much for him to bear. I have a feeling that he has no more tears to shed.

'The killing, it has to stop,' he says.

'Can you help us stop it?' I ask.

He pauses.

'I know the men who fired the rockets and killed my family.'

Jesus.

'Who are they?'

'It does not matter who they are. They are Shias; that is all you need to know. They are my destiny now, not yours.'

'But how can we help you if you don't tell us who they are? Why do you want to protect them if they're Shias? You're a Sunni.'

'I am also an Iraqi. And I did not say I wish to protect them.'

No matter how hard I press him, he refuses to reveal their names. We're getting nowhere.

'If you won't tell us who they are, then why are you here?'

'I have come to take you to the rockets, Englishman. You will destroy them. You will make sure they are never used against another of my countrymen.' His expression suddenly goes cold. 'And I will seek out the people who murdered my family. And when I find them, I will kill them. Then justice will be done. Then my family will be avenged.'

He strikes me as a gentle, placid man, but I have no doubt that he means what he says. I can see the deep sincerity in his eyes. He's a man of integrity. Once again, I feel humbled by my encounter with him. Once again, I think about Lucy and the girls. What would I do if somebody harmed my family?

I'd like to think I'd respond in pretty much the same way as any other decent human being. I'd like to think I would try to rebuild my life and move on. But I know that wouldn't be the case. I don't think I'd ever be able to move on. I wouldn't be able to forgive or forget. I know I wouldn't sleep until I'd punished those responsible. I would call in every favour and use every skill I had ever been taught to hunt down and destroy every one of them.

Yes, I know exactly where Ali is coming from. I would do exactly the same if I were in his shoes. The lengths I would go to and the damage I would be capable of inflicting would know no bounds.

I head over to Brigade HQ and tell the operations officer about last night's explosion, and the father's walk-in this morning. I tell him that we know where the rockets are and that the father will take us to them.

He's having none of it.

'How do you know we can trust him?' he says. 'How do you know it's not some elaborate trap? You'd have to travel down a long dusty track into close terrain where anything could be lying in wait. You could be ambushed on your way in, or on your way out for that matter—'

I stop him in his tracks. 'This is no trap. The bloke's lost his whole fucking family. I saw them with my own eyes – they were burned alive. And I'm aware of the risks. We're in Iraq. It's a risky place. Fuck it, I'll go in by boat if you like. But the fact remains, if we do nothing there will be more rocket attacks and more innocent people will be killed. Doing nothing is not an option.'

He flashes me a hard look through his blood-red eyes. He's been banging out twenty-hour days and the fatigue is hitting him hard. He's a decent bloke, but he's burning himself out.

'Do it,' he says. 'But be careful.'

Several hours have passed and the radio finally crackles into life: 'Area secure. Deploy ATO now.'

We're going in. The Cheshire Regiment's B Company is in position. They've deployed by vehicle and have established a secure cordon around the cache site. Now it's time for us to do our stuff.

Ali told us the rockets were located across the Shatt al-Arab in a reed bed on the edge of one of the lagoons. We've had a look at the aerial photography, but the area is so overgrown it's impossible to see anything. He's going to walk us in.

The Royal Navy boat handler shifts the drive lever to

full speed and the vessel's powerful engines kick into life. We scream out of the pontoon and dart along the Shatt al-Arab for a further mile, past rich green palm groves and dense reed beds set back into the swamps. Weather-beaten Marsh Arabs in their brown *dish-dashas* watch us uninterestedly as they barbecue their freshly caught fish at the river's edge.

'Twenty seconds!' the coxswain shouts.

We're heading for a clearing in the tree line that opens into a lagoon. I check that my pouches are closed, all my equipment secure, then pull my Bergen on to my back and grip my weapon more tightly.

The fishermen gliding on the mirror-like surface of the lagoon appear to be unfazed by our presence. A couple of wild dogs and a mangy old goat provide the only movement at the water's edge.

'Go, go, go!'

Dan and I step off and the boat does a sharp one eighty before accelerating away. Ali and the B Company commander lead us along a track to a stretch of marsh-land.

'Under there,' Ali says, pointing to a pile of reeds and palm leaves about 20 metres away, at the edge of the reed bed.

'Has anybody else been anywhere near the cache?' I ask.

Right now, it's the critical factor that will determine how I render the rockets safe. If there's been any traffic up to and around the cache, then at least the approach is likely to be safe.

'We've been all over it,' the company commander says.

It's the answer I was hoping for.

'And what about movement? Has anybody shifted any of the rockets or components?'

This is one of the hardest questions for a soldier to answer truthfully. If he has moved something, he knows he's in the wrong, and that he'll be ripped into by his mates for not being Joe Pro. From an operator's perspective, though, I don't give a shit about what he's done wrong. All I want to know is exactly what he *has* done, and most particularly whether anything's been moved, so that I can determine whether it's likely to be booby-trapped.

'No,' he says. 'Nobody's touched a thing.'

OK, so the rockets could have an anti-tamper mechanism. I'm going to move everybody back at least another 70 metres and remove the rockets remotely.

I take the hook and line set from my Bergen and wade through the rancid-smelling reed bed to the target area. True to Ali's word, a cache of seventeen rockets has been dug into the side of the bank. On top of them there's a box containing forty fuses. I search for tripwires and scan the area with my handheld metal detector.

There's nothing. So far, so good.

I take out a roll of plasti-ties and fasten them tightly to each of the rockets, then place more around the box of fuses. Next, I thread the hook and line through the elaborate matrix of plasti-ties and trail it back to the edge of the track.

It's crunch time.

I get everybody under hard cover and give the line a sharp tug.

The rockets and fuses are in pristine condition. We're taking them to the Villa, the home of the Weapons Intelligence Section at Divisional HQ.

Contrary to its grand title, the Villa is one of the most dilapidated buildings in the British sector. But it's perfect. The featureless building has no external markings and is hidden away deep inside Basra Air Station. Inside, Andy, an experienced ATO, and his team of investigators are busy piecing together information on the bombers.

'Make yourselves at home, fellas. You know where the beers are.'

The lads don't need to be told twice. This is easily the best crew room I have ever seen. There's a cooking area, a massive lounge with widescreen TV, Playstations, a

DVD player with surround sound system and, most importantly of all, a huge fridge stacked with cold beers. The lads place the rockets on a sterile drop-sheet then embark on their mission to drink the beer fridge dry.

In the adjacent room Andy is methodically checking and recording all the components that have just arrived. He's a brilliant operator and an outstanding leader. And despite his shrewd Scouse mind and sharp northern wit, he's also a bit of a closet geek. He gets genuinely turned on by technology and is a complete anorak when it comes to electronics and circuit boards, which makes him perfect for this job.

In the next room Gerry, a Royal Signals specialist, is furiously working away on a device.

Opposite him, two RMP investigators are busy doing the bread-and-butter forensic examinations. One of them spends the entire day analysing the tiny fibres left behind by the terrorists. The other guy is analysing IED components. He's using chromatography techniques to test for explosives.

These guys are the dog's danglies.

My lads have barely finished ripping the tops off their first beers when I announce it's time for us to move out. Andy and his team are obviously busy and the last thing they need is us getting under their feet. The boys don't quite see it that way though. There's nearly a mutiny.

Fortunately, Andy walks in and buys them some more drinking time.

'Just to keep you in the Rembrandt,' he says, 'we've cross-referenced our results with the information we already hold on the terrorists. We've analysed every single IED event in our area and looked at every aspect of the terrorists' tactics associated with it. We've been looking at these bastards for weeks now and we're extremely close to determining exactly who the keyless car entry RCIED bombers are and where they're operating from. In fact we're getting closer every day to bringing down Basra's entire bomber network. Pretty soon we'll be ready to start targeting.'

16

Among other things, you'll find that you're not the first person who was confused and frightened and even sickened by human behavior.

J. D. Salinger, *The Catcher in the Rye*

21 May 2004: Day 18

It's no use. I'm restless, on edge. I've been pumped up all day. I head into the Det and begin writing up the incident reports. I can feel the tension ebbing out of me as I type, but it's still not enough. The Sunni bomber team has been ragging us around the city all day. We've been out to three incidents already and even now, as the sun is setting, we can still hear sporadic bursts of gunfire outside the wire. It's going to be a busy night.

I need to go for a run.

The salty tang of the Shatt al-Arab is drifting through the warm evening air. I'm taking in lungfuls. My feet are hitting the ground rhythmically as I follow the dusty perimeter road along the bank of the river. I'm carrying a helmet and body armour in a day-sack on my back. If we get malleted by any more rockets or mortars I'm not going to get caught out again.

The sun's on my face now and the gravel crunches beneath my feet. This is my escape, my release. Mentally I'm a million miles away, in a place where I don't have a worry in the world.

A few hundred metres down the track and I turn inland, along the inside of the fortified concrete walls and guard towers. There are three palaces inside the wire, as well as a shed-load of other imperial-scale Ba'athist buildings, all marble and ornately carved wood – we're talking *Arabian Nights* meets Alcatraz.

I carry on for another mile or so and pick up the pace. I hit the lake, built in the shape of Palestine, and continue around to the main palace entrance, a huge triumphal arch. Saddam definitely had a liking for bling, and he wasn't afraid to let it out of the closet.

I run for about an hour. The pounding of my muscles sends blood rushing through my veins and clears my mind of the stress and anxiety that have been building all day. Sweat's pouring off me. A thick film of dust and sand coats my body. I feel good.

I head back to the Det for a shower and shave. I splash cold water on to my face and try not to pay too much attention to the ghostlike figure looking back at me. I've aged ten years in as many days. There's only one thing for it – a fag and a brew with Will. It's not exactly a day out at Champney's, but it'll do for now.

I stroll over to Brigade HQ then head across the palatial dance floor and into the int cell.

'Hey, Lugsy, coming outside for a brew?'

The scale of Will's fearsome intelligence is matched only by the size of his ears, and I like to remind him of that at every opportunity. He's mega serious, one of those blokes who needs to have the piss ripped out of him from time to time, just to remind him he's still got a pulse.

He also looks as though he hasn't had a decent night's sleep in about a decade.

'Who the fuck are you calling Lugsy, Dumbo?'

He goes into Tourette's mode, but it's a fair one: my ears are not ungenerously proportioned.

Giggling like a pair of kids, we step outside and take our usual places on the bank of the Shatt al-Arab. A dhow is meandering up the river and the fishermen are casting their nets. The deep-red desert sun is setting over the palm trees on the opposite bank and a gentle evening breeze warms our faces.

We're shooting the shit, taking the piss out of each other as we always do, but it's me doing most of the talking today. I'm boring Will about my plans to buy a house and settle in Hay-on-Wye; wanting to bring the girls up in a safe and civilized place, a place where we can go for family walks along the river, where Lucy and I can go running in the Black Mountains or while away our time in the bookshops and cafés. I love it there. I've travelled all over the world, but Hay is special. It's the only place I know where you can walk into a pub packed with strangers – bright, dull, thick, thin, rich, poor – and irrespective of creed, colour or background, everyone will happily chat together. There are no pretences; people just seem to be happy living peacefully alongside one another. Our mates on the bomber teams could do with taking a leaf out of their book.

We sit there in silence for a moment. Thinking about Hay has helped me start to persuade myself that I might be able to share Lucy's future after all.

Will takes a final drag on his cigarette, pulls out another and lights it from the stub of the first. He takes in another huge lungful of smoke, turns to me and says, 'Do it now, mate.'

'Yeah, right. I wish!'

'I'm serious. You've got to go home. You've done enough here.'

I'm starting to think he's been out in the sun too long.

'Are you taking the piss?'

'Look, mate, we've been muckers for a long time, you

and me. We're . . . we're chiselled from the same stone, peas from the same pod. We look out for each other, always have done.'

I can see something in Will's eyes I've never seen before. He looks genuinely pained.

'There's no easy way to say this, mate. You're being targeted . . . by the Shias now as well as the Sunnis. They want you dead, Chris. You've only been here five minutes and already you and your team have captured their weaponry, you've fingered them with forensic evidence, you've neutralized a shed-load of their IEDs, and basically you're making Behadli and his men look like cunts. The word on the street is that they're out to kill the golden-haired bomb man in Basra.'

He does his trick with the cigarettes again.

'Abbs is ginger, and he's operating in al-Amarah. So that, my friend, narrows it down to a field of one. Like I said, you need to thin out, peel, call it a day.'

17

The whole problem with the world is that fools and fanatics are always so certain of themselves, and wiser people so full of doubts.

Bertrand Russell

Day 18

I think about Lucy and the near constant stream of bad conversations we've had recently. I need to speak to her. I need to hear her voice.

I head over to the phones and there's a queue as long as the Great Wall of China. I take my place in it and pull out her photo. Her beaming smile seems so distant, so remote. I miss her terribly. I don't know what the future holds for us, but I know I miss talking to her. I miss laughing with her. I would give anything to hold her in my arms right now.

Eventually, having queued for forty-five minutes in the baking sun, I finally get to a free phone, only to discover she's not in.

I'm gutted.

I take myself on to the roof and spend some time reflecting quietly on what Will told me. We've successfully rendered scores of devices safe and we're close to determining who the keyless car entry RCIED bombers are, so I can understand why I'm at the top of their shit list. And I know Will isn't talking bollocks. That's not his style.

It's all starting to make sense now. A friend from the SF gave me a gypsy's warning a few days ago – there's a price on my head. I suppose it was only going to be a matter of time. I wonder whether the Sunnis or the Shias will take the first pop. My money's on the Shias. We've neutralized more of their devices.

Fuck me. Two groups. It's not a good feeling.

I'm fidgety. I can't stay up here feeling sorry for myself. I decide to take a stroll over to Brigade HQ.

On my way in I notice two new Gucci noticeboards in the palace's reception area. One is headed 'Media Ops', the other 'Intelligence'. The Media Ops board is full of rhetoric about the insurgents and the massive stranglehold they have on the population; about how tribal feuds dating back years are being settled night after night with grenades and AK-47s. Nearly a hundred thousand Iraqi civilians have died since the invasion.

The Intelligence board is more focused. Behadli and

his Mahdi Army have been enforcing their own extreme version of sharia law. Dead bodies are turning up all over Basra every day. Our patrols have found Christian women, their throats cut, dumped at the side of the road or burned alive in their beauty salons. Scores of men have been shot in the head for having allegedly collaborated with the British; others have been killed for their money, or for being members of the Ba'ath party. The bottom line: the Shias were screwed by the Sunnis, and this is their chance for retribution.

But the Sunnis are just as bad. They've been prowling the city with impunity, killing, raping and looting. Kidnapping is rife, and ordinary Iraqis are too terrified to step outside their doors. The insurgents are out of control.

What is it with these guys? Why are they so fucking fanatical? Iraqis are good people. They're educated and intelligent; they're decent human beings. Yet at Friday prayers they have their heads filled with crap, and they believe every word of it.

I head back over to the Det, wondering how I'm going to break Will's news to the team. One of the lads is sitting on the riverbank, staring out across the water. His sullen expression tells me something's up, something serious. I can see it in his eyes. He's a man on the edge.

I quietly take a seat next to him. He turns and nods at

me, saying nothing yet still acknowledging my presence. I look into his forlorn, sunken eyes.

'Are you OK? I know we're all having a bit of a shit time of it right now. Is there anything I can do?'

His face softens for a moment, then his teeth clench. 'I can handle it,' he says brusquely, then turns away. He wants to be alone.

I leave him to it.

What a mess. I'm being targeted, my marriage is in tatters, and the cracks are beginning to show in the team. And I don't have a clue what to do for the best, about any of it.

I wonder what my dad would have done.

For a moment, I am once more that little boy sitting on the end of the bed, watching *Danger UXB*. Did I think I would follow in his footsteps? Who knows? He died unexpectedly when I was fifteen, before I had the chance to ask him properly about his former career.

Dad, if you're there, if you can hear me, tell me what you would do.

He doesn't, of course.

I pull a dog-eared scrap of paper out of my wallet.

Somewhere, a True Believer is training to kill you. He is training with minimum food and water, in austere conditions, day and night. The only thing clean on him is his weapon. He doesn't worry about what workout to do. His rucksack weighs what it weighs, and he runs until the enemy stops chasing him. The True Believer doesn't care 'how hard it is'; he knows he either wins or he dies.

Now, who wants to quit?

I don't know who wrote it; I'm told it was an NCO at a US Special Forces school. But it hits the mark. It gives me the kick up the arse I need.

I'm not going to tell the blokes. They're anxious enough as it is, and this might just be enough to send them over the edge.

18

Day 18

Miracles? Divine intervention? Call it what you will. All I know is I've had plenty of opportunities to meet my maker, and so far we've never done more than nod at each other across a crowded room. If I'm now being targeted, it changes nothing. I'm not going to let it faze me. You die when your time's up. Simple as that.

I go back to the Det, my mind buzzing. I'd had grand plans to stay off the sauce before I arrived in theatre, but I need a drink. We all do. Dan does the honours and fishes around inside the safe, eventually pulling out the fifteen-year-old Glenfiddich left by a very obliging *Sun* reporter who was out a few weeks ago running a story on 'Our Brave Boys' to counter the shit-storm that erupted courtesy of Piers Morgan. He spent each of his three evenings with us necking his whisky while he wrote up his daily reports, and when he went home he left a couple of bottles behind. 'A little something to keep you going until the end of the tour,' he said. Top bloke.

The Glenfiddich tastes good, but we can't kick the arse out of it; one glass, two at most. I'm sitting chewing the fat with Dan, listening to the lads' banter. They're all mercilessly ripping the piss out of one another, trying to upstage one another with outrageous stories of nights on the lash, sleeping with loose women, catching the clap – all the usual sort of stuff.

Vince has been sitting quietly in the corner. Now he extracts himself from the conversation to ring his girlfriend, in full earshot of the rest of the lads. It's a schoolboy error. While he's on the phone the boys are on their best behaviour, listening to him tell her how much he loves and adores her, but the moment he ends the call he's subjected to a torrent of abuse. Now he's fair game. The barrage of insults begins and Vince is taking it well – until one of the lads touches a raw nerve.

Vince is clearly missing his girl, so when one of the lads makes a comment about lasses handing it out like Bombay money lenders, he doesn't see the funny side of it. His face turns red and he picks up the first thing that comes to hand, a bowl of nachos, launches them at his antagonists, then dives over the table himself for good measure. Several of the boys are now getting a real leathering, but they're laughing so hard they can't defend themselves. I know I should be the responsible one at this point and break it up, but it's far too funny to stop, and when Vince says to one of the lads, 'I'm going to give you so many lefts you'll be begging for a fucking right,' it just makes us all piss ourselves even more.

The ops phone rings, and everything goes quiet.

Dan picks up the handset and begins scribbling notes while he talks. 'Yeah, roger that. IED at grid Tango Uniform 7190 7733, two hundred metres south-west of Blue One . . .'

Rob pipes up: 'South-west of Blue One? That's IED Alley. Oh, fucking deep-joy.'

It's a fair one. We're going into Basra's Shia heartland, the place where Behadli and his Iranian-backed army has absolute power. In IED Alley, every night is gelignite.

The Det kicks into life and within seconds we're kitted up and making our way to the team vehicles. We go through the usual ritual. Everyone's running through their last-minute checks, weapons made ready, routes checked, actions-on confirmed. Here we go again. We mount up, adrenalin pumping, and drive out into the night.

Fired up and full-on, we're weaving our way through the city's dark, menacing back streets. The infantry escorts in the front vehicle are providing a radio commentary as we hard-target from one junction to the next, our doors wedged open, weapons in the aim.

At last I can see friendlies; we're approaching the cordon. But we can't let our guard down. We're at our most vulnerable now. The point we fear most. The moment the bomber is likely to detonate the secondary device, hitting us as we turn the corner towards the ICP.

Ollie gets on the radio. 'Boss, half right, there's a TV crew.'

He's not wrong. They're right on the edge of the cordon. Three of them: the cameraman, the sound man – complete with fuzzy microphone – and the presenter. Maybe it's a coincidence, perhaps I'm just being paranoid, but I can't help wondering if this is a come-on. They've never bothered rocking up to one of our tasks before.

Decision time. Do I sack it now and take the team back to the Det? Take a little bit of time to think it over? Let the device soak? Leave the sniper to get bored and go home?

But what's the point? We'd only be putting off the inevitable. Might as well keep going. Get it over with.

We cross the cordon and move into our ICP. No explosions, no shooting. Beyond us the street is eerily silent. Deserted. All the streetlights bar one have been shot out. Even the dogs are quiet. I look left, then right, front then back, trying to identify any high ground or likely firing points. My eyes are drawn to a mound of earth 150 metres away, with a rice bag either side of it. Aiming markers. This is definitely a come-on; I don't even need to ask. I'd bet a year's salary the device is directly opposite it, secreted somewhere on the other side of the road.

Rob and Dan are sorting out the ICP while the rest of the team are carrying out searches of the immediate area for secondary devices. I don't need to remind them to be thorough. They know this job stinks.

Dom, the infantry cordon commander, comes over to the ICP to brief me. He's a mountain of a man. I've worked with him on a number of tasks now and I like him a lot. I ask him for background info and he switches into briefing mode.

'At around sixteen hundred hours, unknown local residents claimed to have seen four unknown males planting an IED at the side of the road and reported the matter to the Iraqi Police Service. At around twenty-one thirty an

IPS callsign set up a cordon and satellite patrols, and a team from my company was tasked to attend the probable IED incident.'

'That's a lot of unknowns and probables, Dom. Did you interview anyone who reckoned they saw the device?'

He shook his head. 'The IPS had let them all go by the time we arrived.' Now that the brief was over he was speaking like a normal person again.

'Did you get to speak to anybody who saw these unknown males planting the device?'

'No. The IPS said they'd interviewed all the witnesses and released them before we got there.' He hesitated. 'Are you thinking what I'm thinking?'

'What? That the IPS can't be trusted? That the snidey bastards are all secret members of the Mahdi Army? That they're trained, equipped and funded by the Iranians to kill British troops? That they almost certainly planted the device themselves? That this is a come-on and the pricks think we're so stupid we can't see through it?' I paused. 'Yeah, that's pretty much what I'm thinking.'

'They weren't particularly happy when we rocked up and I told them I was taking over the cordon. They said they wanted a British ATO to come and deal with the device, but insisted that they were going to maintain control.'

'Funny, that. So how did you persuade them to stand down?'

'I said you only come out on the ground when British forces are running the show and politely but firmly suggested they should take their circus elsewhere.' He grinned. 'In other words, I told them to fuck off.'

'Those pricks are to policing what Myra Hindley was to childcare. I don't trust them one bit. I wouldn't be surprised if there wasn't an IED there at all.'

'Well, actually, Chris, there is. My lads confirmed the device was a likely RCIED. The callsign drove up and noted that it was contained in a yellow cardboard box, covered in sand.' Dom can't quite look me in the eye. 'You're not going to like this bit. The patrol commander then moved some of the sand by hand and spotted several wires attached to a white electrical box with an antenna extending from it. At that point he figured it was a bomb and requested EOD assistance.'

'Fuck, Dom! What the hell are your blokes doing moving sand off a suspected IED? They shouldn't have been anywhere near it.'

'I know, I know. But don't worry, it's all under control. I've had a word with the patrol commander and given him a fucking good rifting.'

'And what about lines of sight into the area for a sniper?'

'Unfortunately there are loads of them.'

At least he's being honest with me.

If they presented themselves as targets – assuming the bomber or sniper could see them – they obviously weren't the intended victims. That narrows it down. The bad guys are waiting for a specific target.

'Has anybody else approached the device since?'

'Nope, you'll be the first.'

A TV crew; no streetlights; a cardboard box; no witnesses; an excessive police presence; their insistence on manning the cordon; their insistence that a Brit ATO deal with it; Will's little pep talk; the rice sacks . . . It's not looking good.

'Dom, this is a come-on. They're trying to target me. I'd like you to maximize your company's presence on the cordon. Wherever there's an IPS callsign, I want one of your blokes all over him like a rash. I want all lines of sight into the device covered too. And I want a couple of your Warriors positioned next to our EOD vehicles, just in case. Does that sound workable?'

'I can put a man on each of the IPS, and I can give you as many Warriors as you want to protect your team. But covering all lines of sight into the device? There are too many potential firing points. We'll just have to do the best we can.'

Dan is sitting in front of the monitors in the back of the

Duro. He's loaded up the wheelbarrow and moved it to the front of the ICP, ready to deploy it to the target. He's holding the remote control unit.

'OK, Dan, it's time to get the barrow down there and give it a good snotting. The device is in a yellow cardboard box, probably on the right-hand side of the road.'

Dan's in his element. He sends the robot trundling down the road. The 3-foot-high miniature tank's cameras transmit fuzzy pictures back to us at the ICP. It makes for compelling viewing. We are both glued to the grainy monitor screens. This should be an easy job, but on this particular stretch there are at least twenty boxes and it's impossible to identify which one is tonight's star prize. I spark up a cigarette while Dan does the business with the barrow, trying to determine which of the boxes contains the IED.

I'm getting a tingling feeling between the shoulder blades. I feel like I'm being watched. I look behind me. There, on the cordon, I see a familiar face – a face I really don't want to see tonight. Behadli has appeared with his stooges and is chatting with the TV crew. He glances towards me and peels back his lips to reveal a collection of tombstone-like teeth. I guess it's as close as he gets to smiling.

'What are you up to, you bastard?' I say under my breath.

The penny drops.

I tell Dan the device will be directly opposite the rice sacks. He brings the barrow level with the mound of earth and turns hard right. Sure enough, there it is. He extends the boom and the cardboard box begins to fill the black and white monitor screen.

'Thought I'd use a pig stick for this, boss. What say you? It's only a cardboard box. Should get through it, no probs.'

The disruptor is soon in position, its water-filled steel tube aimed at the heart of the device. Dan looks at me and I give him the nod. He yells out a one-minute warning, pans the camera away from the device and selects the firing circuit.

Even though we're 150 metres away, we can hear the crack of the controlled explosion and the thud as the pig stick's high-velocity water jet smashes into its target. Dan pans the camera back on to the box. There's an empty space where it once stood. He then scans the surrounding area with the barrow for secondary devices, and finds nothing.

Now I have to confirm that the device has been completely disrupted, find the detonators and separate them from any explosive. Then I can hand the whole lot over to WIS and make one hell of a dent in what remains of the Glenfiddich.

I wait for the soak time to elapse and decide to crack on with a manual approach. Before I do, though, I'm going to use the ace up my sleeve. I call in a heli to over-fly the area with infrared cameras. The Shias hate helis, particularly at night, and especially when they know they're equipped with IR. If there's a sniper waiting for me, the heli is going to flush him out. And he knows it.

The bird swoops down low and hovers a few hundred feet above the road. The locals begin to run around like lunatics. It's working a treat.

The pilot eventually pulls off. It's time for me to get stuck in.

I begin the walk. I'm carrying the world's biggest array of EOD weapons, tools and electronic counter-measures, and all I can hear is the heaving of my lungs and the sound of the blood rushing in my ears. I'm back in the zone. Ollie and Vince come with me for the first 50 metres, to provide a bit of extra firepower should the shit hit the fan. I fancy my chances.

At the halfway point, Ollie and Vince give me a nod and peel off into their fire positions. I approach the target area, feeling the sweat coursing down my back. I hear the gentle rustle of the palm trees. I have to remind myself to breathe.

Fuck. The boxes – I can see them now. They're made of metal, not cardboard. The bomb was never in a cardboard box – it was in a metal tin. The pig stick will have done sod all to one of those. The bomb must still be up and running somewhere. Bollocks.

I'm starting to get a little bit excitable now. We thought the device had been snotted. We thought we'd seen it with our own eyes. We were wrong. And now I'm here in the middle of a deserted street, trying to find the bastard thing. It's like a bad dream. But I can't exactly turn around and leg it back to the command vehicle. I'd look like a prize twat. And it would really make Behadli's day. My heart is thudding like a jackhammer. This is insane.

I take a few deep breaths and begin the search, slowly, systematically, methodically. I look into the top of each of the boxes, one by one. Nothing. Then, as I approach the area in front of the rice sacks, I see a metal box set back from the others. That's got to be it. The force of the disruptor must have pushed it back a few feet. I can't believe I lost it. How do you lose a bomb? It's hardly a set of fucking car keys. What a tosser. Still, I've found it now . . .

I can literally smell it. I'm that close. I shuffle forwards. I can see part of the TPU. The brains of the bomb, daring me to make a mistake. Willing me to. I'm standing there, sweating in the darkness. The small white box is half hidden under sand and I have to resist the impulse to pull it clearly into view. More and more sophisticated electronic sensors are flooding into Iraq every day. This device could be fitted with any number of novel anti-handling sensors. The last thing I'm going to do is give it a tug.

I switch off my radio and edge forwards. My gaze is transfixed by the yellow metal container. I hate the thing. It's the root of all evil. I'm leaning over it now, examining the white box inside, up close and personal. My hands are shaking; my breathing is deep and fast. I can really feel the fear now. Perversely, it feels good. I feel alive.

I drag the tripod slowly up to the edge of the bomb. I extend its steel legs one at a time, and then I manoeuvre the disruptor over the top of the container. I'm going to take a downward shot into the device. I'll use the disruptor to shatter the firing pack, separating it from the explosive. But I have to be quick. I'm kneeling over a bomb that's already been given the good news by a mini howitzer and moved several feet. It's angry and unstable.

The disruptor's in place and I'm making my way back up the road to the ICP. Dan hands me a lit ciggie and a bottle of iced tea. I strip off my body armour to let the air dry my skin. I take off my helmet, too, and run my hands through my sodden hair. Then I throw my kit back on and give Dan the nod.

'Stand by . . . firing!' he shouts, and a second later he's pressing the tit on the Shrike firing device. The sound of the hotrod – a deep roar – pummels the night air. I can feel it through my boots as the disruptor delivers its low-pressure blast into the bomb's circuitry. This time I know it's done the trick. The high-pressure jet will have smashed into the device and torn it apart – instantly neutralizing it.

I make another manual approach. As I re-enter the target zone I can see the shattered TPU and explosives spread across the road.

First things first – I need to find the detonators. Most bomb-makers use only one per device, but the Shias do things differently. They're good – they use two detonators in case one fails. Their MO bears all the hallmarks of a state-sponsored group – I suspect they've been trained by the Iranians and Lebanese Hezbollah. I put my hands gingerly into the container and remove a block of Iranian C4 with the detonator still in it. I'm walking on eggshells. I may have disrupted the device, but there are components all over the place. If a battery comes into contact with the detonator's leads, I'll be blown to bits. I ease the detonator from the block of high explosive and twist the ends of the det leads together.

One down, one to go.

I begin searching for the other detonator. I find it

deep inside the metal container, hanging off the remains of the TPU, surrounded by TNT and C4 explosive. The TPU has been blown open and I can see all the components inside it. Good, I can do this by hand.

I know I won't be cutting into a collapsing circuit, but I still think twice – force of habit. I rummage in the tool bag for a pair of snips. The twin-flex wire attached to the detonator must be cut precisely. If the bare copper strands touch each other and complete the circuit, it's game over. I'll sever one first, then move an inch further down the line and deal with the second. That way, there's no possibility of the two arching together.

I take a breath, hold it for a few seconds, exhale, and make the first cut. Nothing. Good.

My heart is racing.

I move the snips an inch to the right and repeat the process. Still nothing. Even better. I cut the second detonator out of the explosive and pull it free.

I lay the components meticulously on to a forensic drop-sheet and hand the area over to the WIS team.

As I head back to the ICP, the team is busy packing up the kit. I tell Dan we're leaving in five minutes; there's something I need to do first. I make up some nonsense about going to debrief the incident commander, but instead I make my way over to the edge of the cordon. Behadli is looking seriously pissed off now. We make eye contact. He treats me to a look of utter contempt. He's a powerful man. A man used to getting his own way. I can feel the anger boiling up inside me. I stare into his cold dark eyes.

'You're a lucky man,' I say. 'I'm surrounded by witnesses and constrained by the rules of engagement. But one day, I'm going to come back for you. And when I find you, I'll kill you.'

19

The great blessings of mankind are within us and within our reach; but we shut our eyes, and like people in the dark, we fall foul upon the very thing we search for, without finding it.

Seneca

22 May 2004: Day 19

The thudding of the approaching Chinook resonates through our bodies. As the giant helicopter swoops low over the Det and down on to the HLS the distinctive beat of its rotor blades echoes around the palace walls like cannon fire.

I drop to one knee and pull on my Bergen, turning to avoid the clouds of dust and grit being churned up by the heli. The ramp lowers and the loadmaster gives us the thumbs-up. Dan and I shuffle rather than run towards it. We're carrying 100lb of EOD equipment each.

The engine's scorching downdraught sears our faces as

we scuttle under the rear rotors and into the chopper. Inside, weary-looking soldiers from a previous pick-up are buckled into their seats. Most of them are asleep, sedated by the engine's hypnotic vibrations, hunched over their rifles, barrels pointing to the floor.

Seconds later the aircraft begins its rapid ascent. The two door-gunners train their gympies on potential targets, taking in every detail of the urban maze beneath us. We're at our maximum risk of being destroyed by enemy rocket fire during take-off and landing. The pilot banks hard left, drops 100 feet then executes a sharp 90-degree right turn. The airframe judders violently as he conducts a series of evasive aerial manoeuvres. In the back, twenty bronzed soldiers are rapidly turning green. One throws up into a paper bag. More follow suit. After the world's longest rollercoaster ride the pilot tweaks the cyclic and levels off the aircraft. Moments later we're powering high over the desert, heading north to al-Amarah.

Only an hour ago the SO2 phoned out of the blue to inform us that we'd be covering for Abbs and his team 'with immediate effect'.

I've got no problem covering for Abbs, despite the short notice. He's a brilliant warrant officer, and he and his team have been getting ragged senseless recently. There's no two ways about it, they all need to decompress. Abbs has been the PWRR battle group's ATO in al-Amarah for several weeks now and they've been involved in some seriously dangerous operations. During one particularly cheeky incident he was dealing with a device outside the police station when insurgents broke through the cordon and began engaging him with small-arms fire. It escalated into a massive fire-fight and he was caught right in the middle of it. Abbs took it all in his stride, calmly stopped what he was doing, climbed into a Warrior and emptied a magazine of 5.56 into the enemy from its back door. Then, as soon as there was a lull in the fighting, he jumped out of the Warrior and finished neutralizing the device. The guy's an awesome operator.

As I said, I don't have any dramas with him and his team being given forty-eight hours off to soak up the sun in Sh'Ibetha. I'm just a little concerned about the mechanics of it.

'What if there's a device in Basra while I'm away?' I asked. 'How am I going to get back?'

'Oh don't worry,' said the SO2. 'I'm sure we'll work something out.'

Fuck me. What could possibly go wrong?

The loadmaster is sitting on the floor, his feet hanging over the edge of the ramp. As the Chinook beats across the sky I look past him at the billiard-table desert terrain and think about the task ahead. We're deploying to two IEDs that have apparently been recovered from a school in al-Amarah. What concerns me is that the devices have been recovered to the police station in the centre of town. I'm instinctively suspicious. It's where Abbs came under fire. Manned by Shia police loyal to the Mahdi Army, it has a reputation for being one of the most dangerous places in the world.

To say I feel slightly uneasy about this job is a bit of an understatement.

There's a flurry of activity. The loadmaster has just held up three fingers. Three minutes to landing. All around us, people are frantically replacing their helmets and donning their kit. They know what's coming. The pilot lowers the collective and pushes the cyclic forward and we plummet towards Camp Abu Naji at breakneck speed.

I hear an explosion and see flashes of light outside. My heart misses a beat, but it's nothing, just the pilot firing off some decoy flares. Moments later we're on the ground, stumbling down the ramp and across the HLS, tripping over one another as we wrestle with our Bergens. As the last man exits, the pilot is already beginning his ascent. Within seconds he's gone.

Second Lieutenant Rich Deane is a larger-than-life Ulsterman in his mid-twenties with the kind of beaming smile that can light up the place – which is strange, given that he was in banking before going to Sandhurst. He's also had a career's worth of combat in the few months he's been commissioned. His tour has been full-on. He and his platoon have been involved in numerous engagements with the enemy and he's already been hospitalized after being hit by an RPG.

I warm to him from the word go. He knows his onions and has an air of infectious optimism.

He's accompanied by Chris Broome, his platoon sergeant. Like Rich, Chris is a gladiator of a man who has also seen plenty of action this tour. The rest of their team has gathered around the Warriors; they take Dan and me across to meet them. Despite their bronzed faces, they look drained and emotionless. Each set of bloodshot eyes tells its own story.

We go through our plan with them in detail. Basically, we're going to scream into the centre of al-Amarah in four Warriors, park up outside the police station, pile inside, render the devices safe, then drive home via a slightly different route, in case the Mahdi Army decides to lay an ambush.

Nothing like keeping it simple.

Rich's driver, Johnson Beharry, shows us around his Warrior and helps us load up our kit. Private Beharry joined the British Army as a Commonwealth recruit from his native Grenada. Until he came to Iraq he was one of the battalion's bad boys. But out here things are different. He loves his job and he's proved himself an outstanding soldier. He even saved the life of his platoon commander – and about thirty other guys – a couple of weeks ago.

The platoon was tasked to rescue a foot patrol that had been pinned down by enemy fire in al-Amarah. Beharry's Warrior, Whiskey Two Zero, was hit by six or seven RPGs. He had no comms, a vehicle in flames, a wounded gunner and commander, and God knows what carnage in the back. In spite of all this, he drove over a mine and pushed on through the ambush, leading his own crew and five other Warriors to safety. He then extracted all the wounded from Whiskey Two Zero, one at a time, while under intensive enemy fire.

I'm glad to be going out with these guys. They give me a warm fuzzy feeling.

'Just one other thing, boss,' Beharry says with a slightly mischievous grin. 'The air-conditioning unit in the back is broken. The temperature outside is around fifty degrees, but in the back of my Warrior it's closer to seventy.'

I take it all back. I'm rapidly going off them.

Rich plugs his headset into the socket behind him. 'OK, Chris,' he says, 'the transit time is going to be about fifteen minutes. There's probably going to be a bit of two-way traffic en route, but that's par for the course up here, so don't be too alarmed.' His Ulster lilt makes it sound as though he finds the whole situation rather amusing.

The Warrior's steel blast-door clunks shut. We trundle out of camp and head towards al-Amarah. The feeling that violence is about to be visited upon us at any moment is disconcerting at the best of times, but the fact that we're stuck in the back of an iron coffin makes the experience a whole lot less enjoyable. Dan and I exchange despairing glances. While Rich and his crew are chatting on an all-informed net, neither of us has a fucking clue what's going on outside. It's not their fault, of course; there simply aren't enough headsets to go around. They're not passing any information back to us, so I guess they've got more important things to concentrate on right now.

'Care for a piping hot beverage?'

Dan reaches into his Bergen and passes me a bottle of scorching hot Lipton's Iced Tea. Beharry wasn't joking. It's redders in the back of his wagon.

I'm not sure what's worse, the extreme heat or the feeling of complete helplessness that comes with being squeezed into a 6-foot-square compartment like bully beef in a tin. At least we can see when people are shooting at us in the Duro. The dismount compartment of the Warrior only has a tiny 4-inch by 2-inch letter-box set into the back door, and that's completely obscured by the thick clouds of dust churned up by the tracks. If we're hit, the first thing we're going to know about it is when the RPG's warhead comes punching through the armour, and by that stage it's all going to be a bit late.

We've been travelling for ten minutes. I don't have a clue where we are, although I guess we've just entered the town. I try to imagine exactly where, based on my memory of the route. The plan was to turn out of Camp Abu Naji and head along Route 6 towards al-Amarah, then, as we dog-legged into the town, to continue north along Red Route. This part of the journey is the most dangerous, because it's long and straight and the insurgents can see us coming for miles. A mobile phone call is guaranteed to be made the moment we leave camp, informing every insurgent with a weapon that we're on our way.

The journey is relentlessly uncomfortable, and the roar of the Warrior's engines is deafening, but in spite of the noise I can still hear the unmistakable sound of bullets hitting the vehicle. The look on Dan's face confirms it – we're taking incoming. Beharry is already accelerating out of the killing zone as Rich traverses the turret left and his gunner fires off a long burst from the chain gun.

I look out of the rear window, trying to get an idea of what's going on. I can still hear rounds pinging off the side armour, and now I can see them clipping the stony road behind us. I so hope the boys with the RPGs are having a day off today.

There's another long burst from the chain gun above us, and then silence. The insurgents' fire has stopped.

We turn hard right. We must be crossing the river on to Blue Route.

'Two minutes,' Rich shouts from the turret.

Thank fuck for that.

Blue Route is a huge boulevard that runs up through the centre of the city. We're almost at the objective, but we're not quite out of harm's way yet. This is where the Mahdi Army is most heavily concentrated.

After two of the longest minutes of my life we screech to a halt and the back door opens. The automatic mechanism broke several weeks ago, so Rich has jumped out to open it by hand.

As I climb out of the Warrior, I'm blinded by the brilliant sun. The stench of rotting garbage and crap is all too familiar now, but it still makes me want to puke. It's just like being back on the streets of Basra. I'm beginning to wonder whether every city in this country smells of shit, or if they've just saved the best ones for us.

Among the two-storey flat-roofed buildings and palm-lined boulevards I can feel the simmering tension. It's as if somebody's about to light the blue touchpaper and the whole place is going to explode any second. This is supposed to be the location of the Garden of Eden, and to those that live there I'm sure al-Amarah is the most wonderful place on earth. But as far as I'm concerned, this collection of fly-blown hovels in the middle of nowhere is one of the most violent, shit-reeking slums I've ever visited.

My mother-in-law told me Iraq would be one of the most beautiful countries I'd ever set eyes upon. She must have meant a different Iraq. It may have set the gold standard in biblical times, but right now the place is in rag order. Burned-out cars, festering rubbish and piles of bricks and rubble litter every street. Centuries-old buildings have been destroyed by insurgent mortar and RPG fire. Al-Amarah is a city in ruins, and the people who live here don't give a damn.

As Dan and I enter the solid, flat-roofed police station through a small flagstoned courtyard, I find myself momentarily contemplating all the possible scenarios we might encounter inside.

The interior of the building is bustling with blue-shirted policemen sporting Kalashnikovs and shouting into their handheld radios. They watch us through beady, suspicious eyes.

The police chief steps into the corridor and shows me through to an adjacent room. Two of his men are sitting on the sofa, chain-smoking furiously. I can hardly see through the smog that surrounds them, but at least it gets in the way of the smell.

'The bombs are ready for you to take away – we have made them safe,' he says, full of bravado.

I now realize why these two maniacs are puffing away as though their lives depend on it. The IEDs are there on the table; they were obviously ordered to make them safe before we arrived. They're not trained bomb disposal operators, so now the poor guys are complete nervous wrecks.

I can't say I blame them. Hollywood bombs always have ten seconds left on the clock and curly-wurly wires. There are always curly-wurly wires. Real devices often look crude, but they're usually far more complicated than the movies would have us believe. Very occasionally, removing the detonator is all the operator needs to do to make a bomb safe. More often than not, though, it's a complex, scary, time-consuming process.

'I need you to tell me everything you know about these devices, and what actions you carried out to make them safe.'

They tell me they found the devices outside a school in the centre of town. The circuits worked pretty much as they were designed to do, but the devices failed to detonate because the bomb-maker had neglected to scrape a thin layer of paint off the drawing-pin terminal on the clock face. It makes sense. If the bomber modified a clock with a drawing pin and some wire, the device would spark up as soon as the minute hand made contact with it. In this case, the paint acted as an insulator and inhibited the electrical contact.

'Go on,' I say.

They tell me they tore out the wires by hand, then removed the detonators from the explosive.

Fucking hell. Tearing the wires out by hand – it's hardly a textbook job. I definitely wouldn't recommend trying that at home.

'How many detonators did you remove?'

'Two.'

'Is that two from each device, or two in total?'

'Two in total.'

I nod. These are Shia devices. The Shias always use double dets, yet Tweedle Dumb and Tweedle Dumber here have removed only one from each.

Decision time. Worst case, this is a come-on. An anti-handling device or long-delay timer may have been inserted to detonate the explosive when it's in my possession. Best case, these clowns genuinely did try to dismantle it, but didn't know what they were doing and left a det or two behind. Either way, I'm still going to have to completely dismantle both IEDs to remove all chances of them initiating accidentally.

I thank the two policemen, and after lots of back slapping and shaking of hands, I get Dan to usher them out.

When they're gone, I place a film cassette behind the devices and position my portable X-ray machine a couple of metres away. I step behind a wall, take the shot and hand the plate to Dan.

'If I was a gambling man, I'd bet a month's salary there's still another detonator in each of those explosive main charges,' I tell him.

He smiles and inserts the plate into the small laptop-sized processing unit he's been lugging around on his back since we left Basra. He waits patiently for thirty seconds before removing the positive from the unit and handing me the finished radiograph. The faint grey mass of plastic explosive is fairly difficult to distinguish, but, sure enough, the detonators, their wires and the 9-volt batteries that are still inside the charges are perfectly visible.

Fuck me. If I'd taken these back to Camp Abu Naji in the Warrior, the transmissions from Rich Deane's HF radio would have been more than enough to induce a current into the detonators and cause the charges to explode.

I don't have a robot with me – we could only bring what we could carry on our backs – so I'm going to have to remove the detonators by hand. I take out my scalpel and begin to shave away small strips of the wax-like explosive. As I take each slice, I look back at the radiograph so I can keep track of the exact position of the det and the batteries. The last thing I want to do is cut into them.

Beads of sweat soon form on my face and arms. It seems to take me hours to cut my way far enough to remove the dets and render the devices safe, but eventually we're done. We pack up the kit and head back to Camp Abu Naji without incident.

Having said our goodbyes to Rich Deane and his platoon, Dan and I sit on the pan quietly reflecting on the task.

Half an hour or so later the silence is shattered once again by the tumultuous engines of the Chinook. It's dark now, and tiny granules of sand glitter on the tips of the giant rotor blades, creating giant luminescent halos.

As the ramp lowers, I see that the loadmaster is wearing night vision goggles. I take out my infrared torch and flash it twice. He responds by giving me two flashes with his own. We're clear to board.

It's pitch black inside. There's no room to move and both of us are struggling to crawl over the rows of Bergens tied down in cargo nets. Chinooks are normally used for troop and load carrying. The fuselage is massive, large enough to carry two Land Rovers, but tonight the bird is full to bursting.

We drop into the canvas seats and begin buckling up. The pilot is already making his rapid ascent. We pull up hard and fast, and I'm thrust into the back of my seat. I can see the lights of Camp Abu Naji fading as we scoot up and power out over the desert. So far, so good.

A quarter of an hour passes, and Dan is already fast asleep. I crane my neck to look out of the window at the streetlights of al-Majar al-Kabir. It's another Shia stronghold, the place where six Royal Military Police were murdered last year and a Chinook was shot up as it tried to pick up the wounded. Flying over this place makes me feel uneasy. Maybe I just have an overactive imagination, but even the visceral whining of the engines fills me with foreboding.

There's a loud bang. Lights are flashing inside the aircraft and there's an incessant wail from the missile warning receiver. The sensors on our chopper have detected a SAM launch and fired decoy flares. The

MWR has detected the incoming missile's thermal signature and has given the pilot an idea of its incoming direction. Now the pilot's following a pre-defined set of tactics to evade the missile. But time really is against him. The missile's travelling at Mach 2.

He puts us into a near vertical corkscrew dive. My head smacks into the elbow of the guy on my left. I'm lying on my side. I think I'm upside down – saved only by my safety belt. I've got no idea which way is up. It feels like my brain is parting company with the inside of my skull.

The pilot's already triggered the counter-measure systems – ejecting flares and chaff. Now he's trying to confuse the missile's sensor further by lessening our own heat signature. He's simultaneously reducing the engine temperature, deflecting the exhaust gases, injecting water into them and losing altitude heat from the engine by dropping several hundred feet.

A young soldier opposite me retches into a bag. I'm amazed he can even find a bag at a time like this.

The world is spinning as the pilot struggles to keep the 15-ton Chinook airborne and control its torque. Our lives are completely in his hands. He pushes the cyclic forward and drops the collective, sending us into another nose-dive. We're twisting and turning so violently that rifles and loose items of kit are being thrown all over the cabin. My kidneys feel as though they're going to burst and my brain is being scrambled all over again. The pilot sweats over the glowing instrument panel, fighting to shake off the predator on our tail.

Another warning receiver lights up on the cockpit console, adding to the cacophony of tones already indicating the missile's approach. The aircraft banks, groans and then corrects itself.

The loadmaster's pulled himself up off the floor. He's saying something to the pilot.

And then there's silence.

Nobody moves. Nobody makes a sound.

He's done it. The pilot's evaded the SAM. I swear I'll never slag off the RAF again.

20

The web of our life is of a mingled yarn, good and ill together. Our virtues would be proud if our faults whipped them not; and our crimes would despair if they were not cherished by our virtues.

William Shakespeare, *All's Well That Ends Well*

23 May 2004: Day 20

A new face has arrived in the Det. Mick Brennan, a corporal from the Royal Signals, has been with the team for some time now but he left to go on leave the day I arrived, so today's our first actual face to face. The lads tell me he's a storming bloke with a cracking sense of humour but that he talks incessantly.

When I sit down to interview him I see exactly where they're coming from, but despite his unrelenting chatter the first impressions are all good. Just talking to him, I know immediately he's a team player. He spends the entire conversation asking after the blokes and wanting to know what they've been up to. He genuinely gives a shit. He's the archetypal British NCO. Tall, fit and brimming with enthusiasm, he's like Zippy on speed.

I ask him if he's got family.

'I certainly have, boss,' he says proudly. 'Two beautiful kids and the most stunning wife in NATO.'

He tells me that one of his daughters needs round-the-clock healthcare – she's got a hole in the heart. I wonder how I would cope being out here with that sort of pressure playing on my mind, but he doesn't seem at all fazed by it. He just takes it all in his stride.

Later, a group of us are outside the Det playing touch-rugby in the blazing sun. A stream of staff officers heads over to bollock the blokes for having their shirts off – until they notice I'm there and execute a swift about-turn. After a good hour or so things are brought to an abrupt end by a tasking. Two minutes later I'm briefing the blokes.

'We've been tasked to sort out a device outside the OMS. It stinks of a come-on and it could very well go noisy. If it does, be in no doubt, those fuckers are going down. Whatever happens we're all coming home today.'

Some of the lads flash me a look that says 'What's with the dramatics?'

Then Tom pipes up: 'Boss, what's the OMS?'

Here I am, trying to fire the blokes up, and they don't

have a clue what I'm babbling on about. It's a fair one:
I still haven't mentioned the warning about being
targeted yet.

'The Office of the Martyr al-Sadr,' I reply. 'The HQ of
Behadli's Mahdi Army.'

I decide to try to put it into context.

'Have you served in Northern Ireland, Tom?'

'Yes, boss.'

'Think of the OMS as Sinn Fein, and the Mahdi Army
as the IRA. They're kind of on a par. So what we're about
to do is go out for a day trip in the middle of the Falls
Road.'

'Fucking hell,' he says.

The heat is paralysing. It's 40 degrees plus now and it
feels like someone's wedged my face inside an oven. The
sweat's pouring down the inside of my helmet and into
my eyes.

I look to my front. The lads are covering every possible
threat, aiming their rifles at houses, cars and pedestrians
as we speed past them. I feel confident. I'm definitely on
the winning team with these boys.

I continue to scan the route, searching for signs
of IEDs.

'ICP two hundred metres right at the next junction,'
Rob's voice crackles over his radio.

Good, we're nearly there.

But as we approach the junction, a voice inside my head tells me that something's not right. It's a busy lunchtime in central Basra, yet for a couple of hundred metres in every direction the streets are deserted.

'I don't like this, boss,' Dan says. 'Everybody's fucked off.'

As we turn towards the cordon outside Behadli's headquarters an al-Jazeera crew films us from the corner. They're between us and the ICP, panning the camera as we scream towards our target.

As we pull into the ICP, I notice another crew on the roof of the OMS building. They're not the media. They look more like an amateur crew, possibly freelance guys, who have turned up all over Iraq – the ones who film attacks on coalition troops for the insurgents to post on the internet. I fix them in my rifle sights. What I'd give to be allowed to remove them from the equation . . .

As I scan the sights along the parapet I see someone else I'd like to pull the trigger on. Behadli is looking down at us. I have a feeling things are about to get very unpleasant.

Everyone knows what has to be done. Some of the lads are busy carrying out their 20-metre checks, while others scan the rooftops and tree lines for suspicious movement. They take in every possible enemy fire position, every potential IED site, and make eye contact with every person they see. They're doing everything by the book, sending out a message to any would-be aggressors: don't mess with us, because if you do, you're going to get hurt.

A few more Iraqis have rocked up on the cordon position. I wonder what they know that I don't. Rob scans their faces, daring them to go for a weapon.

While the lads are carrying out their drills, I go to the edge of the cordon. I don't feel at all happy about this job.

'How's it going, mate?' a young artillery gunner asks me.

I realize my rank slides are hidden beneath my assault vest.

'Yeah, good . . . mate,' I reply.

We start chatting. He tells me about the patch and about Behadli and his cronies. He fills me in on the murder squads and their fanatical methods of enforcing law and order. It's useful to get the gen from somebody who walks these streets every day.

Then he asks me if I've heard about the ATO being targeted. It knocks me for six. For the past couple of days I feel like I've been living in denial, but here, finally, the reality hits me.

I head back towards the team, trying to put the gunner's words behind me. Then I see something that really makes my blood boil. Mick's carrying out his 20-

metre checks, but instead of searching the bushes by hand, he's kicking them with his feet.

Fucking hell. I can't believe what I'm seeing. I know some of the lads are more motivated than others, and some are more disciplined than others – as civilians. But out here, on operations, everyone's expected to screw the nut. Everybody has to stay switched on. We're supposed to be professionals. We're supposed to set an example. That's how we gain the respect of our companions, and that's how we gain the respect of the Iraqis. Out here you can't just do what you like, when you like. You can't bimble around with your thumb up your arse. The pressure of continually having to remain vigilant is extreme, but that's what we're paid for, and that's what we're trained to do. A slack attitude just leads to premature death.

I fight the urge to rip his head off there and then. My first boss taught me a valuable lesson: never lose your rag. Take a deep breath, say, 'Never mind, that didn't turn out quite the way I'd hoped,' and move on. It's sound advice. Now definitely isn't the time or the place; we'll have words later.

I make do with giving him a scowl. He looks back at me sheepishly. He knows exactly what it means.

I need to move on. I start planning how I'm going to render the device safe. It's conveniently located about

150 metres away, in the middle of the central reservation just off the crossroads, next to the OMS building. I'm going to send the barrow down there, shoot it, and then I'll walk down and hoover up the forensics.

Within sixty seconds of me briefing Dan, the barrow is bombed up and trundling out of the ICP. We're monitoring the screens. I glance up at Behadli. He hasn't moved an inch, and we're still being filmed from the roof. I get on the phone to Brigade and request a heli for some aerial top cover, but it's not our lucky day.

I bite back my frustration.

Then I have an idea.

'Rob, I want you to get the blokes to start taking photos of those pricks up on the roof.'

Within seconds Behadli's Shia militiamen are running around the roof, arms flailing. They're going bananas. I'm not sure quite why they're so camera shy, but it's certainly touching a nerve.

Things seem to be going pretty much according to plan, but about 60 metres outside the ICP it all suddenly goes to ratshit. The barrow's frozen, for no apparent reason. The monitors have gone blank.

'What's going on?' Dan asks. 'What's happened to my barrow?'

Behadli.

'They're jamming us, Dan. The barrow's radio-control mechanism has been inhibited.'

'They couldn't have that sort of hardware, could they?'

'Dan, this isn't the MO of some fucking numpty outfit. These are specialist skill-sets. This is the real thing. It's state-sponsored, and unless I'm gravely mistaken, there's only one outfit supporting al-Sadr who has the capability.'

'Iran?' he says.

I nod.

Rumour has it the Iranians are funding the Shias, as well as training and supplying them. It's certainly not beyond the realms of feasibility. Iran is the only country in the Middle East with this level of sophisticated electronic warfare equipment at its disposal. And Behadli is their man in southern Iraq.

'So if your conspiracy theory is right, boss, what are we going to do about the device?'

'*We* are going to let it soak. Then *I* am going to walk down there and place a weapon on it.'

'Boss, with all due respect, have you completely lost the plot? They've jammed the barrow for a reason. They obviously want you to walk down there. The place is completely overlooked. There are hundreds of firing points and literally thousands of places they could secrete a device. Walking down there would be suicidal.'

He's right. These lunatics are no casual wannabes. They're not amateurs with 'born to lose' tattooed on their foreheads. They're the hardcore; highly trained, highly motivated terrorists hell-bent on killing us. If I'm going to come out of this in one piece, I'm going to have to use the ace up my sleeve.

Once again I look up at the men on the roof. Now I know why they were going mad the moment we started photographing them. Half the fanatics up there are probably Iranian Special Forces working undercover.

'That which does not kill us . . . eh, Dan?'

I set off out of the ICP. I've worked out a plan with the team and now it's time to get cracking.

'Yeah,' he says. 'And on the plus side, when the bomb does go off, it'll explode faster than your nervous system can react, so you won't feel a thing.'

Now I'm heading towards the device. I've decided to bin the EOD suit with its heavy armoured plates. They may well protect the front and rear of my torso, but with the toughened helmet and the soaring temperature, wearing the suit is far more likely to result in me becoming a casualty than actually saving my life.

I clutch my jammer in one hand and my tool bag in the other. For the last few seconds I've thought about nothing but the array of possible surprises Behadli's men have lying in wait for me. The bomb's just a lure. I'm the target now.

I can't afford to take anything for granted. I want more information. I want to know more about the bombers. I want to get inside their heads. I want to know what's around that corner. But nobody here is talking.

No ATOs have been deliberately targeted in Iraq before. The rules have changed, like they did in Northern Ireland in the early seventies.

The road is still deathly silent and empty. Yet all around us, from the windows and the roofs, people are watching, waiting. Unusually, there are no piles of rubbish or debris in the street. At least that's one less hiding place for a bomb.

I'm getting closer to the crossroads. I know something nasty is on the cards, I just don't know whether it will be a sniper, an RPG or an IED. Maybe it will be all three. Another 30 or so metres down this dusty boulevard and I'll be completely exposed. If someone pops up with a weapon, there will only be a split second to drop him before he fires. My two infantry escorts will know what to do.

I turn the corner and sweep the area, looking for command wires, shooters and potential IED positions. The dual carriageway is bare except for the grassed central reservation. Thankfully there are no drainage culverts. I look left, then right. I can see the device, a plastic shopping bag flapping in the gentle breeze. Hundreds of sets of eyes are burning into me from the roofs and windows.

I start to think of Lucy, but stop myself immediately. Now is not the time or the place. I erase her image from my mind. I can think about her later.

Now all I feel is fear. It's a killer, the one thing that can destroy a man's soul. I have to force it out.

I look over at Ollie and Vince.

'Ready?'

They acknowledge me, dropping to one knee and slipping the Bergens from their backs.

'Now!'

Ollie and Vince remove dozens of smoke grenades and begin tossing them into the street. Within seconds, the whole place is filled with thick green and orange smoke. Scotty is jamming the airwaves, and the smoke is obscuring any would-be aggressors' vision. The boys have just trebled my chances of getting back to the ICP alive.

I begin running blind towards the device. I've got a rough idea where it is, but I only have a few minutes to locate it and place the disruptor before the smoke clears. Seconds later I stumble on the package. In my eagerness to get to it, I almost end up giving the sodding thing the

Jonny Wilkinson treatment. Mick's bad habits must be rubbing off on me.

I do a final scan of my surroundings. The sun's rays are still burning through the smoke, but that's about all I can see. OK. I'm still overwhelmed by an incredible feeling of loneliness and isolation, but I'm safe enough for now.

I drop down on my haunches to examine the package. I can't see the entire contents of the bag, but I can see the explosive, some wires and a receiver. It's an up-and-running RCIED. I take a deep breath to get the adrenalin back under control, then drop to my knees and lower the disruptor on to the edge of the bag.

Now I'm racing back out of the smoke cloud towards the ICP. I turn in mid-stride, give Behadli and his cronies a look of defiance, and replay Will's most recent briefing in my head: 'Sheik Abdul-Sattar al-Behadli, the Jaysh al-Mahdi leader in Basra, commands an unknown number of JAM members who specialize in IED operations and assassinations. Sheik Sattar owns and operates the al-Ghadir media office and *al-Ghadir* newspaper in Basra. He is an artist and has a background in acting.'

Well, he's certainly enjoying some theatre today.

Dan hands me a cigarette as I arrive back at the ICP, but my hands are shaking so badly he takes the lighter and, without saying a word, passes the flame under the tip.

Moments later he fires off the disruptor. The crack of the exploding jet resonates along the street.

I finish my cigarette and prepare to head back. All I've got to do is make one more manual approach, confirm disruption of the device, collect the forensics and I'm on the home straight. This time the boys have decided to go large. Ollie and Vince have blagged the world's supply of smoke grenades from the infantry and have cleaned out our own vehicles in order to provide me with maximum cover.

I move through the sweet-smelling smoke towards what's left of the device. I lift a corner of the shredded plastic bag and there, in the middle of the shattered bomb, is a thick, viscous yellow liquid.

I'm fucked. The bastards have put out an improvised chemical munition. And I've just touched it.

I can feel the bile rising in my throat. Mustard gas has played a central role in my nightmares since well before I became an ATO. It often featured in my dad's war stories.

I try to calm myself, to think back through what I've just done. I'm wearing latex forensic gloves. Have I touched any exposed skin?

Yes. Shit. I wiped my brow with the back of my hand. This is definitely not good. I've seen the pictures. Your skin becomes red and blotchy then the blotches turn into bulbous yellow blisters. You feel irritation and swelling in your eyes, which if left untreated will result in blindness. In an hour or so your nose starts running, then haemorrhaging. Severe abdominal pain, shortness of breath, diarrhoea, nausea and vomiting follow . . . On the plus side, only 5 per cent of mustard gas casualties die.

I'm going to need to move fast if I don't want to become one of them, but since I've already touched the stuff, there's no point in sacking it now. I quickly locate the dets and remove them from the main charge. I photograph the device then slip the plastic explosive and the remains of the radio-controlled firing circuit into a transparent forensic bag. I turn back towards mission control and call Dan on the radio.

'Mate, I'm not fucking about, I think I've been contaminated with mustard gas.' My voice sounds alarmingly brittle. 'I need you to fire up the chemical agent monitor and crack open the blister agent decontaminant. I'll be back in the ICP in one minute.'

'Roger that,' he says, without a hint of panic.

By the time I arrive, the team has prepared everything I asked for.

Dan approaches me cautiously with the CAM. It looks more like a handheld vacuum cleaner than a highly complex piece of diagnostic equipment, but I have total confidence in it. The kit issued to British forces has come in for quite a lot of stick recently, but this is the business. It's Swiss-made and does exactly what it says on the tin. And right now I'm its number one fan.

He sweeps the device meticulously over the contours of my body, systematically checking my arms, legs, torso and head. The CAM's processors whirr quietly as its nozzle sucks up every particle in its path. Two minutes later Dan checks the reading on the small LCD screen. There's no chemical agent present.

Having done my best to hold it all together, perversely I'm shitting myself now. 'Are you sure? Are you absolutely certain it's working properly?' Suddenly I'm being bombarded by irrational doubts.

'Absolutely certain. I check it every Monday morning.' Dan looks offended. How could I even consider questioning his professionalism? 'But if it makes you any happier, I'll run a quick sensor confidence test.'

Without waiting for a reply he digs into the CAM box, whips out a block of what looks like snooker cue chalk and runs the nozzle over it, to make sure that the device is working properly.

It is.

He checks me again, from head to toe. The LCD readout remains blank. To say I'm relieved would be the understatement of the century, but it has completely thrown me. I still don't have a clue what that yellow liquid was.

We're not taking any chances, though. The lads help me to remove my assault vest, body armour and combat shirt before double-bagging them. I should take every-thing off, but I decide to keep my trousers and boots on. If we get hit, there's no way I'm going into combat wearing nothing but my boxers. They cover my hands, arms and face in Fuller's Earth to absorb any droplets of the stuff that might have touched my skin. Finally they empty their water bottles over me.

Once every part of my body has been decontaminated, I start to breathe easily again. I look up at Behadli. Maybe next time, eh?

I shrug on some more kit as the lads prepare for the off. But there's one last thing I need to do before we go.

'Mick?'

I take him to one side, out of range of the team, and out of sight of our friends on the rooftop. It's been a tough morning and I don't want to lay into him too much, but he needs to hear this. I tell him we've all got enough on our plate without having to babysit him as well. 'So do me a favour and get a fucking grip. You're an NCO, for Christ's sake. These pricks are watching and recording everything we do. Now they've seen you kicking that bush, the next time it will be booby-trapped

– I can guarantee it. Worse still, it's likely to be a different callsign that deploys, and there's a good chance the poor sod sent to search for it will get fried. Now start fucking sparking. I mean it, Mick. I don't ever want to see a member of this team pulling a stunt like that again.'

It's not news to him. 'I'm really sorry, boss. I don't know what I was thinking. It won't happen again.'

Technically, I should still discipline him, or at the very least kick him out of theatre. But I don't. I feel sorry for him, and I give him a second chance.

I hope like hell I won't regret it.

21

We tend to meet any new situation by reorganizing and a wonderful method it can be for creating the illusion of progress, while producing confusion, inefficiency and demoralization.

Gaius Petronius, AD 66

24 May 2004: Day 21

The troops from the Nuclear, Biological and Chemical Defence Regiment look like astronauts. They're dressed from head to toe in protective suits. They've been carrying out tests on the yellow liquid for close to twelve hours now, working through the night to avoid the fierce desert heat. Now it's morning and the sun is rising. They can only work for twenty minutes at a time otherwise their oxygen tanks run out and their body temperature rises to a dangerously high level. You couldn't pay me to do their job.

I stand watching from a safe distance as they

continue their painstaking work in the protective airtight tent. They take minute samples of the liquid and transfer each one into the spectrum analyser, then wait as the machine carries out its electronic examination. I'm interested, almost to the point of obsession, to know what it is Behadli and his crew cooked up in that device yesterday.

The troop commander eventually makes his way over. He peels off his protective hood and face mask and gulps down a lungful of cool air. I can see he's knackered.

'We've identified your yellow liquid.'

He steadies himself on the sandbag wall. If I didn't know better, I'd think he was trying to stop himself laughing.

'I have to say, though, I'm surprised you boys weren't able to identify it yourselves.'

He finally allows himself a wry smile.

I'm lost, and, I realize, feeling more than a little defensive. I've spent several years training to defeat terrorist weapons of mass destruction and I know my onions when it comes to chemical agents, but I defy anybody to be able to recognize one a hundred per cent without having proper scientific diagnostic equipment. But maybe the heat and the constant pressure have taken their toll. Maybe I'm just losing it.

'Sorry, mate.' I can feel my ears burning. 'I'm more of an explosives type of guy.'

'Exactly. That's why I'm surprised you didn't recognize it.'

He's not being arsey, but he's grinning like an idiot. The suspense is killing me.

'You've lost me,' I say.

'Your liquid isn't a chemical agent, my friend. It's an explosive. It's rocket fuel.'

The blood rushes from my ears to my cheeks. I feel completely inept. How on earth did I miss that? It's the first thing I should have thought of. It's a bog-standard accelerant; Behadli and his mates just wanted to give me an extra kick in the nuts. And I've just had these poor bastards working all night to identify a substance I should have cracked in twenty seconds flat. I suddenly realize just how rattled I must have been.

'Look, I'm really sorry for wasting your time. I fucked up. I don't know how I managed to miss it. I just saw the liquid and it completely threw me.'

'Hey, no worries,' he says. 'And don't beat yourself up about it. The boys were chuffed to bits to get a real shout, and so was I. We've been here for two months and we've done fuck all. We hadn't had a single tasking until you dragged us out last night. Trust me, it was good, even if it did turn out to be a false alarm.'

A couple of hours later and I'm still thinking about what just happened. I appreciate his generosity but he leaves me feeling pissed off and annoyed at myself. I need to let it go. At the very least I need to imagine that I'm somewhere other than here.

I take myself off for a wander over to the lake where I sit and think about home. I recall the hikes Lucy and I did together through the narrow valleys and along the heather-clad ridges of the Black Mountains; the crystal-clear air, the breathtaking views of the Brecon Beacons, and the final drop down to Llanthony Priory. In the late twelfth century, Giraldus Cambrensis described the priory as being 'fixed amongst a barbarous people', but as far as we're concerned its cellar is home to the best scrumpy in the world.

I picture Lucy looking at me over the rim of her glass, eyes shining with mischief and delight, at that time a kaleidoscope of shared moments. I ache for her right now. But maybe the ache is a different kind of pain. I'm wondering if those memories have become distorted in some way, if I've somehow recreated them, rewritten our own personal history and made it more enjoyable than it really was.

Maybe I'm in denial. Maybe I just need to accept that our marriage has finally broken down, that I've put in everything I have here – the adrenalin rush, the camaraderie, the satisfaction of a job well done – before my promise to her. I've spent seven years of my life piecing together bomb fragments, but on a personal level I've never been one to pick up the broken pieces and try to glue them together again.

Another image swims to the forefront of my mind: Lucy and the girls on a picnic rug in Richmond Park, the sun shining, fooling around, laughing and joking, without me. Maybe it's time I started . . .

I reach into my kit for Lucy's photo. I hold it almost reverently. Perhaps it's my terrible need for her that makes the image appear so vivid. It's as if she really is here, sitting right in front of me. She tilts her beautiful head to one side and whispers in my ear, 'Don't be an arse, honey-pie. It's me, remember?' She leans back a moment, those blue eyes glowing, that unforgettable smile, saved for me alone.

I have to call her.

When she answers, her voice sounds harried and impatient. I just put it down to the kids playing up and go straight into permanent-send mode, drip-feeding her sanitized extracts from the daily diary, trying to kid her it's really safe and that the press just likes to make everything look worse than it really is to increase their ratings.

She stops me in my tracks. 'I'm surprised you've not

phoned before now. The kids have really missed you.'
Her voice is ice-cold.

'The kids? What about you?'

I didn't mean it to come out like that, but it's too late.
Lucy goes straight on the offensive.

'What do *you* think? What do you want me to say? Yes,
darling, I miss you terribly. I sit here every night with my
head in my hands and sob uncontrollably. Is that what
you want to hear? Or would it make you happier if I told
you I'm glued to the television, constantly watching news
footage of British soldiers in Iraq, praying that your name
doesn't appear on the list of today's deaths?'

She pauses for a moment and apologizes to somebody
in the room with her.

'I'm sorry, Luce, I didn't realize you were entertaining.
Have I interrupted something?'

I mean it genuinely, but even as I'm saying it I sound
terminally sarcastic. I'm trying to calm the situation and
all I seem to be doing is exacerbating it.

'No, you're not interrupting anything. Ed was passing
by and popped in to say hi.'

'Ed?'

I feel a pang of unnecessary jealousy. Ed's a mutual
friend; he and Lucy have been pals since long before she
and I first met. I know full well they're nothing more
than mates, but he's a good-looking bloke and I'm not at

my most rational right now. Instead of taking a deep breath, I leap straight in at the deep end.

'Lucy, it's eight o'clock in the morning. What time did he arrive?'

The green-eyed monster has made an unwelcome appearance. I know I'm being totally unreasonable, but I just can't keep it at bay.

There's silence at the other end of the phone.

'He popped in for supper last night, and yes, he ended up staying over in the guest room.'

'He stayed over?'

The conversation goes from bad to worse. Even when one of us tries to say something to placate the other, it just seems to end up coming out completely wrong and all that happens is things get more complicated. We love each other, we live for each other, yet we seem to be completely incapable of opening our mouths without hurting each other.

My head says I need to get to grips with the impossibility of her high-wire act; that the combination of missing your loved one and getting on with your life is virtually impossible for those we leave behind. Just coping day to day is hard enough. She has to use these four months as an opportunity to do the things she's neglected for so long. Like catching up with old friends . . . But my heart says something more alarming: perhaps my greatest fear isn't that she'll leave me, but rather that I'll come back to find a wife who's doing just fine without me.

I tell her I'm sorry and that I miss her terribly. But my apology falls on deaf ears. It's come too late.

'If you were that sorry, you'd come home now.'

She starts to cry. Now I can't help myself.

'Don't be ridiculous, Luce, you know I can't. You're missing the big picture here. Even if I did come home now, it wouldn't be the end of it. They won't give up. They're going to keep going until they find me.'

There's an awesome silence at the other end of the line.

'What do you mean, they're going to keep going until they find you?' Her voice is shrill. 'Who are *they*, Chris? What on earth's going on?'

I've said too much.

'Nothing, I don't mean anything by it. Look, I'd better go . . .'

Once again I've taken the coward's option. As I come off the phone I can feel my hands shaking. I really am losing it. I'm making stupid mistakes – first the liquid, then Lucy. God only knows what I'm going to fuck up next. I've allowed this whole targeting thing to cloud my judgement. It's making me paranoid, and I need to get a grip. The only way I'm going to end this is to find these bastards and somehow pin enough evidence on them to justify killing or arresting them.

I go back to the Det with a heavy heart but a newly strengthened resolve. I get my head firmly into the reports, looking for any clue or pattern that might so far have been missed. I want to get a better understanding of the men who are trying to kill me. I'm looking for information about the equipment they're using, their infrastructure, their support mechanisms, tactics, techniques and procedures. When I've established those key components, I can start to drill down and predict what they're going to hit us with next.

If I take it a stage further, and fuse that prediction with technical and tactical intelligence, then I'll be in a position to help the int staff produce detailed targeting information packs containing, among other things, high-definition satellite imagery of the target dwellings and digital mugshots of the terrorists. At that point, the infantry will be in a position to start seeking out and eliminating the Shia and Sunni bomber teams that are so intent on nailing us.

If we can build up a decent enough intelligence picture, then it may even be possible to identify and recruit somebody on the inside. Conflict zones have always been magnets to spooks, and this one is no different. There are a number of agencies in theatre doing similar work already. It takes a little bit of effort to turn somebody, but here, everything's possible. Ideology, ego, revenge, money – it's a volatile mixture. If we can run somebody on the inside, we'd be able to disrupt their logistics capability, possibly even bring down the entire network. We could get in the way of the whole chain of events before the next IED is even emplaced.

Mark, one of the brigade's staff officers, wanders into the Det before I take any more leaps of imagination. He's a pleasant enough bloke, and his heart is in the right place, but professionally I've never really rated him.

Despite having no experience in counter-terrorist bomb disposal, he's been given the job of coordinating all EOD operations in theatre. His lack of specialist knowledge can be frustrating at the best of times, but just lately he's really been winding me up.

'I've been chatting to Colonel Sanderson,' he tells me brightly, 'and we've decided it would be a good idea to rotate the teams.'

'Rotate the teams? You mean us swapping with Abbs's boys up in al-Amarah? Mark, are you fucking insane? What can you possibly hope to achieve by us rotating?'

'Well, for a start, you both need a rest, and you know what they say about a change being as good as . . .'

He tails off, seeing the look on my face. He's convincing nobody.

'Have you really thought this through? Have you honestly considered the full implications of taking us both out of our own back yards? Places we know like the back of our hands? For a start, we're both starting to get closer to the bombers in our respective areas. We're getting more of a grip on their MOs and bomb-making signatures with every passing day. We're within a gnat's whisker of making a breakthrough. And you want to rock the applecart now? Abbs is happy where he is, I'm happy where I am. If you move us, all that work is going to be wasted and more lives will be lost. It's sheer lunacy.'

'I hear what you're saying,' Mark mutters, 'but the decision's been made. Trust me, it's for your own good.'

For my own good? That's a joke. I'm not giving up that easily.

'Have you spoken to Abbs about this?'

'Well . . .' He looks mildly sheepish. 'Not as such.'

'Not as such? What the fuck does that mean? You either have or you haven't. Which is it?'

His mobile rings. He holds up his hand, motioning me to shut up – which just makes me want to rip it off.

'You've got a task,' he says, relieved. 'And when you get back from it, you'll need to start preparing for your road move to al-Amarah. You're leaving tomorrow morning.'

22

Without a measureless and perpetual uncertainty, the drama of human life would be destroyed.

Winston Churchill

25 May 2004: Day 22

'It's beautiful, isn't it?' Dan says.

We're heading up Route 6 and I'm completely taken by the contrasting scenery. To our west, the road is lined with dusty concrete single-storey bunkers, set against a backdrop of featureless desert. But the other side is breathtakingly beautiful: hand-built houses in lush, tree-lined gardens irrigated by the clear blue waters of the Tigris. Exotic birds fly between the palm groves, and canoes glide elegantly along the mirror-surfaced serenity of the lagoons. It really is the Garden of Eden. Maybe my mother-in-law was right after all.

'Absolutely amazing . . .'

'Well, don't let it lull you into a false sense of security, boss. This is one of the most dangerous stretches of road on earth and it's about to become more so. We'll be driving through Qalat Salih in about five minutes.'

This is Dan's third tour in Iraq and he's driven this route a few times before. It's good to be with somebody who knows the ground.

'What's Qalat Salih got to offer then, Dan? Twenty-four-hour party people?'

He gives me a sideways glance to see if I'm taking the piss, then realizes I don't have a clue. 'The lion's share of attacks on Route Six take place in Qalat Salih – probably because it's the last town you pass through before you reach the relative safety of the city.'

It makes sense. This is the primary route for convoys travelling from Basra to al-Amarah and I'm told the whole thing is a target-rich environment.

We were supposed to be free-wheeling – travelling on our own before first light. It's the safest time, when most people are still in bed and the bad guys are too fatigued to be seriously effective. But it's all gone to ratshit. We've been ordered to tag along with a long, slow-moving convoy of supply trucks instead, and they're as vulnerable as a tramp steamer on the run to Murmansk. This epic road move has been organized by some of the divisional support troops from Shai'ba Log Base and it's turned into a total cake and arse party. The forty-vehicle convoy set off four hours late, way after first light, and now we're going to be passing through several militia strongholds as well as vast stretches of empty wasteland at the worst possible time of day.

I still can't believe we're being sent to al-Amarah just for the hell of it. We've been messed around something stupid and to make matters worse Scotty was poached by Div HQ last night. They needed somebody to manage all ECM operations in theatre and he's the best there is. The chief of staff personally selected him so there was no arguing the case. It was all done very suddenly and I'm told his replacement – Neil Heritage – has already been flown into al-Amarah to meet us on our arrival.

Still, at least we'll have a change of scenery. It will offer us some respite from the lunatics we've been working with in Basra Province. Yesterday we were called out to another device under a bridge in the Danish AOR, about 10 miles north of the city. And because they mixed up their grid references yet again, our team drove straight over the top of the bomb to get to their ICP.

To make matters worse, the position was completely exposed – another gift of a shot for a sniper, *and* I had to deal with the device manually. We were also being dicked for the entire operation – under observation by hostile locals loyal to the Mahdi Army – so I did the smoke trick again. This time I decided to deploy more powerful red phosphorus grenades to mask my approach, prevent the render-safe procedures from being compromised, and get the troops off the ground as quickly as possible.

The upshot of this, so I've heard from several mates, is that the EOD head-sheds back in the UK are beginning to question my judgement. Apparently the use of smoke to mask an operator's manual approach has sent them into a flat spin. It isn't a procedure taught at the school and I don't think it's been used in Northern Ireland either, so the old and bold just can't bring themselves to accept it.

This is the one thing that really bugs me about the system: there are far too many people who just cannot find it within themselves to accept change. They're too busy reminiscing about past conflicts to think about present or future ones. Many of them go into meltdown if you even begin to suggest anything that's outside their comfort or experience zones.

'OK, boss, two minutes.'

I snap back to the present and get on the net. 'Stand by, stand by.'

The boys know what to do.

As we enter the outskirts of Qalat Salih, the Iraqi menfolk seem to be lounging around the side of the road doing next to nothing. Some are smoking, others are sleeping, some are reading books – letting the world pass them by as they sit outside their mud houses and tin shacks. It seems to be a place at peace with the world. Children are playing football in the street and wild dogs roam around, scavenging for food.

A sultry breeze is gusting gently through the vehicle, goading me to switch off and relax. I have to make a concerted effort to remind myself where I am.

And then it comes: the combat premonition. That unexplained presentiment soldiers experience when something is out of place.

I feel my heart rate increase as I turn my head left and right.

Something is wrong. Again, it's unusually quiet. The street is suddenly void of life. I look up at the buildings and can see eyes staring back at us suspiciously from the windows. There's nobody, nothing, on the street. It's our first combat indicator.

We don't get another.

Three or four shots crack open the air above our heads and kick up dust as they ricochet off the pavement. My thoughts slow for a split second, and then I feel the familiar wave of adrenalin rush through me. I shout into my mouthpiece: 'Contact right, contact right!' But this isn't an ambush; we're being shot at by a lone sniper.

'Here we go again,' says Dan.

We're both surprisingly calm. This time neither of us feels the need to hunch down into his seat and assume the fetal position. This time it just feels like a drill.

Dan floors the accelerator and the Duro lurches forward, its engine whining. He's in a trancelike state, blocking out the noise around us as he focuses completely on the road ahead. But almost as soon as we begin to build up momentum, he has to stand on the brakes. The convoy in front has slowed almost to a halt; one of the drivers must have panicked and hit the wrong pedal. We jerk forward in our seats, cursing loudly.

The first rule of being in contact is to return fire, to match aggression with aggression. But we can't. There's nothing to shoot at. My safety catch is off and I'm looking over my rifle sights, scanning the area in search of the sniper. But he's good. No one has located him yet.

Another shot punches into the road behind us.

'Has anybody seen him yet?' I yell into my radio.

We can't debus and move into proper cover; the vehicles would start moving again the moment we did.

My eyes flick back and forth over the area, trying to identify where the bastard's shooting from. He may not be a crack shot, but he's a brave little bastard, I'll give him that. But right now I just want to get him in my sights and drop him.

'Boss, the convoy's moving again,' Vince says.

As Dan guns the accelerator again and we finally pull out of the town, I can still hear the sniper popping off sporadic rounds at us despite the fact that we're now well out of range. This whole episode has lasted no more than fifteen seconds from start to finish, yet time just seemed to stand still.

As the adrenalin starts to subside, I begin to feel slightly nauseous. Dan hasn't said a word. I give him the once-over, worried that he might be doing his usual trick of getting shot and not mentioning it to anybody.

'Are you OK?'

'Livin' the dream, boss, livin' the dream.'

He's grinning from ear to ear. And with that he sparks up a cigarette and begins puffing himself to death.

We're halfway to al-Amarah, completely enshrouded in our own dust storm. The wipers have long since given up trying to clear the windscreen; now they just smear it with a film of shitty brown mud. We're travelling blind.

'Is al-Amarah really as bad as everybody makes out, Dan?'

He pulls out his packet of Lambert and Butler, sparks up another cigarette and draws deeply before eventually answering the question. Dan is very much a thinker, and the whole Lambert and Butler routine is one of the quirky rituals he needs to complete before answering any question that requires a sensible answer.

'In terms of IED activity,' he says, 'there's not much going on, but I read yesterday that the battle group up in Camp Abu Naji has had around two hundred and fifty contacts with the enemy since they arrived six weeks ago. They're averaging around five contacts a day. They've fired tens of thousands of rounds at the insurgents so far and are on the receiving end of indirect enemy fire virtually every night. In short, if you think Basra is bad for rockets and mortars, al-Amarah is ten times worse.'

I can hardly wait.

As the windscreen wipers do their best to swish from side to side, I find myself falling into a zombie-like trance. I'm struggling to keep my eyes open and I allow them to close for a fleeting moment.

When I open them again, we're two hours further north, approaching al-Majar al-Kabir.

'Welcome back, Rip Van. Thought we'd lost you there for a minute or two.'

'Er, sorry, Dan. You should have given me a nudge.'

'You looked so peaceful, sat there dribbling on yourself,' he says. 'And anyway, there was fuck all going on between Qalat Salih and al-Mak, so I thought you'd appreciate the shut-eye.'

I did appreciate it, but still feel Jack none the less.

Outside, the dust storm has cleared and the sky's a brilliant pale blue.

'This place is beautiful. Where are we?'

'Looks can be deceptive. We're on the outskirts of al-Mak. It's where those RMPs got killed last year. Remember? In the police station?'

I nod gloomily. 'Yeah, I remember reading about it at the time. It sounded fucking horrendous. Six of the poor bastards against a few thousand angry Iraqis . . .'

The press reckoned they didn't stand a chance. The locals were massively pissed off about the British military's heavy-handed approach; apparently a young Iraqi had been shot by some Paras earlier that day, and his mates were going bananas. They badly wanted to even the score, and the six redcaps just happened to be in the wrong place at the wrong time. They were on their way to al-Majar al-Kabir Police Station when the mob surrounded them. Two of the boys tried to defuse the situation and were killed on the spot. It seems the remaining four lads managed to leg it to the station house, but one of them was killed in the doorway. The other three battled it out with Iraqi gunmen for two hours. They finally surrendered when they ran out of ammo. The poor fuckers must have been terrified. They were murdered with their own weapons, alone, without any military back-up, unable to defend themselves or to summon help. Each one of them took at least two rounds in the head. Between them they'd been shot over thirty times.

Dan sparks up another cigarette.

'That's why all vehicle moves between al-Amarah and Danny Boy, the checkpoint on the outskirts of al-Mak, have to be escorted by Warrior,' he says. 'You'll need to radio through to the PWRR battle group to get an armoured escort to come and pick us up.'

As we arrive at the checkpoint, which is nothing more than an unmanned outpost marked by some sand-filled blast walls, there's a Warrior escort already waiting for us.

'Which one's the ATO?' shouts one of the commanders.

'Me,' I reply.

'OK, sir, if you want to travel with us, then the rest of the vehicles can follow on behind.'

I'm about to get in, assuming they want me to travel with them to brief me about current ops. But then the penny drops. I'm considered a high-value target.

Even if I did want to, travelling in the back of the Warrior because our soft-skinned vehicles are too dangerous to use doesn't exactly send the right signal to the team. So I politely decline their offer.

It's one in, all in, or not at all.

And besides, Warriors don't have aircon.

23

*People do not see; they only recognize. And what they do
not recognize remains invisible to them.*

Simon Leys

26 May 2004: Day 23

The combination of oxygen-starved air and the stifling
heat makes running around the camp almost unbear-
able. That, plus the fact I've got my body armour, pistol
and helmet on my back. As the fierce desert sun does its
worst, I realize why the world's best runners come from
its hottest countries. The dusty track that runs around the
inside of the perimeter wall is only a few miles long, but
completing a single lap feels like a test of endurance. I'm
trying to orientate myself and unwind at the same time,
but as my feet pound the soft sand, the whole miserable
experience feels anything but therapeutic.

I complete a second lap and glance in the direction of
our new Det. The single-storey bombproof building is

made from reinforced concrete, and has an ops room, a crew room and several four-man bedrooms for the lads. We're told it can withstand a direct hit from a mortar – which is handy as we're going to be receiving incoming on a daily basis. It's perfect. I just feel a bit Jack, because most of the guys on camp are living in canvas tents with virtually no ballistic protection.

To add insult to injury, the Det is also conveniently situated opposite the medical centre. As far as the lads are concerned, this is even more important than being mortar proof, as the Med Centre happens to house 95 per cent of the females on the base.

As I pound further along the track, my feet beating rhythmically into the dust, I decide to up the pace. I'm really going for it now.

I notice a pair of ISO shipping containers to my right that have been turned into a large internet café. Behind them, more containers have been converted into a laundry, some ablutions and a NAAFI shop. I try to make a mental note of what's where. If I get called to the battle group headquarters at night, I'll have to take this route and it will be pitch black. The use of white light is banned after last light to prevent enemy mortar crews from accurately targeting us. At least that's the theory.

As I reach the main gate I take a left, through the shadows of the heavily fortified watchtowers and concrete blast walls protecting us from the outside world. My concentration is suddenly broken by the thunderous roar of a Chinook taking off. Seconds later a Warrior armoured vehicle hammers past me, churning up a cloud of thick dust in its wake. Now I'm blind as well as unable to breathe.

Thank Christ I've only got half a lap to go.

I continue past the RMP Det and the Battle Group HQ and on towards the tank park. It must house close to a hundred armoured and soft-skinned vehicles. It's also full of huge flying beasts. No matter how fast I run, the insects swarm around me, feeding off my head, neck and arms as I try to swat them away.

Just when I think things can't get any more unpleasant, I hear two loud bangs resonating in the distance, followed by the unmistakable whistle of incoming mortars.

My guts turn to water. It's impossible to know where a mortar is going to land; it's not until you hear the bang that you know whether or not you're safe. And right now things aren't looking particularly good. I'm completely exposed and at least 200 metres from the nearest cover.

Fuck it. I need to do something.

I turn in my tracks and begin to sprint towards the nearest parked Warrior. The only sound I can hear is the subsonic whistling of the mortars as they drop towards the earth. I've left it too late; I'm running for my life.

I dive into the dirt as the first of the two deafening explosions resonates around the camp. There's a bright orange flash 100 metres away. It's still far too close for comfort. I feel a wave of heat and blast pressure shoot across my body. Two seconds later it's followed by another massive bang. This one's closer, maybe 80 metres. The mortar plunges into the scorched earth, flinging great lumps of debris high into the air. Small pieces of rock and earth fall from the sky like hail.

I feel like I should be reacting differently. I should somehow be more professional and emotionally detached, but I'm not. I'm shitting myself.

I wrestle frantically with my pack and struggle to put on my body armour and helmet. There's a third explosion, followed immediately by another; their blinding pulses of brilliant white light stun me and their blasts suck the air from my chest. My ears are ringing from the detonations and I can taste the bitter metallic tang of burned cordite.

I'm rooted to the spot. It's too dangerous to move. Even if I wanted to I couldn't. Every new blast makes me jump involuntarily. I'm paralysed by fear. I want it to end. I want the earth to open up and swallow me.

Another gut-punching explosion pierces my eardrums. Fuck me, that's five now. How much longer is this going to go on?

I wait for the next explosion. I feel numb. But this time there's nothing. My brain races as I lie there, rooted to the ground. Still nothing.

A military policeman runs out of a building shouting, 'Incoming!' I appreciate the sentiment, but he's a bit late.

I stand up, giddy but alive. The flood of relief is overwhelming.

My first response is to check the family jewels – all OK on that front. Then I run my hands down my arms and legs, checking to see if I've been fragged. I'm pumped up on adrenalin and probably wouldn't feel it even if I had been. There's nothing.

The episode now feels completely unreal. It's only because my ears are still ringing and I feel a strong urge to vomit that I know I'm not dreaming. And the fact that I'm covered in a thick layer of dirt and dust.

Now I know first-hand why Camp Abu Naji is known as 'Camp Incoming'.

A short while later the team and I are sitting in the battle group briefing room. Randsy, the battalion's intelligence officer, is giving us his Welcome to al-Amarah speech.

'I'll begin with friendly forces,' he says, getting straight into the meat of the brief.

He explains that the battle group consists of a squadron

of Challenger 2 tanks, a company of fusiliers and two further armoured infantry companies from the Princess of Wales's Royal Regiment – his battalion. Y Company, the battalion's fire support company, is also part of the battle group, although it's based forward in the centre of al-Amarah, about six clicks away.

'We have a policy of smile – shoot – smile,' he says. 'One moment we're trying to win their hearts and minds, the next we're engaged in a ferocious fire-fight with them, and a day or so later we'll be back to the softly, softly approach. It's insane really.'

It sounds about par for the course. Nothing's clear cut in al-Amarah.

'The town's witnessed a fearsome amount of anti-coalition activity. Since the end of April, almost every patrol we've sent out has been ambushed, and the police we're here to support are more often than not involved in some way. You have to see it to believe it; we've experienced everything from mortars and rockets through to RPG ambushes. Virtually all attacks are carried out by the Mahdi Army. There are at least three hundred members in al-Amarah alone.'

He concludes by telling us that the place is a total fuck-up and that the operating environment is at best completely unpredictable.

*

As we all bimble back towards the Det, Rich Deane pulls up in his Warrior.

'Good to see you again, mate. We're about to be crashed out to a terrorist heavy weapons cache, at a farm about ten clicks south of here. We've asked for ATO assistance, so if you've not had it already, you should be getting a formal tasking any minute.'

We get some more background to the task. Our primary target, Bravo One, is a godfather-type figure and senior player in the insurgency. He's also a supplier of weaponry to a number of terrorist groups. His son, Bravo Two, lives on the farm with him and is effectively his chief of staff.

Despite the fact that these are hardcore terrorists, it's only a search assist op, so I can afford to leave the majority of the lads behind. We've been on the go since early o'clock and they need as much rest as they can get. Dan and I reckon we can manage this job between us. We get the boys to help us transfer some EOD tools and equipment into a couple of Bergens, then, grabbing the ECM kit from the new bleep, we chuck the whole lot into the back of a Warrior.

We pull out of the camp and through the fortified chicane designed to stop suicide car bombers, and head across the barren wasteland towards Route 6. Dotted around this short stretch of billiard-table desert are derelict buildings, destroyed during the war by American J-Dam aircraft bombs.

As ever, the journey in the back of the Warrior is anything but pleasant. The heat's so strong you can taste it.

We turn on to Route 6 and begin the short journey south towards the target area. Five minutes later the Warrior screams to a halt, its ear-piercing engine leaving us temporarily deaf as we debus and make our way over to Rich Deane's vehicle. At least this time nobody's shooting at us.

Rich and his platoon are already busy conducting a rummage search of the farmhouse. They've been on task all of about two minutes and the so-called terrorists are bending over backwards to help us. As soon as we ask them if they have any weapons, the oldest son, Bravo Two, leads us straight to the cache.

The intelligence we've been given proves to be bang on. There's a stack of mortars and other weapons in the middle of their field. But it isn't quite the high-profile haul we'd hoped for. It's nothing more than a pile of knackered old mortar tubes and a couple of rusty gun barrels lying among a heap of assorted junk and scrap. The weapons are covered in thick lumps of mud and concrete and look like they've been dredged up from the bottom of the ocean. Bravo Two tells us the weapons have been there since the first Gulf war.

Bravo One is clearly no more of a terrorist than my granddad. Our primary target is nothing more than a gentle old man, with a greying beard and bark-like skin. A young child, his grandson, sits on his knee listening to the old man's stories. As he passes on his lessons in life I recognize the look of unconditional love and patience he lavishes on the child. It's the same affectionate look my grandfather used to give me as a young boy. The old man's kind blue eyes and deep-lined face tell me that he's anything but an insurgent. It's obvious to anyone who can locate his own arse with both hands that we won't be finding any terrorist weapons here today.

What concerns me right now is that C Company has had a particularly ferocious time since they've been in Iraq and Rich Deane's platoon in particular has taken numerous hammerings from the insurgents. I've not worked with them long enough to know how they go about their business, and if I'm honest, I'm feeling slightly anxious in case they decide to get a touch heavy-handed.

'What do you think, Chris?' Rich asks.

'Bag of bollocks, mate,' I reply. 'In fact, it wouldn't surprise me if the source that provided us with this int just happened to be involved in some sort of personal vendetta with the guy. Seems to me like he's been stitched up good and proper.'

But this is Rich's op and I'm interested to see how he's going to play it out. Winning the hearts and minds of the population is the first principle of counter-insurgency. Separate the insurgent from his popular support and you've won. If this sort of situation is handled correctly, and the farmer is treated with dignity and respect, there's every chance the old boy and his son will become supporters of the coalition. If we fuck it up, and somehow end up shaming or offending them, all we've done is provided more recruits for the Mahdi Army.

'Bag of bollocks it is, Chris. If this old boy's a terrorist then I'm Father fucking Christmas.'

I can't believe I doubted him for a second. If an Ulsterman doesn't know what to do at a time like this, nobody does.

Later that night I dart across camp to the ablutions, wearing a towel, helmet and body armour – it's the al-Amarah look. Inside, a group of young platoon commanders are exchanging stories about the day's patrols. I take a ship's shower: covering myself in just enough water to get lathered up, then repeating the process to rinse off the dirt and grime that's accumulated over the course of the day. Water discipline is really important here. If we waste the stuff, it means we either go without or some poor bastard in a slow-moving logistics convoy has to brave the rigours of Route 6 to resupply us. Neither option is good.

As I make my way back, I think about the weapons cache incident. I still question the logic behind our teams rotating, but I'm chuffed to bits to be working with these guys. On paper, Rich may be a second lieutenant not long out of Sandhurst, but people like him make me proud to be an Army officer. He's living proof that the system works. One of the reasons we've had so much more success than other members of the coalition, especially with hearts and minds, is because of our Northern Ireland experiences. Ulstermen like Rich Deane are a unique breed. What's more, they possess that one quality no amount of officer training can teach – common sense. After all he and his men have been through, he could so easily have made a bad call, but he didn't. And he wouldn't.

It's been a good day.

Back in the Det, I lay out my kit on a chair in the tiny ops room which doubles as my bedroom and crawl underneath the mozzie net and on to my camp bed. I open a copy of Michael Ondaatje's *The English Patient* and allow myself a moment to stare at the makeshift bookmark – a photo of Lucy and the girls.

I lie back on the pillow but struggle to read even the first line. Being on immediate notice to move, expending so much nervous energy and never getting any quality sleep has left me in a zombie-like state of fatigue. The critically injured Count Almasy will have to lie, hallucinating, in his Tuscan villa for another day.

24

There are moments when, faced with our lack of success, I wonder whether we are failures, proud but impotent. One thing reassures me as to our value: the boredom that afflicts us. It is the hallmark of quality in modern men.

Edmond de Goncourt

1 June 2004: Day 29

The boys are starting to get bored. In Basra we had so many call-outs there was hardly time to eat, let alone sleep. But here we're experiencing long periods of tedium, waiting for the call that never seems to come. We've been out to a couple of crude command-wire incidents, but the fact is there's very little going on here, IED-wise.

I've had the lads preparing kit, cleaning weapons and conducting training tasks. They've even been filling sandbags to help fortify the camp's defences. They're used to living with danger and uncertainty and they accept it, but I can't keep inventing tasks for them just for the sake of it. Besides, on immediate notice to move, we're severely limited in what we can do. For now they seem content to sit in the crew room and watch DVDs.

Dan and I chat at the back of the room as he packs up boxes of Viagra.

'It's twenty times cheaper on the black market here in Iraq than back home,' he says cheerfully.

And enterprising soldiers like Dan have been buying it in bulk – for personal consumption of course.

Unfortunately for Dan, this will be his last consignment of Vitamin V – at least until we leave al-Amarah. Up until last night, the supplier ran a busy shop on camp, selling sweets, drinks, cigarettes and novelty mosque-shaped alarm clocks. From under the counter he also traded in contraband Viagra, pornography and whisky. But yesterday everything changed. The shopkeeper, popularly known as Bob (due to his unpronounceable Iraqi name), had been a familiar sight in camp until he decided to expose himself to one of the lads then ask him for a blow job.

'It wasn't Bob's smartest move,' Dan says. 'The bloke he propositioned ran back to his bunk, grabbed his rifle and chased him out of the gates, threatening to kill him if he ever returned. We've not seen him since.'

The air shakes in mid-sentence and our conversation is brought to a sudden halt by a powerful sonic jolt. We're under attack again. For several minutes a concentrated and accurate mortar bombardment rains down into the compound. Another mortar whistles overhead, but the lads are so engrossed in *Love Actually* they hardly seem to notice the colossal explosion shattering the night air.

Then another. I swear the bangs are getting closer. I can picture the insurgent listening on his mobile, adjusting the dials on his mortar to correct his fire. And seconds later another barrage of bombs hits the compound. Once again the boys duck involuntarily but all eyes remain fixed on the TV as the thunderous booms echo around the camp and out across the desert. The duct tape-lined windows shudder with each new blast.

There's another explosion in the distance. I stop and listen. A short pause, followed by another three, in rapid succession.

It's payback time. Puff the Magic Dragon is giving it back to the bastards. Laying down some serious counter battery fire. The AC 130 Spectre gunship is an airborne artillery firebase armed with twin 20mm multi-barrelled Gatling guns, a 40mm cannon and an automatic 105mm artillery piece. Its onboard computer allows the aircraft to fly around in a huge arc as the fearsome weapons suite engages targets on the ground. It can hit two insurgent positions simultaneously within a kilometre, and with pinpoint accuracy. The beast is fearsome. 'You can run, but you'll only die tired,' is the Spectre crews' mantra.

The 105mm opens up another deadly volley on the unsuspecting mortar crews below. Now its twin Gatling guns are cleaning up, unleashing a formidable storm of lead on any surviving militiamen.

I bet they weren't expecting that tonight.

'Fire mission complete – you had love from above,' a Texan voice drawls over the net.

There's a loud cheer.

Later, I'm sitting outside in the darkness, shooting the breeze with the lads. The tips of our cigarettes glow orange in the shadow of the Det's vast concrete porch.

The sapper EOD teams are with us too – a hardy collection of Jocks, Scousers and Brummies, and a storming bunch of lads they are. They've been sent here to destroy the vast stockpiles of artillery shells still littering the country. An estimated 650,000 tons of explosive ordnance was stockpiled by Saddam's forces prior to the war. Some 250,000 tons of this was looted by insurgents. The rest is being destroyed in controlled explosions every day by these boys. It's going to take them years.

R&R is the principal focus of the conversation, and they're taking no prisoners.

'I'm going to find myself a nice big-breasted Mark F and get some Etch-a-Sketch action.' In case any of this was lost on us, the Brummie mimes drawing a smile on the girl's face by twiddling both of her nipples.

Tom leans towards me. 'What's a Mark F, boss?' he says in what he thinks is a whisper.

The Brummie helps out. 'A larger lady, man – one dress size up from a marquee.'

'That reminds me of a wedding I went to when I was on leave,' one of the Jocks pipes up.

I prepare myself to start laughing out loud. There is nothing quite like a squaddie wedding story.

'The bride was the size of a fuck'n whale,' he says. 'And she was no looker, either. Although to be fair, she was the first girl the groom had met that didn't look like a bloke in drag.'

The Jock carries on reciting the story, telling us how the bride's parents also happened to be worth a few quid and that it was apparent they weren't overly chuffed with their daughter's choice of husband.

'Pity they didn't get to choose the best man either. Total fuck'n heed-case.'

At the reception the servicemen, including the best man, were all sat at the standard twelve-man squaddie table – the one closest to the toilets and furthest from the bride. When it was time for the best man's speech, he was as pissed as a parrot and could barely stand. He set the tone immediately by shouting at parade-ground volume, 'You lot on the back table, keep the fucking noise down!' That was when the first batch of guests got up to leave.

He then staggered over and put his hand on the groom's shoulder.

'Before I launch into my speech, I've got a small announcement to make. Billy has told me the happy couple are preparing to start washing a few nappies.'

'Aaaaaahhhh,' the guests chorused, thinking that perhaps the best man had a shred of decency after all.

'Apparently all the muscles in her arse have packed up.'

Of the hundred or so guests remaining, only twelve were laughing. Another group got up and left in disgust.

'Now this is a very special day for the happy couple,' the best man continued, 'so I'd like to finish on a high – with a wee ditty about the groom.'

By this stage, Billy's head was firmly in his hands.

The best man proceeded to tell the guests about his mate's fearsomely smelly feet. How by the end of the previous year it had all got too much – the smell was killing them.

'After a week of threatening to beat him like a ginger Welsh stepchild,' he said, 'we still couldnae get the grotty bastard to change his socks, so we locked him in the drying room for three days. You know, so he could sort himself out. The poor wee bastard lost three stone in there, but when we let him go back to his bed space it still smelt like something that's crawled up your arse and died.'

He rocked back on his heels and gave his dwindling audience a huge grin.

'Anyway, turns out it wasnae Billy after all. Someone had shat in one of the empty lockers, and it had gone off.'

At that point the bride burst into tears, the mother-in-law fainted and Billy leapt up and began punching the best man into unconsciousness.

It's the oldest wedding story in the world, but the Jock's given it everything. We're laughing so hard, I think I'm going to need surgery.

After another batch of stories about offending parents of potential brides, the lads dart from subject to subject, eventually ending up in a semi-serious discussion about the rights and wrongs of the government's decision to invade Iraq. After much toing and froing, they resolve that even though no weapons of mass destruction were found, 'Saddam was a cunt who had it coming'. With the complexities of the situation now fully resolved, they go back to one of their favourite subjects – FIPAC.

Fighting in pubs and clubs is one of the British squaddie's most popular pursuits. The lads reminisce about how after an evening of FIPAC they'll put on their beer coats (the invisible garment worn when walking home at three in the morning) and navigate with the aid of a kebab compass (the edible course-plotting tool used by squaddies to find their way back to camp). 'Failing that, we'll go for fish and chips,' one of them says. He's referring, of course, to fighting in someone's house and causing havoc in people's streets.

Suddenly one of the other Jocks lets out a loud, piercing scream. 'Aaaaarrrgh, get off me, ya wee bastard!'

'What is it, what is it?' says another voice.

'A fucking camel spider! You should see the size of the bastard! It's just run over my fucking flip-flop! The fucking thing coulda killed me!'

'AAAAARRRRGH! AAAAARRRRGH!'

Now everybody's jumping around screaming. All of a sudden these rufty-tufty airborne warriors don't seem quite so tough. It's hilarious.

In all my time in Basra I didn't see a single creepy-crawly but this place is brimming with the little rascals. What's worse, Camp Abu Naji seems to have a particular appeal for camel spiders. They turn up anywhere – boots, Bergens, cupboards – that's dark and warm.

Members of the Solpugid family, they are a cross between a spider and a scorpion. They're extremely aggressive and only come out to hunt at night. When they bite, they inject you with a chemical that instantly numbs the skin and the surrounding tissue. If it happens when you're sleeping, you can't even tell you've been bitten. If the photos are to be believed, you wake up to find part of your leg or arm missing because the camel spider's been feasting on it all night. Worse still, they're the size of a man's hand and can run at about 10 mph and jump several feet. They've been known to chase people.

We're not taking any chances.

'Find the bastard!' somebody shouts.

Nobody has a torch, so the lads start striking matches.

'Up there!'

We all crane our necks, and there it is, on the porch ceiling, right above us. More screaming. Until someone appears with a can of deodorant. He presses the button and, in true James Bond style, lights the vapour, turning it into a handheld flame thrower.

'Yeah, have some of that, ya bastard!'

The arachnid jumps off the ceiling and begins running around the floor. There's more screaming before the little bastard finally runs off into the desert, still on fire. The boys dissolve into fits of nervous laughter.

I decide to turn in for the night. But before I get my head down I spend an extra five minutes checking my bed space for any sets of beady eyes that might be staring back at me. I'm going to be having nightmares about spiders for weeks now.

25

Our greatest glory is not in never failing, but in rising each time we fall.

Confucius

3 June 2004: Day 31

As the sun crouches low over the dust-fuelled horizon we take the 100-metre walk across the stretch of waste ground known as 'the runway'. We clank over its distinctive metal tracks, past the diesel generators and on towards the cookhouse. Outside, an Iraqi in coveralls is topping up the anti-bacterial gel dispensers and pouring bottled water into a large boiling vessel. Everybody goes through the same ritual before entering the cookhouse: first washing their hands in the hot soapy water, then applying the gel to help minimize the spread of disease. Once a case of the shits breaks out, it spreads like wildfire in a desert camp like this.

Once inside, Taff and Vince head over to the drinks

dispenser and fill plastic beakers with Screech, a tepid, fruity, squash-like drink made entirely of sugar and chemicals.

'Green or yellow?' Taff asks.

Screech doesn't really have a flavour.

It's good to have some quality time with the boys. In spite of the relative boredom, at least we're getting to decompress and connect properly. We definitely didn't manage that in Basra. Prior to our arrival here, petty squabbles had started to break out and cracks were starting to appear – in all of us. Under normal circumstances, squaddies know exactly when it's OK to gob off and when they need to stay schtum. But when they're living and working in one another's pockets the whole time, it's easy to cross that delicate line. Thankfully, that's not the case in Camp Abu Naji. As each day passes and we spend more time getting to know one another, the lads are definitely becoming more tolerant.

Most of the conversation over lunch is about the RAF flying fighter jets low over al-Amarah to disperse an angry crowd that had gathered downtown this morning. It hasn't really been used as a tactic during classic counter-insurgency operations, but it's been massively successful in Iraq.

I'm mega impressed with the RAF up here. During

one of the command-wire IED incidents we were tasked to earlier in the week, we were sent in with no aerial intelligence (no vital radar imagery or high-resolution photography), no time to conduct a planned operation and no helis, so we deployed by Warrior. When we got back I nipped into the RAF Det. I told myself I wasn't annoyed; it's just much easier to locate command wires from the air and I wanted to get an idea of how we might go about securing helis in future.

After a few minutes' fishing, one of the two pilots saw right through me and started getting defensive.

'Are you implying we'd rather sit about in here than get out and fly?' he said.

Confrontation with these guys was the last thing I needed.

'I'm not implying anything,' I said. 'I just want to know how we can get heli support when we need you, rather than being constantly fobbed off because you've already been deployed on a lower-priority task.'

'You are joking, aren't you?' There was a serious edge to his voice. 'We're desperate to get out and fly, and we've had fuck all in the way of taskings since we've been here.'

Somebody somewhere in the staff chain wasn't doing his job properly. It was clearly time for a brew.

We ran through our respective operational procedures and objectives, and when I explained about the huge

RAF machine we had supporting us in Northern Ireland, it sealed the deal.

'Bollocks to the tasking system,' they said. 'As of now, if you need us, phone or send a runner with a target grid reference, give us fifteen minutes to get the bird turning and burning and we'll take you wherever you need to go.'

And they've been as good as their word.

As the boys and I make our way back from the cook-house, one of the engineers runs up. A task has just come in: a command-wire IED attack ten clicks south of here, on Route 6.

The Puma pilots, Jules and Tim, are flying the twin-engine bird fast, low, and with total concentration. I'm still fiddling with the headphones I was handed when I took my seat. They have a large foam-covered mouth-piece and are connected by a long black curly cable to a socket in the ceiling. Every time the loadmaster hands over a set, he reminds you to take them off before you disembark. Just thinking about that makes me grin.

We're doing over 100 knots, flying 50 feet above the deck alongside Route 6. Inside the sixteen-seat heli you can cut the tension with a knife. All we know so far is that we're being tasked to a partial – some of the command-wire IED's charge has exploded, but not all of it. This is a real swine of a task. You don't know until you're on top of the thing whether it's genuinely malfunctioned or been deliberately modified to lure you in.

But for now I've got a more pressing concern. As we handrail the road, one of my greatest fears is being hit from the flank. The Chechens were the first to realize that it was virtually impossible to hit a moving helicopter with an RPG. They worked out a way of modifying the grenade's fuse and turning it from a device that detonates on impact into a projectile that explodes in mid-air, dispersing high-velocity fragments over a wide area. They no longer needed a direct hit to bring down a chopper. Unfortunately they shared this new-found knowledge with their Jihadist mates across the globe. I've seen *Black Hawk Down*, and as far as I'm concerned it doesn't get much more serious than this.

The pilots continue to scream towards the target and their flying seems to be getting more erratic with each passing second. One minute we're cruising at altitude, the cool desert wind in our faces; the next, we're banging out a suicidal banking manoeuvre, barely skimming the trees and rooftops. Our knuckles whiten as we grab the edges of our seats.

I'm directly behind the door-gunner. Dan, my number

two, and Steve, the commander of the Royal Engineers Search Team in al-Amarah, are both with me. The remainder of our teams are moving to the target by road, escorted by Rich Deane's Warrior platoon.

About a kilometre out, the pilots put us into a steep climb. I can feel the bird reducing speed as we ascend then bank hard right over the road. Only my seatbelt prevents me falling out of the door.

There's a rice sack in the central reservation beneath us.

'Jules, I think that might have been an IED back there. Can we go back and have a look?'

'IED? Where?'

I can hear the alarm in his voice.

'Back there ... three hundred metres ... our six o'clock – in the central reservation.'

I unfasten my seatbelt and position myself next to the gunner. As he sweeps the M60 back and forth across the target area, I grab the cross-bar above the door and talk the pilots towards the rice sack. Moments later we're hovering about 200 feet away from the thing.

'Can we get in a bit closer? Maybe use the down-draught to blow off the sack? That should let us know what's underneath.'

'You're joking, right? You did say you thought it was an IED?'

'I think it could be,' I reply.

And so begins five minutes of debate about the risk to the airframe if the thing detonates, versus the need to identify whether it's a device or somebody's lunch. I can see their point. If it's in the central reservation, it's likely to be a radio-controlled device; if we get too close, it could be detonated against us. But right now I'm more concerned about the team that will be travelling along this stretch of road any minute.

I take a deep breath. 'It's your call, fellas.'

'In that case,' comes the reply, 'I really think we should pull off.'

Bollocks. That wasn't the answer I was hoping for. I go for Plan B: Jedi mind tricks.

'I thought you fuckers were supposed to be the best of the best.'

The fact is, they are. These guys are totally fearless, but this isn't World War Two, when airframes were expendable. The RAF is curiously averse to destroying multi-million-pound aircraft these days.

They don't even bother to respond. They can't resist a challenge. We drop down so fast my stomach is in my mouth. The brown-out from the dust-cloud is so severe that neither the door-gunner nor the pilots can see anything below them, but after a few seconds' hovering just a few feet off the ground the area is clear and the sack – along with most of the central reservation – has vanished.

There's no device. The pilot offers me a smug look, followed swiftly by his middle finger.

We continue towards the target site, scanning the faces of people below us as we soar towards the prearranged RV. A British patrol from nearby Camp Condor, a dusty outpost stuck right in a stretch of featureless desert where the Iraqi Army is being trained by the Brits, is waiting at the ICP. They happened to be in the vicinity and responded as soon as the explosion was reported.

When we get there the bird will circle to give us a better idea of what's lying in wait for us on the ground, then swoop on to the landing site, drop us off – while still in the hover – and move into a holding pattern to provide us with some protection from above. After the task, Dan and I will drive back in our own vehicle.

'ETA five minutes.'

I hold up five splayed fingers. The other two lads repeat the signal to acknowledge they've understood before re-fastening their helmets and weapon slings.

'Three minutes.'

We begin to circle the target and I can clearly see the command wire dug into the scorched earth. I point it out to Dan and Steve and tell the aircrew via my microphone.

We drop down again, ready to begin the final run in.
'One minute.'

We're travelling low and fast again. Really low and fast.
I remove my headset, replace my personal-role radio and
helmet, and slip my goggles over my eyes. Then I reach
under my seat, grab my Bergen and slide it over one
shoulder. I don't put it on properly in case we get
bumped and I need to get it off in a hurry. Out of the
door I can see cars racing past in the opposite direction.

The bird flares, banks 180 degrees and then drops into
a hover, facing back the way we've just come. I suddenly
feel vulnerable. I'm not bothered so much about snipers,
more the possibility of a landmine at the side of the road.
Route 6 is supposed to be clear, but with 250,000 tons of
ordnance still unaccounted for, how can they be so sure?

'Go, go, go!' the loadmaster shouts.

We toss our safety-belts to one side and throw ourselves
out of the door. A wall of dust and sand belts us in the
face. Grit and phlegm begin to fill my lungs.

As the last man exits, the heli pulls off.

As the roar of the Puma's engine fades, I begin to
recover my equanimity. For a moment there's silence; all
I can hear is my own heartbeat, and the blood rushing in
my ears. I'm covered in a thick blanket of sweat and dust.
The place reeks of shit, just like Basra and al-Amarah,
but in case our lungs weren't getting enough of a

hammering, there's also the stench of chemicals from the brick factory a couple of miles north.

We've been dropped about 150 metres away from the contact point, a huge roadside crater surrounded by scorched earth. Dust and debris are spread across the tarmac in front of it. I look around the shimmering desert, trying to piece together the terrorist's tactical design, to work out exactly where he sited his firing point, what type of IED he used, his intended target, and, most importantly of all, what else he might have lying in wait for us.

The platoon from Camp Condor is manning road-blocks on the barren plain 200 metres either side of the bomb crater. I do a quick threat assessment to determine the possible location of any immediate dangers. There are a couple of small mud hut villages overlooking this position. They're set back on the horizon against a backdrop of straggly trees. I take out my binoculars and have a good look around for snipers. I see more friendly troops on the ground, lying on top of sand berms or taking up fire positions in roadside ditches. They're Argyll and Sutherland Highlanders. It gives me a warm fuzzy feeling seeing these blokes looking alert and instantly ready to return fire. They're good, and they need to be: we're very exposed here. Apart from the thick riverside vegetation along the banks of the

Tigris to our east, the terrain is largely open desert.

The Argylls' platoon commander introduces himself and explains the background to the incident.

'One of our patrols was stopped by some locals who told them there had been an explosion and took them to the crater. They saw scorch marks and a bit of shrapnel, then a couple of intact shells. At that point, my men pulled off target rather sharpish and we called you guys in.'

I ask him to describe the shells, their exact location inside the crater, when they were found and what else was seen or heard that might have aroused his suspicion.

'Has anybody approached the area?'

'Yeah, the lads were escorted to the end of the command wire by the locals, then traced it all the way back into the contact point. We've been all over it.'

'Have you got both ends of the command wire under control now?'

His face goes ashen. 'Er, no. Should we have?'

It's normal to take control of the command wire, otherwise you're effectively allowing the terrorist to go back and trigger the device. But I don't want to make this guy feel an arse in front of the blokes. He seems like a decent guy and his boys have been lying here waiting for us in the baking heat for the last hour.

'It's nice, but not vital,' I reply.

I ask him a few more questions, and then chat to the lads who actually walked up to the device.

I drop into some cover, spark up a cigarette and take a moment to work out a plan. The Argylls have been here an hour already. We don't want to hang around much longer. Any more than two hours on the ground and we can definitely expect to be bumped. We'll clear the firing point – remove the command wire, and then we'll clear the contact point with the barrow.

There's a rumbling sound behind me. The lads from the PWRR are rolling into the position with my team sandwiched between them. Two of the Warriors peel off to take over from the Argylls' soft-skinned Land Rovers manning the roadblocks. They'll double as our flank protection. As our lads park up the team vehicles in a protective V and get straight into their arrival drills, Chris Broome, Rich Deane's platoon sergeant, brings his Warrior, Whiskey Two Two, into the ICP to act as our protection.

I brief the lads concurrently and set about completing my RSP.

I tilt my head in the direction of our new bleep. 'Neil, can you grab me an ECM kit?'

'Roger that, boss.'

I don't know Neil all that well yet, but he strikes me as a grafter. He's going to fit right in.

He and Mick Brennan dive into the back of the ECM wagon and begin configuring the kit, frantically screwing antennae on to the metal briefcase-like device. The two of them are muckers of old and have become inseparable since Neil's been on the team.

Neil reappears a moment later and hands me the ECM set. I grab the rest of my kit.

'And, boss?' he says. 'Those who live by the sword get shot by guns, so try to look unimportant while you're down there. You never know, the sniper may be low on ammo.'

I give him a grin. The fact is, I don't intend to hang around. This RSP is going to be something different. Something nice and quick. Dynamic IEDD with a twist.

'Sergeant Broome, is there any chance I could borrow one of your Warriors, please?'

'Certainly, sir,' he says, with a mischievous smile. 'Where would you like to take it?'

I read him out the ten-figure grid reference given to me by the two lads from the Argylls who first found the firing point. 'It's at the furthest end of the command wire. The trouble is, because the wire's at right angles to the road we're on, we have to travel from our ICP along Route 6 until we reach the contact point, then make a left and follow the command wire all the way to the firing point.'

He knows as well as I do that route isn't ideal as we'd have to drive past the live devices in the crater.

'Alternatively, because we have a grid reference, we could just vector straight on to the target, navigating diagonally, across country, using the GPS.'

Broomstick, as the lads have nicknamed him, remains impassive.

'Personally, I prefer Plan B,' I say.

'No problemo,' he says. 'Cross country it is.' He yells in the direction of the nearest Warrior. 'Beharry, you're on!'

I don't know what it is Beharry says or does, but quick as a flash the platoon sergeant replies, 'Genius does what it must, talent does what it can, and you'd better do what you're fucking well told, Beharry.'

He turns back to me. 'You know how it works, sir. We fight for democracy, but we don't have to practise it.'

Moments later I'm trundling across the desert in Whiskey Two Zero. We're battened down, heading towards the firing point, so I'm holding the GPS receiver out of a tiny gap in my hatch and giving directions to Beharry over the radio.

'So, how do you enjoy driving these things, Private Beharry?' I ask him.

'I like it,' he says. 'But some days, you know, some days you the bug, some days you the windshield.'

If anyone should know, he should. When he rescued

his team from that ambush five weeks ago, his vehicle was hit by more RPGs than you could shake a stick at. At one point he was shot in the head by a 7.62mm bullet which penetrated his helmet and remained lodged on its inner surface. You can still see the scar.

'Are they difficult to drive?'

'Not bad,' he says. 'Trouble is, they make somet'ing idiotproof and someone just make a better idiot.'

I like this guy, and I can see why Rich Deane does too. When Rich was hit by the RPG, young Beharry waded through the incoming fire and pulled him bodily out of the top of the Warrior.

I glance at my GPS. We've been travelling for around three minutes but only covered about 100 metres. For some reason Beharry's driving Whisky Two Zero as if he was negotiating it through a minefield.

'You can afford to speed up a bit if you wish, Private.'

'You sure?'

'Yeah. Drive it like you stole it.'

He doesn't need telling twice. He sets off like Lawrence of Arabia and within seconds we're approaching the firing point.

'Fifty metres . . . right a bit . . . thirty metres . . . a touch left . . . OK, now you should take it slowly. 'Ten, nine, eight . . . three, two, one. Stop!'

I get out and there, in the lee of the berm, is the end

of the command wire – the firing point. Technology – I love it. This is definitely the way to do bomb disposal.

I complete a search of the area, using the natural cover of the sandbank to protect my right flank and Private Beharry's Warrior to protect my left from sniper fire. A shell scrape has been prepared at the firing point. The shallow 6-foot-by-3-foot dugout has been constructed to offer the bombers some cover from view as well as to provide protection should they be compromised and come under fire. It has all the hallmarks of a well-trained group. The attack has been meticulously planned and patiently executed. The remains of food and drink suggest the bombers were lying in wait for some time. There's also a mountain of cigarette butts and bits of chewing gum strewn all over the position. Forensically, it's a gift.

When I've finished bagging everything up, I tie the end of the command wire to a line and attach it to the back of the Warrior. I get everybody on the cordon and back in the ICP to take hard cover in case the command wire is booby-trapped, and then climb aboard. I ask Private Beharry to roll slowly towards the ICP. We pull the wire as we go. This is remote neutralization made easy.

Back in the ICP, Dan and I prepare for phase three, clearance of the contact point, while Mick and

Neil pack up the 400-metre length of command wire.

'Seen this, boss?' Neil asks.

Dan and I are busy fucking about trying to get the barrow configured with a special robotic arm called the manipulator – a highly dextrous mechanical hand. Trouble is, you need a highly dextrous mechanical hand just to get the bastard thing on.

'It's probably nothing,' he continues, 'but it might be better than a poke in the eye with a frozen turd. This command wire? It says "Made in Iran" on it.'

It's no smoking gun, but this is definitely going to raise a few eyebrows back at Divisional Headquarters.

The rest of the job is pretty uneventful. From the back of the EOD vehicle, Dan guides the barrow and its manipulator on to the edge of the contact point, then, extending the robotic arm, he removes the live artillery shells one by one from the crater. It's like a big boys' version of one of those arcade games where you try to win yourself a fluffy bunny with a small grappling iron.

We've been on target thirty minutes – the shells have been cleared. We need to get a shifty on. There are 300 known members of the Mahdi Army here, but they can increase their numbers tenfold at the drop of a hat. I don't want to be on the receiving end of one of their attacks. But we need every bit of evidence we can get – components, explosive residue, fragmentation, clothing, fags, the whole shebang. I've searched the firing point but we need to search the contact point.

The team cracks on, the usual smattering of banter belying their absolute understanding that this is potentially the most valuable phase of the task.

Neil pipes up again: 'Boss, I've found something.'

I head over to where he's standing. He points to a trail of tiny footprints. They're children's footprints, and they're spread along the entire length of the command wire. I don't believe what I'm seeing. The bastards are using children to dig in the wire to minimize their chances of arrest or capture. This needs to be reported immediately. If coalition forces see somebody digging in a command wire, they'll shoot them on the spot, or, worse still, call in an air-strike. Most enemy sightings are made from several hundred metres away and the last thing a soldier would think if he sees somebody planting a bomb is that it might be a child.

I glance at my watch. We've been on the ground for about forty-five minutes now.

'OK fellas, saddle up. We need to get back.'

I feel completely shagged. I don't know whether it's the intensity of the tasks or the cumulative build-up of pressure, but I'm feeling more and more exhausted at the end of every job.

*

As we head back to camp in convoy, Dan is back at the wheel of our vehicle while I sit manning the radios and sparking up the fags. The featureless desert around us is punctuated only by stray dogs and the occasional cloth-covered hut. The lead Warrior, Whiskey Two Three, is about 50 metres in front of us. Sergeant Adkins, the vehicle's commander and a veteran senior NCO from the PWRR, has only recently been posted into the platoon. His predecessor was hospitalized after receiving terrible burns during a contact: a couple of kids on a balcony lobbed a Molotov cocktail down his hatch.

We're travelling north along Route 6. As we pass through the outskirts of a small village, ragged, malnourished children wave to us. We've got about another 6 kilometres to go before we reach the gates of Camp Abu Naji.

I'm running the last job through my mind. It's the first task that has really gone like clockwork from start to finish. Every phase seemed to go without a hitch. As we drive through the dust-cloud churned up by the lead Warrior, my eyes are focused on the middle distance. Thumb up arse, brain firmly in neutral.

Call it luck, call it intuition, but something causes me to snap out of my daydream and shift my gaze to the side. I do a double-take. There's a device dug into the side of the road. We're right next to it. Literally a couple of feet away from the fucking thing. Jesus.

Then the terror takes hold. I wonder if this is going to be the last thing I ever see before I'm engulfed in flames and torn to pieces by the blast.

Everything goes into slow motion, but the bomb doesn't detonate. Because of my daydreaming, we just drive straight past it.

Fuck! What if they're waiting to hit the back of the convoy?

My blood runs cold, and bile burns at the back of my throat. I look in the wing mirror. The vehicle behind us will be approaching the device any second. I've got to stop it.

I grab the HF radio and get on the net.

'All Whiskey Two callsigns, hold your position! I say again, hold your position!'

I see Chris Adkins's vehicle stop in front of me. More importantly, the vehicle behind me has stopped – just short of the IED.

Thank Christ for that.

Fucking hell, how lucky are we? It's a miracle the thing didn't detonate. It must have been placed there to catch us on our way back to camp.

Dan and I drive up to Chris Adkins's Warrior and I brief him on the device. He looks gutted. When these guys are pulling convoy protection, their primary job is to act as lead scout, to look out for freshly disturbed earth or anything suspicious. As far as he's concerned, he's just failed on both counts. I can see he's beating himself up about it. He gets on the radio and briefs the rest of the lads. Then he turns and looks me square in the eye.

'Do you want me to shoot it with the thirty mil?'

I try not to laugh. 'Tempting, but if I let you do that I'd be sacked instantly. We'd destroy all the forensics. We need to catch these bastards.'

I still can't believe the neck of the fuckers who've emplaced this device. They obviously did it after our team passed through on our way to the first tasking.

Now it's payback time.

We leave the soft-skinned vehicles where they are and scream into the village, hull down, in the Warriors. We need to completely dominate any likely firing points so that the insurgents can't trigger the device while I'm neutralizing it. We pull into the cluster of one-room mud houses and find the end of the IED's command wire, but the insurgents have legged it. The place is just full of 'innocent' civilians who saw and heard nothing.

'What's your plan, boss?' Chris asks.

'We need to get out of here,' I say. 'I'm going to need to get this cracked quickly.'

If we hang about too long, there's bound to be another device waiting for us further along the route.

Grabbing the snips, I run to the roadside IED and start

frantically chopping wires. Then I attach a line to the charge, trail it back behind the warrior and give it a tug.

Nothing.

We're in business. I give it a quick once-over, then throw it in the back of the Duro.

The whole task has taken less than five minutes. It's the quickest I've ever neutralized a bomb.

As we continue north, trying to complete the final 4 kilometres of our epic journey, we roll alongside the River Tigris. Marsh Arabs canoe across the calm water and old men sit fishing from the banks. They don't have a care in the world. On the opposite side of the road, people watch us from the windows of flat-roofed houses festooned with red Shia flags.

Whiskey Two Three slows again. Fucking hell, now what? But deep down I know.

The radio crackles into life. 'I was feeling a bit left out,' says Chris, 'so I've found another one of the little buggers. It's identical to the last two.'

I'm beginning to wonder if we're ever going to make it back to camp. This must be the longest journey in the history of bomb disposal.

'Where?' I ask.

'I'll show you.'

Chris reverses alongside our Duro. I climb out of the

cab and on to the back of his Warrior. He hands me his binos as it lurches forwards again.

And there it is, another command-wire IED, glimmering on the side of the road.

This is getting silly now. It's like something out of a Roadrunner cartoon. I have an image of small, dastardly, bewhiskered men planting bombs nineteen to the dozen all the way up the road ahead.

'How accurate are those things?' I ask, pointing at the 30mm cannon on the front of Chris's Warrior.

'Very,' he says.

'OK, do it.'

Sergeant Adkins mutters something to his gunner, then shouts, 'Stand by!'

I brace myself.

A single shot rings out, then . . . nothing.

He's missed.

'Just bringing the gun on,' Sergeant Adkins says.

There's another ear-splitting crack as the 30mm cannon fires a second high-explosive round at the 2-foot-long artillery shell.

Nothing again.

'You couldn't hit a horse's arse with a fucking banjo,' Chris says to his gunner. 'You're sacked. Let me have a cabbie.'

They climb out of their respective hatches and swap

seats to a chorus of abuse from the other Warrior crews.
A few seconds later a third shot rings out.

Ping!

I don't believe it. The armour-piercing 30mm projectile has just bounced off the artillery shell.

'Do it again,' I urge him.

There's another loud ping. But still no explosion.

Great. We've got an artillery shell that's been knocked
around so much it's now effectively a 'blind' – an angry
piece of unexploded ordnance. What's even more frustrating is that if we do this by the book, we're going to
have to wait an age for any explosive in the shell to cool
down before I can get close enough to make it safe. And
we just haven't got the time.

On the flip side, I've already broken every rule in the
book by trying to shoot it in the first place, so is breaking
one more really going to hurt? And any semblance of
professional credibility I may once have had was
destroyed the moment I said it was OK to start shooting
bombs with cannons.

Fuck it.

I run down to the edge of the road and grab the shell.
It's still hot. Then I double back to the wagon and hand
it to Dan.

'Stick this in the boot would you, mate?'

'Boss, are you insane? We're not honestly going to

drive to Abu Naji with that in the back, are we?'

'Dan, trust me,' I say in my best Delboy Trotter voice. 'What could possibly go wrong?'

'Well, if it goes bang and we both get killed,' he replies, 'don't say I didn't warn you.'

26

Research has shown that boredom is closely related to frustration and that the effect of too much frustration is invariably irritability, withdrawal, rebellious opposition or aggressive rejection.

Fritz Redl, *When We Deal With Children*

11 June 2004: Day 39

Life in Camp Abu Naji continues to be an excruciating combination of boredom mixed with rare spurts of exhilaration. I wake up, scratch my balls, then shit, shower and shave. Then I have to try to think of something interesting to occupy us.

We've had a few interesting jobs, but no real excitement since we drove back from the command-wire IED with the shell in the back of the wagon, and even that turned out to be pretty much a non-event. We took the thing to an isolated corner of camp and rigged it up with a couple of plastic explosive charges before giving it the good news.

Otherwise there's been little to write home about. It's dire. I can live with the night-time mortar attacks, the camel spiders and the sandstorms; in fact I've actually started to look forward to them. But the waiting around, the mind-numbing boredom, is sucking the life out of me.

Until a week ago, supply convoys were getting hit by roadside command-wire devices on pretty much a daily basis, so having had some initial success finding one from the air, the RAF pilots and I came up with the idea of daily clearance flights along Route 6, starting with a sortie first thing in the morning, before the log convoys drove the route. The battle group commander seemed a bit reluctant at first, but eventually gave us the go-ahead.

The following day we found our first fully intact device. And the day after that, we found another. Our last job was four days ago when we discovered another roadside command-wire device, only this time the Mahdi Army had thrown in a few funnies, just to keep us on our toes. The cheeky bastards had placed anti-personnel and anti-tank mines all around the command wire and firing point. The mines – small, but powerful enough to blow off a man's lower leg and kill him with his own bone fragments – are among my least favourite devices. What's more, thanks to internal military politics, if we do get caught neutralizing them, the engineers tend to get all precious.

I decided that this task was the perfect opportunity for a bit of inter-cap-badge diplomacy. It was crying out for what we call the Joint EOD concept: Royal Engineers search the area, an RE bomb disposal operator carries out the de-mining, and an ATO (me) concentrates on dealing with the IED and coordinating the overall operation.

It worked a treat. It was so effective that the insurgents haven't put out any devices since. So now we're sitting around with fuck all to do, forcing ourselves to daydream about the future just to make the present seem more bearable.

'Anyone coming down the Colonel?' Neil asks. 'Colonel Qaddafi' is military rhyming slang for the NAAFI.

'Yeah, I'll come for a wander.' It'll give us an opportunity to chew the fat.

Neil tells me about his fiancée Claire, their two-year-old son and the cracking R&R they've just shared.

'How are you enjoying being a dad?' I ask.

'There's nothing like it,' he says. 'It makes you want to be a better person, doesn't it?'

I nod, but can't help feeling a pang of guilt. *Has it made me a better person? Am I the father I really should be?*

'How about you, boss. Have you got any nippers?'

'Two little blonde bombshells.'

'Daughters? Jesus. I take it you're getting your shotguns ready. "When the military man approaches, the world packs off its womankind" – eh?'

I don't need to be reminded.

'Listen, do you mind if I thin out and give them a call?'

'You fill your boots, boss.'

I make my way through the powdery sand towards the tank park and eventually come out behind the Battle Group HQ building, where a lone Portakabin houses six telephone booths. An entire thirty-man platoon is queuing up to use the phones.

Fuck.

I take my place in the line and spend forty-five minutes baking in the 50-degree sun. I'm tempted to just sack it, but I need Lucy to know that even though I can't always call, there's not a day goes by when I don't think about her and the girls.

The wood-partitioned booths offer no privacy whatsoever. I insert my card and punch in the number. There's a twenty-second delay as the satellite connection is made, and then it begins to ring . . . and ring . . . and ring. There's no reply. I try again. Still nothing.

As I head back along the track I notice scores of infantry soldiers sitting around the place doing nothing. It's an unusual sight at Camp Abu Naji. Some are smoking, some are reading. They seem either too stressed or too jaded to speak to one another. But all are waiting, praying for something exciting to happen soon.

For the clerks and the mechanics, life is even worse. They're so bored they've started reverting to really horrible squaddie games like the 'hard man shitter' challenge. The portaloos, or 'Turdises' as they're affectionately known, get incredibly hot during the day and smell absolutely rank. However, boys being boys, they've invented a challenge: to go for a crap at midday in the fullest portaloo you can find and then try and stay in there longer than anyone else can manage. It's enough to make your eyes water.

As Neil and I arrive back at the Det, having stocked up on cold drinks and cigarettes, I realize why I'm feeling so on edge. The boredom is the least of our worries. Something far worse is eating away at us. Complacency. The prospect of dying in al-Amarah is acutely real. Yet aside from the occasional moments of sheer terror, more often than not we're experiencing grinding, repetitive tedium which I fear will ultimately lead to us making careless mistakes.

We need to get out of here. I need to speak to Abbs.

'Hello, sir, how the devil?'

I've known Abbs for a good few years, and he's straight down the line. He definitely doesn't do first-name terms, especially not with officers. We get on like a house on fire all the same.

'I'm good, Abbs. You?'

We dance around the handbags for a while before I eventually come out with it.

'How are you enjoying yourself there in Basra?'

'Why, what have you heard?'

He's suddenly guarded. I've touched a nerve. I tell him I've heard nothing – which I haven't – but see this as my opportunity.

'Abbs, do you fancy swapping back?'

He asks me if I'm serious, and when I tell him I am, he nearly chews my arm off. I thought he'd be up for it, but I had no idea he was this passionate about the place. 'It's fucking shit down here, boss. I love it up in al-Amarah, and like we said before we swapped, we're both far better off running our own patches. I don't have a clue who's who down here. And having to deal with the brigade staff officers is hardly my idea of fun.'

That's settled, then.

'When do you want to do it?' I ask.

'How 'bout tomorrow? I'll go and brief numb-nuts tonight.' He's referring to Mark, the EOD staff officer. 'And if he disagrees, we'll shoot him in the head and bury him in the desert on the way. We'll be there first thing.'

*

298

'OK, Tom, what does CSMO mean?'

'Clear shit and move out, boss?'

'Correct. We're going to pack up tonight then we'll hit the road early doors tomorrow. We're going back to Basra.'

There's a loud cheer.

'For the time being, though, we're going to do a couple of hours of training.' We need to do something interesting.

'What sort, boss?' Dan asks.

'Counter-suicide bomber training, Dan.'

'Cooool,' the lads reply in chorus.

We find a suitable training area out the back of the Det and Mick grabs one of the old cars. Until a few days ago it belonged to an insurgent, but he won't be needing it any more.

I start by explaining that the most important aspect of dealing with a suicide bomber, whether the bomb is vehicle-borne or worn on the terrorist's body, is to separate the device from the person. If you can do that, it's pretty much like any other IED incident.

'What's the best way to stop the suicide bomber?' Tom asks.

'A five-five-six to the head,' I reply.

I can tell by the look on his face that he thinks I'm being crass.

'Seriously, Tom, I'm not taking the piss. A high-velocity bullet shot through the head will sever the brain stem and kill the perpetrator instantly, before he has a chance to fire off the device.'

Ollie asks me what the chances are of the bomber setting off the device if you try a 'soft arrest' – without using lethal force.

I explain that these boys are religious fanatics, intent on committing suicide at all costs, and wanting to kill as many people as possible in the process. The chances of them giving up are next to nothing. It has happened, but it's very rare. 'The fact is,' I conclude, 'as long as the device and bomber are still together, there's a massive risk of detonation, even if the bomber appears to be cooperative.'

'Not being funny, boss,' Neil says, 'but surely it's the infantry who should be focusing on these tactics, rather than us?'

Dan says, 'It's not quite as black and white as that. Even if the infantry shoot the bomber in the head, there's still an up-and-running IED that needs to be rendered safe. And besides, when we're out on the ground, we're all soldiers together. It could be down to any one of us to take the shot.'

I tell them to bear in mind that there's a very high like-lihood of a back-up timer or radio-control firing switch being incorporated into the device. In 1993, the Iraqi Intelligence Service plotted to assassinate former US President George Bush and the Emir of Kuwait with a suicide car bomb containing both back-up timers and RC initiation.

The lads are soaking it all up.

We rattle through a series of different scenarios: shooting a live suicide car bomber and neutralizing the device he's wearing; dealing with a device when the suicide bomber has had a change of heart; sorting out a bomber in a car that's broken down.

After a couple of hours we have a fag break.

We're about to switch our focus to vehicle-borne IEDs when there's a deafening roar. Scores of Warriors scream past us, churning up a huge cloud of dust and sand as they race out of camp.

Something's going down. Something big.

'Boss,' Dan says, 'you'd better head down to Battalion Ops. I'll make sure the vehicles are ready to go in case we get a shout.'

I've been waiting around Battalion HQ for hours. Something really is going down, but it's been a closely guarded secret until now. All we've been told is that a major operation was going on tonight.

But in the last few minutes the place has gone nuts.

The ops room is manic. There's a live radio feed booming out of the speakers transmitting the battle group and company radio traffic. The signallers are scribbling frantically, trying to log the activity while the ops warrant officer tries to get a feel of the battle picture. On an adjacent table, the ops officer and his team are poring over maps, planning fighting withdrawals and counter-attacks. Outside the ops room, the QRF are waiting for the next imminent call-out.

It's chaos. The Mahdi Army has been going crazy and the battle group has been taking hits left, right and centre.

And then I hear a medic talking about Whiskey Two Zero. Rich Deane's Warrior. My ears prick up.

'They're both P1,' one of the medics says to the doc.

Fuck me. P1 is the highest medical priority. It's only assigned to cases requiring resuscitation or immediate surgery. P0 doesn't exist, but if it did, it would mean you're dead.

I'm stunned. While we've been sitting around chuntering about being bored, Rich Deane and his platoon have been getting a serious hammering. And two of them are at death's door.

'Who's been hit? Give me their fucking zap numbers,' shouts the ops warrant officer to one of the signallers.

The signaller reads out the unique alphanumeric code

used to identify a casualty over the net. The medic is going through his regimental nominal roll trying to marry up names with numbers.

'Mr Deane and Private Beharry, sir,' he replies.

This is terrible. I know the initial report is almost always incorrect, but things aren't looking good. It sounds as though they were ambushed and took a direct hit from an RPG.

Several minutes later a full sitrep comes in.

'Sir, Beharry has received serious head injuries and Mr Deane has also been badly injured. Several other members of his vehicle crew have been hurt as well. Their Warrior was hit with multiple RPGs. They're all in a pretty bad way.'

A cloud hangs over the ops room.

Then more reports come in.

'Sir, I've just had another update on Whiskey Two Two.'

The room goes silent. You can hear a pin drop.

'Apparently Mr Deane's platoon was ambushed at Red Eight and the entire crew was knocked unconscious by the first RPG detonation. All except for Private Beharry. Despite suffering severe head injuries, he crashed through a roadblock under a massive weight of enemy fire and drove the team to safety.'

'Fucking good lad,' someone says at the back of the room.

'But as soon as they were safe, he lost consciousness himself. He's in a bad way, sir. He's still alive, but he's only hanging on by a thread.'

I'm speechless. All I can hear now is Johnson Beharry's cheery Grenadian voice in my head: 'Some days, you know, some days you the bug, some days you the windshield.'

27

Believe nothing, no matter where you read it or who said it, not even if I have said it, unless it agrees with your own reason and your own common sense.

Buddha

12 June 2004: Day 40

As the early-morning sun blazes through the cab of the Duro I try to imagine the conversation between Abbs and Mark the EOD staff officer yesterday. Abbs is a gentleman through and through, but he can be a tenacious bastard when he wants to be. I'd love to have been a fly on the wall when he suggested to Mark that we swap back.

Whatever he said obviously did the trick. We've been travelling for the last five hours and we're all on our chinstraps. We're finally within reach of Basra.

I wonder how Rich Deane and Johnson Beharry are doing. I imagine the poor buggers will still be lying in the operating theatre in Shai'ba.

I call through to Brigade HQ to let them know we're approaching the outskirts of the city.

'Roger that, stand by for tasking,' the watch keeper replies.

'Did he just say what I thought he said?' Dan has been fantasizing about a fry-up for several hours now and it looks like he's going to miss out. 'I don't believe it. We've not even arrived back at camp yet and already the bastards are sending us out on task.'

I get back on the net and ask the watch keeper if he's got any further details. He tells us some RMPs have been hit in southern Basra, on the Red Route, IED Alley. This six-mile stretch of potholed tarmac is probably the world's longest bombing range right now. Vast stretches of dusty wasteland lie along each side of it, at the edge of which sit rows of two-storey flat-roofed blocks. The nearest buildings are at least 100 metres away and provide perfect cover for snipers and RCIED triggermen.

We screech to a halt, cursing as a goatherd ushers his flock across the tarmac in front of us. We've come to rest next to a street vendor. The aroma of freshly ground coffee and warm pastries fills our nostrils. And we're famished.

'Get out of the fucking way,' shouts one of the top cover men, motioning with his SA80 for the young farmer to move.

He gets the message.

As we scream down the dual carriageway, using the rubbish-strewn hard shoulder to weave in and out of the pockets of congested traffic, we see a platoon of redcaps manning the cordon up ahead.

'ICP fifty metres,' Rob bellows over his radio. 'Located between a Sunni enclave and the Shia Flats.'

Seconds later we're pulling into the ICP and getting stuck into the task. The sun is barely above the rooftops but it's already sweltering.

Stood at the side of the ICP, I immediately recognize one of the victims. The RMP officer who was hit by a device just before we left for al-Amarah has just been blown up for a second time. She originally joined another branch of the Adjutant General's Corps, but chose to transfer to the RMP because she wanted to see some action. I'm not sure this is quite what she had in mind.

The poor girl's understandably jumpy, as any of us would be.

'How are you feeling?'

'Oh, you know . . .'

There's an unusual but somehow familiar musty aroma in the air. It's the smell of fear. Large saddlebags of sweat have formed under the armpits of her combat shirt. She's still visibly shocked.

'Can you talk me through what happened?'

She explains how she and one of her platoons were travelling south in convoy when a device exploded between her Land Rover and the vehicle in front. 'The noise was excruciating. I thought someone had ripped out my eardrums. The blast felt as though it was going to shake the flesh off my bones.'

She's a highly professional officer who's spent years conditioning herself to keep her emotions under complete control – but she sounds like she's going to burst into tears any second.

'Were you carrying ECM?'

She wasn't. There wasn't enough equipment to go round, so she'd given hers up to some of the other members of the platoon who were on the ground more regularly. 'I just can't justify using it three times a week when I've got soldiers going out three times a day—'

The conversation is interrupted by an ear-splitting explosion which sends a tremor across the southern part of the city. A whirlwind of flames engulfs the road as the artillery shell's detonation sends a wall of fragments into surrounding cars and buildings.

We all dive for cover.

A Land Rover comes screaming into the ICP and Andy jumps out. 'Fuck me, that was close!' he yells. He and his team of investigators from the Weapons

Intelligence Section have arrived to carry out the post-blast investigation.

'Jesus, mate,' I say. 'Do you always have to make such a dramatic entry?'

'It's outrageous. I can't believe the fucker just tried to hit us with a secondary.'

The bomber missed them by a whisker. I look across at Andy's team and see Scotty's familiar face in the vehicle. I give him a nod.

So now the insurgents are deliberately targeting first responders with secondaries. Had to happen.

We've been very lucky. Because we were returning from al-Amarah, we approached the scene from a different direction to usual. I can't help wondering if the bomb was meant for our team, and if they chose the WIS vehicle instead because we showed up from the opposite side of town.

Maybe my paranoia is getting the better of me. Basra is a bloody big place, and there are scores of different routes through it. By the law of averages, whichever road you choose, there's eventually going to be a bomb waiting for you at some point.

What makes it so damn hard is that there's so little you can do to defend yourselves against the bastard things. You could be the most highly trained soldier on the planet, but no amount of training, skill or judgement can protect you from the random and indiscriminate effect of a bomb. It's nearly all down to luck.

The sound of nearby gunfire makes everyone jump involuntarily. For some strange reason, it doesn't register with me at first. I'm so preoccupied with firing questions about the bomb that I seem to miss the bullets whizzing past.

We duck. The firing seems close, but we have no idea exactly where it's coming from. Some of the boys are cocking their weapons; others dive for cover.

'Where the fuck is he?' one of the military policemen shouts.

'Fucked if I know,' comes the reply.

We're all scanning the rows of houses, trying to locate the shooter. Then one of the RMPs on the edge of the cordon fires two rounds at a man standing at the window of one of the houses. There's no more shooting. He must have got the bastard. But time is definitely against us now.

One forensic clearance task has now effectively become two, so I deal with each bomb scene quickly and sequentially. I'm just about to hand Dan the sealed forensic bags containing the pieces of bomb debris when we have another major result. Two young boys come running up to us with a pair of key-fobs – the RCIED transmitters used in the two attacks that have just taken place, confirming that these are keyless car entry system IEDs. They said the bomber was sitting in a car, watching us, and after he detonated the devices he threw the fobs out of the window. They even gave us a description of him and his blue saloon. I speak to a couple of other witnesses who confirm the boys' story.

This is brilliant. We should be able to cross-match the components with the other forensic evidence we've been gathering.

'Fuck me, you look rough,' Will says, clearly unmoved by my boyish good looks. 'You've got a face like a freshly slapped arse.'

'Er, hello, pot. Kettle calling . . .' He doesn't so much have bags under his eyes as two outsized matching Bergens.

As the boys are enjoying eggs and bacon back in the palace, Will and I sit on the edge of the Shatt with our rock star's breakfast: twenty Marlboro Reds and a bottle of vodka. Only we're all out of vodka, so we settle for fresh coffee. We shoot the shit for a while, and he has a good bitch and whine about some of the mince and triv that's been bothering him over the last couple of weeks. Then we get on to the serious stuff.

He tells me the initial intelligence reports suggest that this morning's secondary device *was* intended for the team. The insurgents just didn't know Abbs and I had temporarily swapped, so hadn't expected us to approach the ICP from al-Amarah.

So there's still a price on my head. Fuck it, you've got to die some time. Roosevelt was right. When you come to the end of your rope, you tie a knot and hang on. I realize I'm way past the point of worrying any more.

'What else is happening then, Jock? What's the long-term prognosis?'

'Not good, mate,' he replies. 'Six months ago we were averaging eighteen attacks per day across the country. Today there are ten times as many. The country is closer than ever to civil war.'

'What about the city? Much changed since we've been away?'

He tells me that IED incidents are occurring every day in Basra. Of these, only one a month is usually successful.

I interrupt him. 'Define successful.'

'A death,' he replies matter-of-factly.

He goes on to explain that since we've been away the insurgents have attempted several close-quarter attacks on British troops, and both sides are employing highly organized cells, operating in small numbers. 'The bastards are employing sophisticated S&R techniques to identify targets and determine the optimum attack methods. Some of the ones we've caught actually worked on coalition bases in the city.'

'What about the bomb-makers, Jock? Do we know any more about them?'

'Only what you know already: that they're designing and mass-producing IEDs of all types, including time-initiated and victim-operated devices. By far the greatest threat is still the well-camouflaged radio-controlled road-side bomb. And before you ask, no, we've still not caught the second bomber team.'

Will's one of the hardest-working blokes I know. I've come back in from jobs at three a.m. and he's still sat there hunched over a laptop, taking coffee intravenously to keep himself awake. But he's hugely under-resourced. He's also working very much at the strategic level. He's looking at intelligence covering the entire political, economic and social piece, not just the military battle picture.

The WIS team are good, but they're more focused on the technical make-up of the device. To counter the IED threat properly, we need somebody to fuse all the strands of intelligence reporting together. The trouble is, we just don't have anyone.

'The only other thing worthy of note,' Will says, saving the best for last, 'is that we've got teams carrying out surveillance, as well as helicopters and unmanned aerial vehicles carrying out reconnaissance of potential bomb-maker positions.'

I feel a wave of excitement. 'That's fucking beezer, mate. The best news I've heard all month.'

'Anyway,' he says, 'enough of the boring bollocks. How's things with you and Lucy?'

I think of her sad, beautiful face, and my gut wrenches.

'I don't think it's going to be happily ever after, I'm afraid.' I hesitate. 'I'm losing her, Will.'

He draws thoughtfully on his cigarette. 'Well, you know how it is, mate. Marriage is a rich mix of sadness and joy. We all have our ups and downs. But life goes on. And so must we. Men are from Mars, women are from Venus.'

And you're talking right out of Uranus, I think to myself.

'Will, she's my life. For me, the sun rises and sets with her.'

His expression suddenly changes. 'Then you've got to change. Give it up. Stop playing cowboys and get a proper job.'

I tell him it probably wouldn't be enough, that I think it's already too late.

He takes a slurp of his coffee and another long drag on his cigarette.

'Can I ask you a serious question?' he says.

'Of course, mate. Shoot.'

'If it doesn't work out between you two, and you do end up getting a divorce, do you mind if I have a crack at her?'

28

Physical courage, which despises all danger, will make a man brave in one way; and moral courage, which despises all opinion, will make a man brave in another. The former would seem most necessary for the camp, the latter for the council; but to constitute a great man, both are necessary.

Charles Caleb Colton

14 June 2004: Day 42

The city is simmering with unease.

We're stuck in nose-to-tail rush-hour traffic on our way back from a bank of rockets we've just rendered safe, and, to make matters worse, the road that would have led us back to the palace is closed. We edge our way through a sprawling mass of slum housing and crumbling concrete apartment blocks under the unwelcome scrutiny of hundreds of pairs of unfriendly eyes.

'Right, boss,' Rob says cheerfully, 'we'll hang a right

in about two hundred metres, zigzag through the back streets for half a mile or so, and then we'll be right back on track.'

As the commander of the lead vehicle, Rob is responsible for guiding the team to and from an incident while I check-navigate.

I squint at my map. 'Are there any better routes available?' I'm trying to make it sound like an oblique question, but failing miserably. The truth is, I don't want us zigzagging through back streets in a four-vehicle convoy if we can help it. It's tactically unsound, and this isn't a nice part of town.

'Not really, boss. I guess we could stay on this road for another two miles and then turn right at the next roundabout.'

'Won't that take us straight through the middle of the car market?'

'Certainly would, sir, and they fucking hate us there. That's why I suggest we make a right in two hundred metres.'

We decide to go with Plan A.

I can't wait to get back to the palace. This is a horrible part of the city and it's just been one of those days.

The two rockets we've just dealt with were on a stuck-fast timer at the Shatt al-Arab Hotel – the Cheshires' Battle Group Headquarters. That part literally went like clockwork, but then some conventional munitions were found outside the hotel and things started going tits up. Instead of tasking us, with all our kit and equipment already on site, the ever-wise Joint EOD Group deployed a Royal Engineers team with less experience and training. Under normal circumstances it would have been the right call. But the Cheshire boys had already spent several hours manning the cordon for us; while waiting for the RE team to rock up, they had to sweat their tits off for several more. When they did eventually make an appearance, instead of dealing with the munitions, they went straight to the cookhouse for their evening meal. Now the Cheshires think all EOD operators are tossers.

'Nil illegitimi carborundum,' Dan says philosophically.

'Sorry, Dan, come again?'

'Don't let the bastards grind you down.' He smiles. 'It's Latin.'

He can read me like a book. And he's got a point. Life's just too short to be getting wound up by minutiae.

But I still feel edgy – more so than usual.

In this part of town you have to have eyes in the back of your head. The place is brimming with criminals and insurgents. And at this time of day the streets are crammed with pedestrians, street vendors and bumper-to-bumper vehicles. As our drivers struggle through the traffic the rest of the team are fervently watching the pavements, the alleyways and the shop doorways, trying to keep track of the several thousand people lining them and praying that the hold-up clears quickly, but knowing deep down that it won't. We're sitting ducks, and it's only a matter of time before one of the bad guys announces that we're today's target.

'Boss, more bad news I'm afraid.'

'What is it, Rob?'

'The right turn we were going to take . . . that road's closed too.'

Fuck. This is the last thing we need.

'What do you want to do, boss?'

If we keep going, we've got at least another mile of this. And if something goes wrong – if the crowd turns nasty – we'll be in serious trouble. But if we decide to turn around – which would be virtually impossible, given the congestion – we'd have to drive north out of Basra, skirt around the city and re-approach it from the south. It would mean a 30-kilometre detour and having to run the gauntlet up the Red Route.

Damned if you do, damned if you don't. It's no accident that we adopted the phrase as our team's motto.

'What do you think, Dan?'

'I'm easy,' he replies.

'OK. Rob, we'll keep going straight.'

We continue to crawl through Basra's biggest car market, and the place is heaving. Street urchins with buckets are busy washing down dusty saloons and running errands for salesmen in neatly pressed suits and crisp white shirts. Hundreds of cars and trucks are parked side by side, several rows deep. Some of the traders have proper forecourts, lined with brand-new Japanese models imported through Kuwait, Syria and Dubai. Elsewhere, private owners are busy trying to sell rickety old crates at the side of the road.

And we're stuck right in the middle of them.

It's not a happy place to be. More and more people seem to be staring at us. Some are chanting and jeering. The atmosphere seems sullen and angry. It's hard to know what is and isn't normal in this place, but it doesn't take a degree in behavioural science to realize we're not welcome.

The crowd is on the brink of kicking off.

I think back to the intelligence brief we were given when I first arrived on the team: 'OK, the final area I want to cover today is public order. Public order is a huge problem in the area and there are a range of triggers, including politics, employment, essential services and security. People can be rapidly mobilized and they're highly volatile. Peaceful activity often escalates into violent clashes . . .'

There's more jeering and frenetic activity around us. Some of the braver ones have started closing in on our vehicles, circling us menacingly, trying to goad us into a reaction. Dan and I stare out individuals, trying to isolate them with our eyes. It's one of the mind games we're taught in training. You're telling your antagonist you know he thinks he's some big-time tough guy in a crowd, but the moment it all goes noisy, he's the first fucker you're going to drop.

I get on the radio.

'Right, fellas, I need you to move the vehicles closer together. Bring them in, bumper to bumper.'

It's easier said than done. The crowd around each of our vehicles is growing bigger by the second. Vince and Ollie are desperately trying to get them to back off.

It's not working.

The noise is like a drug for them. The shouting is getting louder and the mob is becoming more and more intoxicated by the hysterical ranting of the ringleaders, who are screaming commands at them, telling them to isolate the vehicles.

'Fucking hell, boss,' Dan says, 'the bastards are trying to cut us off from one another.'

It's straight out of the insurgent's handbook: a mob of hostile locals block and isolate the patrol, then the really bad guys attack from the safety of the crowd.

I remember Wood and Howes, the two corporals who in 1988 took a wrong turn and accidently drove into an Irish Republican funeral. The crowd surrounded their car and smashed its windows. Corporal Wood produced his pistol and fired a warning shot into the air. The CCTV footage showed the crowd surging back, pulling them from the car and punching and kicking them to the ground. They were tortured, thrown over a wall, and driven to a stretch of waste ground. Wood was shot twice in the head and four times in the chest. He was also stabbed four times in the back of the neck and had multiple injuries to other parts of his body. Howes met a similar fate.

We're not going to go the same way.

I remove my pistol from my drop holster and place it under my thigh. Then I reach down into the door shelf and remove two of the stun-grenades given to me after the ambush. If the crowd turns nasty, tossing in a couple of these flash-bangs might just clear them long enough for us to break out.

My heart is racing. I'm terrified of one of us being snatched by this crowd of fanatics and getting his head cut off on TV.

Shit. Now what? We've stopped moving.

'Keep the fucking vehicles going!' I scream.

'What's the plan, boss?' There's a tremor in Dan's voice.

I'm about to tell him I don't have one when there's a gunshot and the crowd disperses. I see an opening.

'Drive, drive, drive!' I yell into the radio.

There's a break in the throng to our right, leading on to some waste ground. Taff sees it and ploughs through. We follow suit. Bodies are flailing all over the place. I look in the wing mirror, but I can't see the ECM wagon behind us.

'Mick, are you clear?'

'Yeah, roger that, boss. We're through, and so is the Snatch behind us.'

The team bumps its way across the waste ground, towards a group of apartment blocks. Moments later we're weaving our way through back streets. Suddenly it doesn't seem like such a bad idea.

I get on the radio and do a comms check.

'Which one of you geniuses pulled the trigger?' I ask.

'Nobody,' Mick replies. 'It was some old banger misfiring.'

Ten minutes later we're driving under the arch and into the safety of Basra Palace. I ask Dan to drop me at Brigade HQ. I need to go and have a chat with Mark, the EOD staff officer, about today's little episode.

My footsteps echo across the marble dance floor. The place is like the *Mary Celeste*.

'Where is everybody?' I ask the watch keeper.

'The Secretary of State for Defence was here today. The brigadier's debriefing the staff on the visit.'

I need no further encouragement. I head back the way I've come.

In the five minutes since I entered the building, the day has turned to night. A perfect crescent moon shimmers on the lake and the warm night air dries the sweat on my skin. I stand for a moment and watch the palm trees rustle gently in the moonlight. This is a Lucy moment. One of the thousands of idyllic moments I've experienced without her but know she would have loved.

God I miss her. I feel nothing but sadness when I think of her now.

I walk over to the Det with a heavy heart and write up my IED report.

I'm tapping away at the keyboard to Bruce Springsteen's *Greatest Hits* a short while later when I hear a gunshot.

It's close.

I look outside, but there's nothing to see. Moments later the lads walk sheepishly into the crew room.

'Oh no,' I say. 'Tell me that wasn't one of you.'

For a moment they are silent, then Mick steps forward, head bowed.

'Sorry, boss. I jumped down from the Duro and my finger slipped.'

'How the fuck—' I manage to stop myself. There are more important things to worry about right now. 'Did you hit anybody?'

'No, boss. The bullet flew out over the Shatt al-Arab and off into the desert.'

That's something, I guess.

'And did anybody see you?'

'Er, well, yes,' he says awkwardly. 'Unfortunately, they did.'

'How many?'

'Just one. Your mate, the Scottish major in the Int Corps. But there's a bit more to it than that.'

'What do you mean, *more to it*?'

I hear footsteps approaching from outside.

'Wait there, Mick. We're not done here yet.'

I head out to tell whoever our visitor is to bugger off and come back later. It's Will. And I've never seen him so angry.

'That fucking prick nearly blew my sodding head off!'

So that's what Mick meant. I resist the temptation to tell Will that next time he jokes about shagging Lucy I'll get Mick to aim lower.

'Mate, I'm so sorry. I don't know what to say.'

'I do,' he says. 'What are you planning to do to the fucking loon?'

I honestly don't know the answer to that. It's bad

enough when a private has a negligent discharge, but for a corporal, it's unforgivable. But Mick's a good man, and he's got a young family to support, including a daughter with special needs. 'And he's hungry, Will,' I hear myself saying, 'like you and I used to be when we were Toms. He's got the potential to go all the way. He'll be a Corps RSM one day. But if we crucify him over this, we'll effectively destroy his career and his family right now.'

It's true. Mick takes his work very seriously and gives a hundred per cent in everything he does. He's made a stupid mistake, but then so have we all.

'It's your call, Will. It's you he nearly topped. If you want him disciplined, that's what I'll do. But if you're content for me to deal with this discreetly, that's fine by me too.'

'You're right,' he growls. 'We'll achieve nothing by pissing on the hopeless.' He pauses. 'Let me have a chat with the little twat outside.'

As Mick steps out into the shadows, Will treats him to a torrent of verbal abuse.

I leave them to it.

When Mick comes back, it's my turn. He tells me again how sorry he is. I can see he means it, and for a moment I feel a pang of sympathy for him. But he's fucked up big time and needs to be made aware of it.

'Personally, right now, I couldn't give a shit what

happens to you. But like I said to you the last time we chatted, I do give a shit about the team. And this is the second time you've jeopardized the team's reputation.'

He looks mortified.

I tell him that what he did was inexcusable, that I should sack him and have him locked up. But the bottom line is if his career is ruined, so are the lives of his family. 'That's why I'm giving you another chance – for their sake, not yours. But I mean it, Mick. It's time to stop fucking about and start taking life a bit more seriously.'

He's staring at the ground. Then he raises his head and looks me in the face.

'Sir, I promise you I'll never let you or the team down again.'

As we step back inside, Ollie instantly lifts the mood.

'Hey, boss, Sky News interviewed a couple of the lads from my battalion today. Geoff Hoon's been on the TV describing their camp at Umm Qasr as "a city similar to Southampton". When the reporter asked them for their thoughts, one of them said, "He's either never been to Southampton, or he's never been to Umm Qasr." The other lad chimed in: "Yeah, there's no beer, no prostitutes, and people are shooting at us. It's more like Portsmouth." '

29

Never run away from anything. Never!

Winston Churchill

18 June 2004: Day 46

Ollie's Battle Group Headquarters at Az Zubayr is just like any other British Army camp in southern Iraq. There's the same familiar fortified sangars on the main gate, rows and rows of sand-filled Hesco blast barriers, and large concrete walls topped with coils of razor wire.

We're here to negotiate with his company commander.

The major and his Royal Welch Fusiliers have been based at this dusty outpost several miles south of Basra for two months now, and Ollie has been attached to us for that entire period. Now they want him back. Ollie is one of the best snipers in the battalion, and they need him. He's also the only sniper in our team and one of my most capable soldiers.

I need him too.

So I've just spent twenty heated minutes trying to persuade the OC to see reason. It is vital that the team stays together. We're a very tight unit and we don't have the time to keep changing and then re-training new members of the team.

Now it's Ollie's turn.

As he sits getting his ear chewed in the major's office, the rest of us stand around waiting in a bare-walled, windowless room. Emotions have been running high for a few days and Vince has just hurled his mobile across the floor. He's got a face like a freshly dropped pie.

'What the fuck was all that about, Vince?'

I can see by the look on his face and the tiny pieces of telephone beneath our feet that he's in a foul mood.

'My girlfriend, boss. I'm sorry, but she's doing my fucking head in.'

I should be gripping him for his behaviour, having just spent twenty minutes extolling the virtues of my highly professional team. But I can't bring myself to get all anal about it. I know exactly how he feels.

We head outside for a cigarette and he tells me about the argument he's just had with his girlfriend. They've been together for a year, and they're planning to get married when he finishes the tour.

'What do you think I should do?'

I tell him I think he's a cracking bloke and that I'd love

to help, but the last person he needs relationship advice from is me.

'I mean it, boss. I really don't know what to do.' He hesitates. 'How would you play it?'

'Look, Vince, you can take this or leave it, but for what it's worth, if I was in your position and I had a problem back home that I really wanted to sort out, the first thing I would do is take a good hard look in the mirror.'

He looks puzzled. 'Me look in the mirror?'

I nod. 'When we're out here on ops, half the time the problem isn't with our wives and girlfriends, it's with us.'

I'm not about to pretend that I'm the leading expert in this field, so I tell him a fable that I remember my dad passing on to me, about the Cherokee Indian teaching his grandchildren. He says to them, 'A battle is raging inside me. It is a terrible fight between two wolves. One wolf represents fear, anger, envy, sorrow, regret, greed, arrogance, self-pity, guilt, resentment, inferiority, lies, false pride, superiority and ego. The other stands for joy, peace, love, hope, sharing, serenity, humility, kindness, benevolence, friendship, empathy, generosity, truth, compassion and faith.' The old man fixes the children with a firm stare. 'This same fight is going on inside you, and inside every other person too,' he says.

They think about this for a minute, then one child asks, 'Which wolf will win?'

The old Cherokee replies, 'The one you feed.'

'The fact is, Vince, if you've got dramas at home, the only person who can sort them out is you. Don't get me wrong, I think you're a storming fella, but I'm not the one marrying you.'

I don't know if my take on the situation has helped, or if I've made him feel worse. It's difficult for all of us right now, and because we're being called out at all hours of the day, our sleep patterns have gone to ratshit and every-body's tetchy. This has been one of the most exhausting and frustrating stages of the tour.

The day before yesterday we all travelled to Shai'ba Log Base to drop off a robot and Neil's broken-down ECM vehicle. We'd agreed with one of the REME tech-nicians that we'd go and collect the kit early yesterday, but when we arrived the place was like a ghost town. Eventually, one of the sergeants (known unaffectionately by the boys as 'Aquafresh' – the tube with three stripes) rocked up and informed us that they'd all been on the piss the night before and their captain had given them permission to have a lie-in.

It was the second time repairs on our mission-critical kit had been ignored by these pricks and I was absolutely fuming. And it didn't end there. We were called out to another keyless car entry system RCIED attack, this time against a bunch of Motorola engineers in an unarmoured Land Rover Discovery, and I had to carry out the task without essential kit.

Despite the carnage and the chaos, the attack has identified a trend. The Sunni bombers seem to be reducing the number of attacks against British forces – or maybe they're failing because so many British vehicles have now been fitted with highly effective ECM. Either way, they seem to be branching out against civilian support services. That means it's just a matter of time before they hit us with a new type of device. And the destructive power of a new IED is only limited by the bomb-maker's imagination.

Ollie suddenly reappears.

'Well? What did he say?'

He gives us the thumbs-up. 'I can stay – for now.'

We're all chuffed to bits. The team wouldn't be the same without him. We all dive into the cookhouse to celebrate over a spot of lunch. Then Dan comes running in.

'Boss, there's a vehicle-borne IED outside the A&E hospital. We've got to go now.'

Bollocks.

As we gulp down our food on the move, trying desperately to stop it from coming back up, I think about the task ahead.

The A&E hospital is one of the busiest in Basra and it's

only a couple of hundred metres away from Brigade HQ. We still have no ECM and no wheelbarrow, and I'm being actively targeted by both insurgent groups. It would be suicidal to attempt to complete the task with anything other than the robot.

Jesus.

'Dan, I want you to phone those muppets at Shai'ba and ask them if the kit's ready yet. We'll get the vehicles fired up.'

He reappears a few minutes later.

'Good news, boss. The tiffy says the barrow and ECM wagon are both ready for collection. We can pick them up on the way. We're back in business.'

We scream out of Az Zubayr on blue lights and race along the palm-lined highway towards Shai'ba. Minutes later, as we're negotiating our way through the sand-filled chicanes at the Log Base's main gate, I get a call from my friend in the RMP. While the lads are cross-loading the newly repaired kit, I get a brief on some of the background to the incident. She tells me she'll fill me in on the rest at the ICP.

I can't help but wonder whether her being on the cordon is a bad omen or not. Every time she's been anywhere near a bomb it's gone bang.

Minutes later we're loaded up with working kit and heading back towards Basra City.

The ops mobile rings again. I don't recognize the number.

'Captain Dawson here.'

He immediately gets my back up by not even having the courtesy to tell me his Christian name.

'Hi, Chris Hunter,' I reply. 'How can I help?'

'Let this be a warning. The camp commandant and I are unhappy about you speeding and using blues and twos on camp.'

For a moment I'm speechless. I've still no idea who he is, but the clown really is serious.

'I'm on my way to a fucking car bomb,' I say through clenched teeth.

'That may be so, but there are strict speed limits on camp—'

I lose it with him big time and go straight into Tourette's mode. I explain that the task is a Cat A – one which poses a grave and immediate threat to life. I tell him the VBIED is parked outside a hospital and that we were only blue-lighting on his camp because we were en route to the incident but first we had to collect mission-critical kit that would have been ready a whole lot earlier had it not been for the rear-echelon-motherfucker ethos he seems to encourage on his precious camp. 'And by the way, if you or the commandant have any further concerns, please feel free to take them up with the brigadier.'

I can't resist throwing that one in. If the brigade commander hears about this, he'll have the maniac thrown out of theatre. He hates remfs as much as the rest of us.

'Christ, Dan, can you believe that? If ignorance is bliss, that prick must be the happiest person alive.'

'Don't worry, boss,' he says. 'People like him can try to screw you all they like, but they still can't make you love the baby.'

We're soon weaving our way through Basra's back streets, hard-targeting from one junction to the next.

Rob's voice comes up over the net: 'ICP one hundred metres. Check out the camera crew on the corner too.'

Here we go again.

I can see friendlies; we're approaching the ICP. It's on the corner of a junction close to the banks of the Shatt al-Arab. But there's no sign of the RMP officer.

Still, under the circumstances that's not such a bad thing.

As we debus, the team kicks into life and I'm met by Dom, the cordon commander.

'Hello, mate, I wasn't expecting to see you here. I thought the RMP had taken the lead.'

'They had to shoot off. So I've brought a company of Cheshires to man the cordon and the RMP have left us a platoon to back-fill where necessary.'

It's reassuring to know he's running the show again. Dom's an old-school infantry company commander, a broad-chested rugby player who knows his marbles and doesn't take any crap. He's very much on top of his game. We've worked together on a couple of tasks now and the two of us get on like a house on fire.

I take a moment to scan the scene, and immediately spot the suspect vehicle. It sends a shiver down my spine.

Car bombs and booby traps are my two greatest fears. Fears I never discuss with anybody, but they're always there, lingering at the back of my mind. A car is never quite what it seems. Even if it's been subjected to a controlled explosion, there's no guarantee that something nasty isn't hidden away in one of its many recesses. And if it's a come-on that's worse, because it's personal. The bomber is out to get you, and you have to out-think him to survive.

Is this a come-on? Should I sack it now, take time to mull it over? It certainly looks like a standard car bomb. It's an old '73 Chevy, heavily weighted down on its rear axles. Witnesses saw a man, a Shia in dark clothing, drive it into position over two hours ago, park it hurriedly outside the Sunni A&E hospital, and then get into a back-up vehicle before driving off. It could be on a timer, but if the Sunnis in the hospital were the target it would have detonated long before now.

No, this stinks. They want me dead. They've put it outside a hospital; they know I'll have no choice but to deal with it. A bunch of Sunnis are acceptable collateral damage as far as they're concerned. And in case there are any further doubts in my mind, the usual TV crew are right there on the cordon, just like every other time the Shias have targeted me.

Should I let it soak until tomorrow? I'll only be putting off the inevitable. Let's get it over with.

I get Rob to sort out the ICP configuration – a nice, tight, closed V. Then I ask Dom to get everybody on the cordon under hard cover. There's going to be a small controlled explosion in five minutes. He barks orders into his radio and his company pushes the civilians back. The rest of my team are either helping Dan to prepare the kit or searching our ICP for secondaries. If this thing blows, there will be fucking carnage.

Next, there's the little problem of the hospital. It's A&E, so there are going to be people all over the place. They need to be evacuated. The bomb is only 20 metres away from them. I'm going to have to take my balls in my hand and run forward, past the bomb and into the hospital. I don't want to, but I've got no choice. I told the adjutant this was a Cat A task, and I wasn't wrong.

I tell Neil to work his magic with our jammer, then I run out of the ICP and along the hot, deserted street. My eyes are stinging with sweat. I'm running faster than I ever have in my life. I pass the vehicle and feel my stomach tightening.

Maybe it *is* time I got a proper job. I think back to the phone call with my mother this morning. I told her I'd spent an hour catching some rays on top of the roof of the Det, and she was horrified. She gave me a long lecture about the dangers of sunbathing. Was I using factor 30?

I reach the reception area and tell the security guards to shift everybody to the back of the hospital. They don't speak a word of English. Nor, it appears, does anybody else. I go into Basil Fawlty mode, throwing my arms around like a lunatic, shouting 'boom' and 'bang' a lot. Nothing. Can this day get any more bizarre?

I pull out my pistol. Guns they understand. I do the boom and bang routine again and one of the guards finally gets the message.

'Bomb, yes, we evacuate.'

Suddenly they all speak English. It's amazing where you can get with a 9mm American Express. Now it's access all areas.

The guards get to work, pushing everybody back, and I climb out of a side window and make my way round to the ICP. We're in business. Dan has already configured the wheelbarrow into attack mode, fitting it with several disruptors. I tell him to run it on a fibre-optic cable. That way the Muqtada militia won't be able to jam it.

A couple of lads from the Brigade Recce Group have arrived at the ICP. One of them, Bob, an old mucker from a previous life, tells me he's here to look for any players on the cordon. He also asks whether I've been alerted to the fact that I am being targeted. I tell him I have. It's good to know my mates are looking out for me. Especially if they're men in black.

Dom comes back to let me know everybody is under hard cover. We're good to go. We'll crack open the boot to expose the device, then we'll kill the bomb with a disruptor. We'll be home in time for tea and medals.

'Dan, it's over to you now.'

I tell everybody to close in to the back of the EOD vehicle. From there we watch the wheelbarrow race down the street. The Chevy suddenly exudes an air of clinical menace. It's a bizarre sight: a remote and deadly battle between two machines.

We study the monitors. The Chevy fills the screen. We watch the robot close in for the kill. Dan swings it round on its rubber tracks so that it faces the side of the car. He releases the drive buttons and it lurches forward. We hear a whirr as the telescopic arm extends the camera.

We look through the side windows. Nothing. The

bomb must be in the boot. This is going to be a bastard. If we try to get access through the lid and the device is rigged up to the courtesy light or car alarm, it will detonate. Our only other option is to fire a huge directional charge upwards from the ground. If we're lucky, it will scatter whatever's inside hundreds of feet into the air – but it'll probably detonate it. We've got no choice. We're going to go in through the lid.

With the deftness of a schoolkid on a games console, Dan trundles the wheelbarrow around to the back of the car and lines it up to take a shot on the boot-opening mechanism. He's sweating like ten men, in his own private world.

The disruptor is now in place. The supersonic jet will punch a hole through the lock, forcing the boot open and exposing the device. The barrow can then be manoeuvred into the cavity to fire a second weapon at the TPU, shattering its circuitry.

'Boss, I'm on. Are you happy for me to take the shot?'

I go through a quick mental checklist. Everybody is under hard cover; the hospital patients are as well protected as they can be; we're less than 100 metres away from the device, but relatively safe. It's not going to get any better than this.

'Go for it,' I tell him.

He bellows out his one-minute warning, then selects

the circuit and uncovers the firing switch on the control box. 'Stand by . . . firing now . . .'

I hold my breath.

There's a pause, then a blinding, searing flash as the car explodes in a whirlwind of fire and shrapnel. The earth-shaking roar makes the ground tremble beneath our feet, and then the shockwave hits us. I feel my eardrums go and my body judder as I'm smashed into the side of the Snatch behind me. I steady myself. My ears are ringing. There's smoke and flame everywhere. A cloud of flying glass and debris fills the air around us. Distorted metal panels spiral skywards. Rubble bounces off the roof of the Duro. A gearbox lands nearby, the force of its impact burying it right into the tarmac.

And then silence.

Faces begin to appear at shattered windows. People emerge from their houses, shocked and bewildered, but alive. And the silence is quickly replaced with the sound of ambulance sirens and car alarms.

I look at the carnage around me. Shards of hot metal have lanced a car to my right and the air is thick with acrid-smelling smoke and dust. But I can't see any casualties.

What about the hospital?

'I'm going to check on the patients,' Dom says, as if reading my mind.

'No,' I say. Although as a major he outranks me, I have overall control as the ATO. 'Too dangerous. Petrol tanks are going off, and there could be another device.'

'We've got to do something. We can't just stand here.'

He's a good man.

'Just wait, Dom . . . Two minutes . . .'

We wait for the dust to clear. And then both of us run forwards. Bomb disposal is always supposed to be a single-man risk, and though the car bomb has clearly exploded, the incident is still considered 'live' until I've been forward and cleared the area of any secondary devices. The trouble is there's no holding Dom back, so for now it's a two-man risk.

Immediately to our right is the flaming, mangled skeleton of the car. Just in front of it lie the burnt-out remains of the wheelbarrow. Its twisted metal frame is completely wrecked. Forty metres away there's a huge smoking crater where the car detonated, fringed with fiercely burning petrol.

It's outrageous.

The hospital reception area is trashed. Doors and wall panels are hanging off their hinges and the whole place is covered in glass. Thank God we evacuated them. They'd have been cut to pieces if they'd stayed in there.

Two or three hundred people are packed into a huge

room down the corridor. Dom shouts, 'Is anybody here injured?'

An exhausted-looking Iraqi surgeon stares back at him quizzically before replying in perfect English, 'Of course there are injured people here. This is an A&E hospital.' He gives us a broad smile. 'If you mean was anybody injured by the bomb, then the answer is no. We're all fine, thank you.'

It is a beautiful moment. I close my eyes. We've done it. The wheelbarrow has been totalled and there is a bit of collateral damage, but nobody is dead and the bombers have failed again.

This bomb was meant for me, and I'm still alive.

On our way back to the ICP, Dom turns and asks, 'What on earth made you decide to do this for a living? Is it the adrenalin rush, the challenge? Or are you all just barking mad?'

I blurt out some nonsense about it being a choice between this or selling the *Big Issue*. The truth is, I've asked myself the same question a million times, and I still don't know the answer. One thing I do know is that we were lucky again today. And our luck is going to run out soon.

30

God please protect me from my friends and I will take care of my enemies.

Imam Ali

21 June 2004: Day 49
Brigade Headquarters is in complete turmoil. Will and the ops staff are clustered around the bird table, poring over the giant map and discussing military options against Iran. On the plasma screens several news channels are broadcasting pictures of Royal Navy sailors with their hands cuffed behind their backs.

'Have I missed something?' I ask one of the watch keepers.

'Yeah. The mad mullahs have just seized three of our vessels and arrested eight crew – *inside* Iranian waters.'

'Fucking hell.'

'First we heard about it was when one of the translators came in and said it was being aired on Iranian TV.'

He tells me they were arrested by the Islamic Revolutionary Guard Corps, but that nobody knows who's holding them now, or where.

'What were they doing there?'

'They were delivering a boat from Umm Qasr to Basra.' He raises an eyebrow. 'They got lost.'

Jesus. They live in the same Det as us, but because we were out on the ground most of last night dealing with another keyless car entry system RCIED, none of us was aware of it. The lads are all still asleep in their tent.

I hear footsteps behind me.

'What brings you here then, Lugsy?'

'Nice of you to join us, Will. I thought I'd nip over and check you're not getting up to any mischief. And thank Christ I did. We'd probably be invading Iran by now if I hadn't rocked up.'

'Yeah, it's been a surreal day.'

We slope off out of the back door and sit on the wall, looking out over the Shatt al-Arab towards the Iranian border.

Will looks exhausted.

'So, what have you been up to?' he asks. 'I've not seen you for days.'

'Oh, you know, same old, same old . . .' I tell him the pace of life hasn't let up and the team is shagged as usual. We've had thirty-four taskings since we've been in theatre, but when the Motorola technicians were targeted in their Discovery a few days ago, I'd begun to think the bad guys had changed their MO. Two explosions on the oil pipelines in southern Basra the following morning reinforced my theory that the insurgents had stopped targeting our patrols. 'But the loggie convoys have started getting hit again in Basra, so it looks as though nothing much has changed.'

Will takes a long draw on his Marlboro and asks me what we're doing to stop them.

I tell him that about a week ago I spoke with Steve Harrison, the brigade's logistics squadron commander, and an old mucker of mine from Sandhurst, about how to reduce the number of attacks on his vehicles. We agreed the best solution was to stagger the timings of the supply convoys coming over the border from Kuwait. Until then they'd been arriving in Basra every morning between 0800 and 0900. You could have set your watch by them. But if our plan was to stand any chance of being implemented, we needed to get it cleared by Brigade Headquarters.

'So I asked Colonel Sanderson to help us.'

'Brave man,' he observes.

I tell Will I knew the colonel was going to be a tough nut to crack, but despite his fearsome reputation for not suffering fools gladly, he's scrupulously fair. If anyone was going to see the sense of this, it was him. He just asked me to leave it with him and, true to his word, went off and squared it away with the chief of staff. The morning attacks stopped within two days.

'So what went wrong?' Will asks. 'Why are they being hit again now?'

'Unfortunately, someone on the ops staff seems to have missed the point. When they were ordered to stagger the timings, the message must have got lost in translation. Instead of staggering the timings, the lunatics just shifted the eight a.m. slot to nine p.m.'

Needless to say, the insurgents spotted it immediately, and the convoys are now getting hit at night. It comes as no surprise to either of us.

'What about the car bomb?' he says. 'I heard the explosion from my office.'

He's talking about the Chevy outside the A&E hospital. I wondered when he was going to bring this up.

'Yeah, it was quite a rascal.' I tell him how I went back to the palace afterwards, got washed up and went over to the dining room to grab some scoff. Everywhere I looked, people were staring at me. I guess they must have heard the explosion too. 'I felt like a dead man walking, Will.'

His expression hardens. 'That's because you are, Chris.' He takes another long draw on his cigarette before continuing. 'I'm seriously starting to think you've lost the plot. What were you thinking of, running past the car bomb? You might be a guru when it comes to defusing these fucking things, mate, but you're a gold chain short of a Greek if you think you can withstand the blast of one.' He tells me that the intelligence reports suggest the car bomb was intended to kill me. 'The only reason you're still alive is that, because of its proximity to the hospital, the terrorists expected you to deal with it by hand instead of with the robot.'

Perversely, perhaps, I smile to myself, and wonder where I'd be without the support, guidance and incessant lecturing of my wise friend Will.

As I try to work out how to subtly change the subject, Mark the EOD staff officer appears.

'Chris, another task has just come in for you. It's serious.'

There's been an explosion at Shai'ba Log Base. As we drive towards it, I can see clouds of thick black smoke climbing hundreds of feet into the sky. The flames are billowing out of one of the accommodation sites.

I prepare for the worst. I don't know exactly what to expect, but judging by the location of the blast, I suspect there are going to be scores of dead bodies.

We hammer our way through the base, past shops, phone booths and a series of tented sites, then turn into a street stacked with green two-man Portakabins. They're all linked together by acrylic walkways. The acrid stench of burnt plastic catches at the back of my throat.

A makeshift cordon has been set up, no more than 50 metres away from what turns out to be a burning petrol tanker. We pull up alongside two fire engines and an ambulance. Everybody seems in a daze. Nobody's fighting the fire or giving medical aid. They're all just standing around in shock.

I jump out of the Duro and steel myself. A captain from the RMP Special Investigation Branch approaches me with one of her sergeants. Their faces are blackened from the smoke, their distress clear for all to see.

She introduces herself as Lisa.

'What happened?' I ask.

'It's hard to know exactly,' she says. 'It appears the Kuwaiti driver was filling up a generator and didn't notice it was still switched on. One of the storemen allegedly tried to shout a warning to him but it was too late. There was a huge explosion followed by an enormous fireball. The thing went up like a bloody atom bomb. The poor guy was fried.' But they're not a hundred per cent certain what started the fire and can't rule out an IED as the cause. 'If it was an IED, there may well be more, and the fire-fighters aren't prepared to go in if there's an IED threat.'

It sounds a bit chicken and egg to me. I'm not supposed to go and clear an area when there's a threat of petrol explosions, and the fire-fighters aren't supposed to fight fires when there's an IED threat.

'We also need you to clear the body.'

Fucking hell. It just gets better.

'Any more casualties?' I ask.

'No,' she says, 'just the driver. But I should probably tell you he's been horrifically . . .'

The remains of the tanker are still burning fiercely and the column of smoke and flames towers above us. The poor fucker wouldn't have stood a chance.

'Has anyone else been up to the area?' I ask.

'No. Nobody's prepared to approach it.'

'Until it's been cleared of devices, right?'

'Exactly,' she replies.

Dan jumps into the back of the EOD wagon and pulls out a set of white Nomex fireproof coveralls and a fire extinguisher.

'I'd better give you a disruptor, boss,' he says. 'Just in case you find something nasty down there.'

A few minutes later I take the walk. For the first time in a long time I feel a deep sense of foreboding. There's a burning petrol tanker about 30 metres away from me and there could be a secondary explosion any second. My stomach clenches. I'm struggling to see through the miasma of dust and toxic smoke. I forge ahead regardless, trailing the firing cable from the disruptor behind me.

As I get closer, I can hardly breathe. I'm now no more than a few feet away from the gated entrance. The trashed generator and the mangled remains of the tanker stand at the centre of an 80-foot-square steel-fenced compound. The blaze is at its fiercest around the generator and the rear of the vehicle, but it's dying down now.

I freeze.

A smouldering body lies curled in the fetal position on the far side of the gate. The rancid smell of burning flesh is overwhelming. I know I'll carry it with me to the grave.

I scan the area for secondary devices. The compound's concrete surface is charred black apart from two white footprints next to the generator. The poor bloody driver must have been blown from there to where he's now lying.

As I look into his black lifeless eyes I feel a mixture of sorrow and disbelief. I've seen dead bodies before – their images are permanently etched into my mind – but I'm struggling to remain emotionally detached. This morning he rose from his bed, tucked into his breakfast and said goodbye to his wife and children. Just as I would have done. I know how they will react when the shadow of the messenger falls across the door.

I wrench my gaze away and scrutinize the rest of the area, searching for IEDs.

It's clear.

As I make my way back to the ICP, a fireman walks forward to assess the status of the conflagration.

'It's pretty much burned out now,' he says to the RMPs. 'You're safe to go in.'

Lisa asks me to go back with them, to show them where I've been and what I've touched. They still need to carry out a full investigation, and they'll need to know if I've contaminated any evidence.

As we step inside the compound, her sergeant pulls out a foil blanket like the ones used by hill walkers to stave off hypothermia. He shakes it open and lays it over the driver's body. A sudden gust of wind catches it as it touches the body and blows it violently upwards, spraying globules of slimy body tissue over me. My arms, neck and face are covered in scraps of charred corpse. I don't know whether to giggle or be sick. Lisa looks shocked and sympathetic, but her sergeant can't contain himself. He laughs so hard I think he's going to need oxygen. It sets us all off.

I start to feel the tension easing from my shoulder muscles.

Afterwards, when I'm back in the ICP, I realize that some of the younger members of the team have never seen a corpse before. It's covered under controlled conditions as part of the training for first responders in the emergency services, but the military tends to expect us to take these things in our stride. I tell the lads there's obviously no pressure, but if any of them wants to go and take a look before the body is removed, they can. Three or four of the lads wander over. I wonder if it will affect them, but they're all philosophical.

As we pack up the kit, I ask the two medics on the cordon if I can grab something to clean myself up.

'Sorry, sir,' comes the reply, 'we don't really have anything for that on the ambulance.'

'OK. Maybe a bit of antiseptic wash or something?'

They don't do that either.

'What about saline solution? Could I just have a splash of that?'

Again, no joy. It's like trying to push boulders uphill. I'm starting to feel a bit hysterical.

'Dan, you and the guys had better head over to the cookhouse before it closes. I need to go and get cleaned up.'

'Roger that, boss,' he says. 'If we're not in the cookhouse, we'll be in the NAAFI. And we'll make sure the chef plates you up a hot meal.'

I've scrubbed my arms and face and coughed up huge gobs of black snot, but as I sit in the cookhouse I realize it's a whole lot more difficult to eradicate the image of the charred corpse from my mind. As I raise a forkful of hamburger to my mouth, I can still smell bits of burned flesh on my clothes.

I'm struggling here. I don't think traumatic death is something I'll ever get used to. I wonder how the emergency services cope. I can't believe anyone can just shrug it off. The psychiatric nurse Phil Emerson's words echo inside my head: 'Finish each day and be done with it. You have done what you could. Some blunders and absurdities have crept in; forget them as soon as you can. Tomorrow is a new day. You shall begin it serenely and with too high a spirit to be encumbered with your old nonsense.'

I wish.

I'm sitting alone in the dining room, feeling sorry for myself. Suddenly I can feel a malevolent presence behind me. I turn and see another officer walking towards me. He's just grabbed a cake from the dessert trolley and is trying to stuff the whole thing down his throat. He looks like a snake trying to swallow a goat. He wipes his mouth and flashes me a look of contempt.

'You the ATO?' he asks.

'Yeah, I'm Chris. How do you do?'

I offer him my hand but he refuses it. Instead he just stares at me with a wild look in his eyes. I can see his pent-up fury is about to evolve into something even uglier.

'Who the fuck do you think you are, complaining to your CO about the way we do our business?'

So that's his beef. He's not wearing any insignia, but the penny's just dropped – he's an officer from the REME.

I'm tired and emotional, and now is definitely not the time to pick a fight with me. I resist the temptation to strike first and ask questions later, but as far as I'm concerned these fucking lunatics have got a lot to answer for. I can't hide my hostility towards him.

'Listen, pal, I don't know whether you woke up on the wrong side of your mum this morning, but you'd better calm down. I'm not in the fucking mood.'

'What the fuck is that supposed to mean?'

'I didn't speak to the CO; somebody else must have told him. But the fact is we're on the ground twenty-four seven and when we've got mission-critical kit that needs repairing, your blokes are supposed to be around to fix it, at any time of the day or night. So far, every time I've rocked up at the workshops, the place has been like the *Mary* fucking *Celeste*. You lot have more time off than Father Christmas.'

'We deserve every minute of it.' He's going into defensive mode. 'The blokes are working their arses off.

355

And if you and your team aren't getting enough free time, then I suggest you work on your time management. After all, you tossers get paid enough.'

I can hear an edge of trepidation in his voice. Somehow I resist the temptation to stand up and rip his throat out, but I'm still going to give it to him with both barrels.

'We don't get paid a penny extra for doing what we do, pal. Aircrew do, divers do, SF do, but we don't. I get paid as much for risking my life every hour of the fucking day as you do for sitting on your fat shiny arse. But I can live with that. I can accept the fact that the Army doesn't pay me to do bomb disposal. But what really pisses me off, what really riles me about my job, is that I have to sit here and take this kind of crap from wankers like you.'

He stands there staring at me for a moment, doing a pretty passable impression of a rabbit in front of some headlights. His mouth opens and shuts a couple of times, but nothing comes out. 'Oh, just fuck off,' he says finally, then turns on his heel and walks out.

It's over before it even started, but the confrontation has left me even more bewildered. Am I really losing the plot? I look around the cookhouse in a daze, and spot the master chef standing sheepishly by the hotplate.

He's heard the whole thing.

Now I feel really bad.

'I'm sorry, chef. That was totally unprofessional of me. I didn't mean to cause you any embarrassment.'

'You're joking, sir.' He gives me a huge grin. 'It was the best entertainment I've had all tour. That prick's thicker than a whale omelette.'

31

A man never stands as tall as when he kneels to help a child.

Knights of Pythagoras

Day 49

As we pull out of the Shai'ba gates I'm still thinking about the exchange in the cookhouse. I'm trying not to make a big deal out of it. I know it shouldn't have come as a surprise to me. I know that in this sort of pressure-cooker environment, tempers quickly fray. But not far beneath the surface I'm still fuming.

'So, how did the argument kick off?' Dan asks.

'He just came up to me and started spouting bollocks,' I say. 'Someone's obviously just had their wrists slapped so he decided he was going to have a pop. But I wouldn't exactly call it an argument. That would suggest two contrasting yet informed views.'

'Well, I'm glad you didn't take any prisoners.' He

laughs. 'I fail to see how pricks like that ever get into Sandhurst in the first place. He couldn't organize a rock fight in a quarry. Anyway, if it happens again, just remember there are few problems in life that can't be solved by the liberal application of high explosive.'

I love having Dan around. No matter how bad things get, he always manages to make me laugh.

As we continue driving down this long stretch of dusty road, a warm breeze gently blowing through the cab, I can't help but feel captivated by the magic of the desert. For a few moments the two of us sit in companionable silence. But then, a few hundred metres up the track, the magic starts to fade.

We pass one of the most impoverished areas I've yet seen in Iraq. The shanty town is filled with flimsy sack-roofed huts and emaciated children. Some are messing around at the side of the road, others play in fly-infested piles of sand.

I think of Sophie and Ella. Part of me wishes they were here right now to see this hardship and poverty for themselves. If only they knew how lucky we are to have the life we have. These Iraqi kids are starving. They have nothing. They walk barefoot and dress in grubby, tattered clothes. For them, life is nothing more than a daily battle for survival.

We're approaching the T-junction at the end of the

road, but a damaged telephone cable hangs limply across it, blocking our route on to the highway. A couple of Royal Signals engineers are frantically trying to repair it.

I lean out of my window.

'Need a hand, fellas?'

'No thanks, sir,' one of them replies. 'We'll just be a couple more minutes, then you're good to go. A low-loader caught it on the way into camp.'

As Dan and I sit in the cab, the radio crackles into life.

'Boss, incoming,' Neil says.

A dozen or so young children are running towards our parked vehicles, waving and smiling at us. A little girl wearing a tatty red dress stands on her tiptoes, straining to pass a flower up to Dan's window. She can't be more than five years old. She looks up at him with large brown eyes.

Dan and I exchange knowing glances but say nothing. We don't need to. We're both aware of the rules: no interaction with children. We're supposed to ignore them as insurgents have used kids to draw coalition troops into ambushes. But of course they're just as much the victims as we are. They're innocent kids, for Christ's sake. You'd have to be completely heartless to be able to stare straight ahead, stony-faced, and not feel any compassion towards them.

We're both thinking exactly the same thing. We open

our doors in unison and jump down on to the road.

Dan's face lights up as the little girl hands him the flower. Where she managed to find it in this desert waste-land I've no idea, but it's a beautiful moment. She neither wants nor asks for anything in return, but Dan can't help himself. He opens the cab and brings out bottles of water and ration-pack boiled sweets. As he hands them to the children, their faces light up.

And now I'm surrounded too, by little waifs clad in shabby dresses or ill-fitting trousers with no shoes and feet like leather. Despite their withered frames and bloated bellies, swollen from hunger and malnu-trition, no power on earth can stop them grinning from ear to ear.

It's the most beautiful thing in the world, the sound of children's laughter.

These little scamps may have dust-matted hair and rags for clothes, but they still have the faces of angels. And now the whole team is at it. The boys are asking them what they want to be when they grow up. They all want to be doctors. It always amazes me how even kids in a place like this have at least a smattering of English. And they in turn want to know everything about our children and what it's like to live in Britain. One of the lads takes out a photo of his kids and shows them. They're all scrab-bling to take a peek. Their eyes sparkle; they're completely enchanted by the sight of children with blonde hair.

I reach into my day-sack and hand out another ration pack. The children tear eagerly at the wrapping. It's like a game of pass the parcel. They're mesmerized by the sight of the foil-wrapped food and almost reverential as they savour tiny morsels of it. Dan is still busy handing out sweets. His compassion towards these kids is fathomless. He doesn't have children of his own, but he has the heart of a giant. It brings a lump to my throat.

'Okay, boss,' the signaller shouts. 'The cable's clear.'

As we reluctantly drive off, Dan sits for a moment in contemplative silence.

'Life is not measured by the breaths you take,' he says at length, 'but by the moments that take your breath away.'

It sums up the moment perfectly.

Back at the palace I sit at the water's edge, staring into the middle distance. I feel absolutely drained. It's been an emotion-charged day.

I can't stop thinking about the question Dom asked me outside the hospital: 'What on earth made you decide to do this for a living? Is it the adrenalin rush, the challenge? Or are you all just barking mad?' It's bugging me. I've been doing this for seven years, yet I can no sooner put my finger on why I find it so compelling than Joe

Simpson can explain why he keeps on climbing. I don't know if those early memories of my days in Brighton with Dad watching *Danger UXB* influenced my decision. They might have. But Dad died when I was fifteen and I never really got the chance to speak to him much about it.

I can certainly remember *when* I decided I was going to become an ATO. I was at Sandhurst, undergoing officer training. We were on a counter-insurgency exercise and I was standing on a cordon, pissing wet, watching the ATO centre-stage work his magic on the bomb. I was in complete awe. I had no idea what he was doing, but his tradecraft, the way he appeared to be at one with his nemesis, was truly compelling. It fascinated me. I made my decision. That's the moment when I knew bomb disposal was for me. I was twenty-one years old.

But as for the *why*, I still have no real idea. It's certainly not because I have a fetish for taking things apart or understanding how they work. I never had any deep fascination with electronics or model aeroplanes when I was at school and I was crap at engineering and the sciences. I know some do it for the adrenalin rush, others to seek atonement for darker episodes in their lives. But I think most do it out of a good old-fashioned sense of duty – just because they want to make a difference. For me, I guess it's a bit of all three.

I suppose the real question I should be asking myself is, what makes us stay? There's something immensely gratifying about neutralizing a weapon designed to kill and maim large numbers of people. Everybody I know who does it is absolutely hooked. It has to be one of the most interesting jobs on the planet. It doesn't just challenge and motivate me mentally; the fact that we get to save the lives of thousands of people we don't know and will more than likely never meet is massively inspiring on a spiritual level too. Not a single day goes by now when somebody isn't killed by an IED. Every device I can neutralize takes me one step closer to tracing and bringing down the groups responsible.

But I guess if I put my hand on my heart, the biggest, most powerful incentive is the buzz. Rendering safe a terrorist bomb is probably the most exciting thing I've ever done without getting arrested. The rush I get from dealing with a device is fearsome. It's living on the edge. It's truly elemental; a world where everything is black and white; a world of straightforward choices. Life and death.

It comes at a cost, of course. One minute you're standing at the cliff's edge, just you and the bomb, pushing it to the max; the next you're at home with your wife and kids, trying to come down and be normal again. And if you're living on the edge, eventually you're going to go all the way over. If you're lucky, you see the signs and decide it's time to pull back and step away. But maybe by then it's already too late.

'You look deep in thought, boss,' Dan says. 'Mind if I come and join you?'

'Sure, Dan. Grab a pew.'

He offers me a swig of his iced tea. As I guzzle down a mouthful of the cool, sweet liquid, I turn and look at him.

'Dan, why do you do the job? What made you want to become an operator?'

He sits and rolls the question around in his mind for a moment, then quotes that immortal line from *Blackadder*: 'A man may fight for many things. His country, his friends, his principles, the glistening tear on the cheek of a golden child. But personally, I'd mud-wrestle my own mother for a ton of cash, an amusing clock and a sackful of porn.'

32

Change is the law of life. And those who look only to the past or present are certain to miss the future.

John F. Kennedy

25 June 2004: Day 53

We've just got back from neutralizing another bank of rockets. The warm desert air gusts through the palms as a brilliant sunset sweeps across the blood-red sky.

I stand in the doorway, spellbound.

Inside the Det, Tom and Taff are busy preparing the crew room. We're having a movie night, Ridley Scott's *Gladiator*. Dan walks in with a case of Strongbow he's just blagged from the US ambassador's security detail. Furniture is being rearranged, and Ollie is setting up the laptop, focusing the projector on to the bare wall, while Rob sorts out the speakers. Then Neil strolls in with half a dozen pizzas. You don't always have to be uncomfortable in a war zone.

One of the Navy lads walks in from next door.

'Sir, there was a call for you while you were out,' he says. 'Colonel Mayhew. He left a number; said he needs you to call him back urgently.'

I take the slip of paper and thank him.

'By the way,' I add, 'any news on the hostages?'

'Yeah. The Iranians released them this morning.'

'Are they all right? Is there going to be any fallout?'

He tells me they emerged unharmed, but the Iranians refused to return their equipment. 'They put their RIB on display in a museum in Tehran.' He laughs. 'But I wouldn't have wanted to be in their shoes. The Iranians carried out a mock execution on them. The bastards marched our boys into the desert and made them stand, blindfolded, in front of a ditch; then they started cocking their weapons. Not surprisingly, it shitted them right up.'

As Maximus Decimus Meridius unleashes hell on the Germanic hordes, I punch in a number for the UK military exchange. All secure calls back to the UK have to go through the Whitehall operator.

There's a short delay, and then I hear Colonel Mayhew's cheery voice. He's the head of all British IEDD operations in the UK and I'm a huge fan of his. He's an absolute gentleman and I've worked for him for several years. He reminds me irresistibly of Commander

367

Swanbeck, the Anthony Hopkins character in *Mission Impossible 2*. 'This isn't Mission Difficult, Mr Hunter. It's Mission Impossible . . .'

I stop fantasizing for a moment and fill him in on the events of the past couple of days. I tell him about the task we've just completed – another bank of rockets pointing at Divisional HQ – and how we came within a cat's whisker of catching the perpetrators.

'Oh really?' he says. 'So what went wrong?'

I explain that troops from the RAF Regiment were given orders to capture or kill the Shia insurgents responsible for the rocket attacks against the airfield and Divisional HQ. 'They were even given a detailed description of the vehicles and the terrorists, but as the RAF boys were on their way to investigate reports of a pending rocket attack, they managed somehow to drive straight past them.'

'*What?*' He sounds as incredulous as I was.

They were travelling in the two white Dodge trucks that had been spotted at a number of previous attacks, and were all dressed in black. They couldn't have looked more like terrorists if they'd tried. But, amazingly, the muppets let them get away.

'No wonder the RAF are going to disband them,' he comments drily.

He then asks me what else we've been up to. One of

Left: DAY 20: The location of the IED outside the Office of the Martyr al-Sadr, the headquarters of Basra's Mahdi Army. The device was completely overlooked from all directions and I feared I might be targeted by a sniper, so I threw smoke grenades to mask my manual approach to the IED.

Below: DAY 20: This was the second time Behadli's stooges had emplaced a device with the sole intention of killing me. I was beginning to take it rather personally by this stage. The image shows a radio controlled device after I'd neutralized it.

Below: Members of the Mahdi Army watch us from the roof of the Office of the Martyr al-Sadr. Immediately before this photograph was taken they had been filming me and the team – most likely for targeting purposes. Behadli is on the left in the white turban.

DAY 19: Dan and me about to deploy by CH47 Chinook helicopter to a light IEDD task at the police station in al-Amarah. The al-Amarah operator had been given 24 hours off, having been involved in fierce fighting with the Mahdi Army some days previously.

Chinook deploying decoy flares over al-Amarah.

Above left: DAY 31: Dan and me about to deploy on a heli op to hunt for command-wire IEDs. **Above right:** DAY 32: Returning from the 'long walk' to the ICP, having successfully rendered safe an IED. The heat was fearsome: temperatures frequently reached in excess of 50°C in the midday sun.

From top left: DAY 46: The booby-trapped vehicle-borne IED used by the Shia insurgents in another attempt on my life. It contained an estimated 300kg of high-explosive ordnance.

Below: The crater left by the VBIED explosion outside the hospital.

Discussing a surveillance serial with the RAF load-master during a heli-borne weapons-intelligence operation.

Above: All that remained of the vehicle post explosion. Dan was extremely distressed that his beloved robot had been completely destroyed in the blast.

Main picture: DAY 101: Conducting a heli-borne weapons-intelligence task over Basra City following the death of Private Marc Ferns on 12 August 2004. He was killed by a huge improvised claymore mine similar to those used by Lebanese Hezbollah.

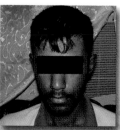

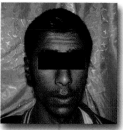

Above: DAY 77: al-Jameat police station following the capture of the first Sunni bomber team. Ironically, we saved the lives of al-Keshti (*left*) and his accomplices, by negotiating their handover from the Iraqi police, who a few minutes earlier were beating them with rubber hoses and threatening to kill them.

Above: Steel door leading into the 'custody suite' where the bomber team was being interrogated. During Saddam's reign the place was known as the Station of Death. Now under Shia control, it seems little has changed…

Above: Note the hook – the Shia interrogators had threatened to hang the bombers from the ceiling and tear off their skin, strip by strip.

Left: al-Keshti's team sit cuffed and blindfolded in the custody suite at al-Jameat while he is interrogated. I could hear their screams from outside the compound.

Right: DAY 102: Post assault. A warrior from the Black Watch company group mans the ring of steel surrounding Alpha One.

Left: 'A man never stands as tall as when he kneels to help a child.' Dan with the kids at Shai'ba.

Main picture: DAY 102: Daybreak following the capture of the second Sunni bomber team in the Hayy al-Muhandisn area of Southern Basra. The photograph is taken from outside Alpha One.

Standing at the Hands of Victory during one of my trips to Baghdad. Saddam had them built in the late eighties to commemorate his perceived triumph over Iran, and insisted that the hands were exact scale-replicas of his own.

The photo of Lucy I kept folded up in my assault vest. I'd removed it from my kit after the ambush, but replaced it the next day. I wasn't prepared to give it up – I'd taken it shortly after we first met.

the beauties of being in the Det is that we've got secure comms back to the UK so we can speak 'in clear'. I tell him about the comedy task we received yesterday at Shai'ba Log Base.

We had another call-out from the Danes. When we rocked up, we kept our eyes peeled for the cordon. What we found instead looked like a casting session for the Village People: half a dozen men in shorts, stripped to the waist, standing around a 1-metre-square taped-off area on their concrete forecourt, at the centre of which was the 'device'. Except it wasn't a device, it was a small radio battery. When I asked them why they'd thought it was suspicious, they said, 'We just wanted to be sure.' Honestly, you couldn't make it up.

'Is there anything else I need to know?' he asks. 'I've got to put together my weekly report to PATO.'

The principal ammunition technical officer is our head of trade.

The only other news I have is that I was summoned to Brigade HQ yesterday to be given a bollocking by Colonel Sanderson for a paper I'd written on enhancing the EOD capability in southern Iraq. 'To be fair,' I say, 'I did expect it to cause a bit of a stir. That's the reason I wrote it in the first place – you know, to shake things up a bit. But it was considered a bit too close to the bone.' The paper highlighted a shortage of the kind of mission-critical kit that's still clogging up the shelves in Northern Ireland, and, crucially, that some of the staff officers out here weren't pulling their weight.

Colonel Sanderson made a few comments about ATOs being in their own little world and gave me the whole 'there's more to fighting an insurgency than just dealing with IEDs' lecture. Then he dusted off the old Churchill line about criticism not being agreeable, but very much necessary.

'He raised his voice quite a bit,' I say. 'But it was all very gentlemanly. Then he completely threw me by telling me he agreed with everything I'd written and that he was going to fight to have every single one of the recommendations actioned. So, to be honest with you, in spite of his ability to give a savage tongue lashing, I've got nothing but respect for the man.'

'Good stuff,' he says. 'Anything else?'

'Well, actually, yes, there is one thing.'

I ask him about the paperwork I need to fill out for destroying the wheelbarrow during the VBIED task last week.

'You won't need to,' he replies.

'I won't?'

It's nearly £1.5 million worth of robot and he's telling me I don't have to fill out any paperwork. I'm astonished.

'It was destroyed during operations,' he says. 'You've

already recorded it in your IEDD report, so you don't need to waste time with any other bumf. Although that does bring me rather conveniently to a more pressing concern.'

He tells me that both my CO back at 11 EOD Regiment and the staff at PATO are concerned about the extent of the targeting here in Basra. Then he pauses. The atmosphere on the line suddenly becomes more highly charged.

'Chris, we're sending another operator out to theatre. You'll need to hand over command of the team to him. We've got another assignment for you.'

I'm gobsmacked. I try to process what he's just said, but I'm lost for words.

'Colonel, I can't do that,' I say eventually.

'I'm sorry, Chris, this is non-negotiable.'

'But, sir, you of all people know I can't leave the blokes halfway through a tour. Not after everything we've been through.'

I know this strikes a chord, but he's having none of it. In his usual calm but firm manner he tells me I'm a British Army officer which means that I not only have to follow orders, I have to serve the interests of those under me as best I can. He reminds me of the Sandhurst motto: 'Serve to Lead'.

'You're going to be a major in five days,' he adds.

'You've got to let go. I know it's hard. The fact is we all have to move on, and you've done your bit.'

For a moment I sit in stunned silence.

'So that's it, sir? I'm being short-toured?'

'Not at all,' he says. 'We've selected you for one of the most challenging new jobs in theatre.'

He tells me he wants me to establish a strategic weapons intelligence cell at Div HQ, responsible for all multinational weapons intelligence assets in southern Iraq.

It sounds grand, but I'm still not sold.

'You'll be working primarily with US military intelligence liaison officers. Specifically, you'll be analysing all terrorist IED attacks in southern Iraq and working with the Americans to identify the bomber networks. We want you to seek out and capture the bomb-makers, Chris, including the ones who've been targeting you.'

I feel guilty and ungrateful. I know it will be a fascinating job, and nobody wants to capture the bombers more than I do, but I feel terrible about having to leave the blokes. And no matter how much he dresses it up, I'll still be a staff officer, and I fucking hate the idea of becoming a Tippex commando.

'Is that it then, sir? The decision's final?'

'I'm afraid so,' he replies.

'How long have I got left on the team?'

'Two days.'

I slowly replace the receiver.

Most of the lads are still engrossed in the film, but Dan's been listening in. He flashes me a look of sympathy and shakes his head.

Fuck it. I spent fourteen sodding months on the ATO course before I could even be considered for employment as an operator. The first six were at the Royal Military College of Science and covered everything from explosive chemistry to nuclear physics. It was horrendous; I was way outside my comfort zone. The majority of my classmates held science degrees, one of them from Cambridge; I'd failed GCSE chemistry miserably at school. Firmly rooted in the class biff seat, I had to work doubly hard and pinned all my hopes on the belief that what I lacked academically I would be able to make up for in practical ability.

Fortunately my gamble paid off. I managed to Forrest Gump my way through the science section and moved on to phase two – a further eight months' training at the Army School of Ammunition in Warwickshire. There we studied practical modules: everything there was to know about ammunition and explosives, chemical, biological, radiological and nuclear weapons disposal, and the most prized module of all, the Joint Services IEDD course. IEDD sounded deceptively innocent. Improvised

Explosive Device Disposal. Counter-Terrorist Bomb Disposal.

Luckily for me, IEDD was a discipline that seemed to come naturally. I had finally found something I was good at. We took well over two hundred exams during the fourteen-month course and were returned to unit if we failed more than three. Borderline cases were never given the benefit of the doubt, the rationale being that if you were unsuitable, the possible consequences of a mistake were highly likely to be terminal. To this day, the standards demanded are something the trade is not prepared to compromise on, irrespective of the need for trained operators.

On graduation, half the course was sent to 11 EOD Regiment as operators and the remainder were posted to other ammunition-related jobs. But the selection didn't end there. For those who wanted to operate in high-threat IEDD environments such as Northern Ireland and Iraq, suitably experienced joint service operators could volunteer for a place on the coveted Special-To-Theatre course. STT has one of the highest failure rates in the British Army, second only to SAS selection. It's probably the most important course an ATO will ever do. Only those who've passed STT and have served as high-threat operators are considered for long-term employment within the IEDD community.

I've amassed years of experience and forfeited promotion to be a high-threat operator. And for what? To be transferred to an intelligence post after only two months. I've worked fucking hard to get out here and I've relished every single minute of it, so to have the carpet suddenly swept out from under my feet has come as a crushing blow.

I think about the spoof intelligence staff recruitment email that's currently doing the rounds on the Army's intranet.

If you played with Action Man from an early age but do not have it in you to join God's infantry, then why not consider a career in the Intelligence Corps? It requires little or no military ability but gives you the chance to read a lot of 'secret' things that nobody else really gives a shit about. Basic training is purely optional but may require you to wear a uniform badly. Entrance is on intellectual ability only and a degree of fluency in a language that no one else can understand.

If you spent your childhood playing either with yourself or a Playstation and locked yourself in a darkened room to avoid any kind of social interaction, then a career in operational intelligence could be just the ticket for you. You will get the chance to travel extensively (weekly to Iraq in some cases) and the opportunity to fill your head with even more irrelevant facts. Slack thinking required. To apply for a career in the Intelligence Corps you must be intelligent. That's it. Anything else is a bonus.

I'm really not sure I want to go back to intelligence. I started my career there fourteen years ago as a Russian linguist. I thought I was going to be James Bond. I was wrong. And it bored the tits off me then.

Still, I'm in the Army, and I'm paid to do what I'm told. If I can't hack that, I shouldn't have signed on the dotted line.

33

The firmest friendships have been formed in mutual adversity, as iron is most strongly welded by the fiercest fire.

Anonymous

27 June 2004: Day 55

The blokes are pissed off.

As soldiers, we are encouraged to be regimented and conditioned to become creatures of habit, so when the status quo suddenly changes, it shouldn't come as a surprise that we often struggle to come to terms with it.

Yesterday, Dan was told he's also on his way out. He was due to finish in a couple of weeks, but his replacement has been sent out early.

We're ending our IEDD tours together. Today's our last day.

While he goes through the equipment handover with his successor, a young lance corporal straight off his High

Threat Number Two course, I'm bringing my replacement up to speed in the crew room.

'Max' Maxwell is a well-built, done-it-all-seen-it-all senior NCO with a reputation for getting things done and not suffering fools. He's the ideal man to take over as the Basra City ATO.

We've spent hours going through the forty-five incidents the team's dealt with over the last two months, as well as those pre-dating my arrival in theatre. He needs to know about every device in minute detail. Not just the technical detail, but the targeting methodology used by the terrorists and the forensics we've gained.

He seems to know his onions. I still hate the thought of having to give up the reins to him, but I'm confident the team will be in safe hands.

'So basically,' he says, 'we're averaging around one device per day. But you've been tasked out to four incidents in the last two days alone.'

I tell him one device a day is only an average; it's not set in stone. Some days there's nothing, other days it goes ballistic. And of course we're not tasked to every incident either. 'We probably only attend two thirds of the IEDs in Basra. Quite often, if it's not too technical the Iraqi Police decide they'll neutralize the devices themselves, and don't report the fact to us. Other times there have been IED explosions in the city and it's just been too dangerous for us to go out on the ground.'

Max thumbs through the remainder of the IEDD report folder until he gets to the final few tasks.

'What about these?'

'Over the last two days we've been tasked to another two keyless entry system RCIEDs as well as a rather cheeky incident in the Arab quarter last night. We also went out to a device this morning, but that was just kids pissing about.'

'What happened during last night's task?'

We deployed to the Old Basra District – a notorious part of town. I had to deal with an Italian anti-tank mine in the road, outside a school. When we got there, the infantry believed it was a come-on. They thought the mine may have been booby-trapped.

'It stank of a come-on. It was very dark and the area was well overlooked. Lots of tall, oak-panelled arabesque buildings with narrow empty streets and people peering out of the windows. You know the sort of thing.'

'How did you deal with it?'

It's important that Max knows exactly what my RSPs are for every single incident, so that if I've inadvertently set any patterns the terrorists can then exploit to attack us – like forgetting to do 20-metre checks when we arrive at a task – he can modify his own RSPs to guard against it.

'I sent down the wheelbarrow to do a bit of remote reconnaissance. Then, having found the mine, I quickly realized I couldn't shoot it. It would almost certainly have detonated, which would have destroyed the school.'

Because I feared I was being targeted, I had to position the infantry tactically in doorways and street corners. I requested helicopter top cover, but that was refused – this time due to the perceived threat from SAMs and anti-aircraft guns – so I fired flares into the sky and used my laser and personal radio to indicate any potential enemy firing points to the infantry escorts as I carried out a manual approach.

'There were three guys watching me from one of the rooftops, and when I lit up the sky with a flare and lased them, virtually every infantryman on the cordon brought his weapon to bear. There were red dots all over them. It was like something out of a fucking Jean Michel Jarre concert. The poor blokes nearly fell off the roof, they were so terrified.'

'And the mine? You defused it by hand?'

I nod. It turned out to be a straightforward anti-tank mine – not one that was booby-trapped – so I nuked it with a couple of X-rays, then I unscrewed the fuse and that was it. Job jobbed.

*

The moment I've been dreading has finally come. It's time to bid farewell to the blokes.

My final forty-eight hours on the team has gone by in a blur. In fact the whole of the last eight weeks has.

As I glance around the room, I feel a warm sense of pride. When the chips were down, it was their determination and support, their incessant banter, and above all their fearless humour that got me through the day.

There's nothing I wouldn't do for these guys. Over the past two months they have become my family. I don't think I fully appreciated it until now, but there have been times when they were closer to me than any friends could ever be. We've lived in one another's pockets twenty-four hours a day, seven days a week, enduring fearsome amounts of stress and tension, yet not one of them has ever put himself before the team. From one desperate event to another, we've fought together, stood side by side together, and when the crunch came were prepared to die together. I'm going to miss them.

They look back at me. They're trying to be upbeat, but their mournful expressions betray them.

Mick walks in.

'Fucking hell, has someone died? I thought we were all going to have a few beers.'

Within seconds the mood has lifted, some heavy metal

is blaring out of a stereo and each of us is cradling a cold can of lager.

Rob and Mick take the floor and say a few parting words. They're short and sweet.

'Dan, you've been an outstanding second in command and a good friend to us all,' Rob says. 'And as Winston Churchill once said, "Never in the field of human conflict have I had a mate like you, mate. May you always party like a rock star, look like a movie star and fuck like a porn star."'

With that, he hands Dan a no-expense-spared Basra spot map signed by the lads.

Dan raises his can.

'Thanks, lads,' he says. 'It's beautiful. And if you get me pissed, just don't make me pregnant. I've got a flight to catch in the morning.'

Now it's my turn.

'Well, boss,' Mick says, 'for once, I'm lost for words. What can I say? A few weeks back you told us we were living in interesting times. I don't think any of us could have imagined they'd be quite *this* interesting. Never a dull car bomb with you, eh? You've not just been a good boss, you've been a great friend as well. And thanks for saving my career. I'll not forget it.'

I feel my eyes pricking.

Rob takes over.

'As you know, boss, I'm an ex-regular, which means I was called up as a reservist to come out here—'

The mere hint of a public admission that he's in the TA is like a red rag to a bull. The rest of the room begin jeering and hurling abuse at him. They're calling him a stab wanker – the affectionate name given by regulars to a member of the Territorial Army. He flashes them a look of disdain, clears his throat and continues.

'I've been running my own business for the past ten years, and when I was called up to come to Iraq I had nightmares about having to work for some jumped-up young Rupert. I thought I was going to hell and back . . . I couldn't have been more wrong. I have enjoyed working for you immensely, and it's an honour to call you boss, boss.' He raises his glass. 'Here's to pussy and gun-smoke. May you live by one, die by the other and always enjoy the smell of both in the morning.'

As I gulp down a mouthful of beer, Rob hands me my spot map. The boys are all clapping and cheering.

'Speech, speech!'

It's my turn. I thank Mick and Rob for their kind words, but as usual, I've been so busy chasing my own arse I've not even thought to prepare anything. I tell them that working with them has been one of the high-lights of my career. I know just how clichéd that sounds, but fuck it, it's true. I finish with a few gems of advice about not being afraid to take calculated risks and always trusting your gut instincts.

As I head for the door, Mick hands me a sheet of paper.

'We know you're pissed off at having to leave the team, but just in case you decide to do anything silly, like sign off, this will dissuade you. Take care, boss.'

I walk into the cool desert night and spark up a cigarette. Underneath one of the streetlamps, I read the slip of paper. It's a twelve-step programme for leaving the Army.

I am in the military, I have a problem. This is the first step to recovery.

STEP 1. Speech:

- Time should never begin with a zero or end in a hundred. It is not 'zero five thirty' or 'fourteen hundred'. It is 'five thirty' or 'two o'clock'.
- 'Fuck' cannot be used to replace whatever word you can't think of right now. Try 'Um'.
- Grunting is not talking.
- It's a phone, not a radio. Conversations on a phone do not follow a set procedure and do not end in 'out'.

STEP 2. Style:

- Do not put creases in your jeans.

- Do not put creases in the front of your dress shirts.
- Do not iron your collar flat.

STEP 3. Women:

- Being divorced twice by the time you're twenty-three is not normal; neither are six-month marriages, even if it is your first.
- Marrying a girl so that you can move out of the barracks does not make financial sense.

STEP 4. Personal accomplishments:

- In the real world, being able to do push-ups will not make you better at your job.
- Most people will be slightly disturbed if you tell them about people you have killed or seen die.
- How much pain you can take is not a personal accomplishment.

STEP 5. Drinking:

- In the real world, being drunk before 5 p.m. will get you a reprimand and formal warning, not a pat on the back.
- That time you drank a full slab of beer and pissed in your wardrobe is not a conversation starter.

STEP 6. Bodily functions:

- Farting on your co-workers and then giggling while you run away may be viewed as 'unprofessional'.
- The size of the dump you took yesterday will not be funny, no matter how big it was, how much it

burned or how much it smelled.

- You can't make fun of someone for being sick, no matter how funny it is.

STEP 7. The human body:

- Most people will not want to hear about your balls. Odd as that may seem, it's true.

STEP 8. Spending habits:

- One day you will have to pay bills.
- Buying a £40,000 car on a £20,000-a-year salary is a really bad idea.
- One day you will need health insurance.

STEP 9. Interacting with civilians:

- Making fun of your neighbour to his face for being fat will not be appreciated.

STEP 10. Real jobs:

- They really can fire you.
- On the flip side, you really can quit.
- Screaming at the people who work for you will not be normal. Remember they really can quit too.
- Taking naps at work will not be acceptable.
- Remember, 9 to 5, not 0530 to 1800.

STEP 11. The law:

- Non-judicial punishment does not exist and will not save you from prison.
- Your workplace, unlike your command, can't save you and probably won't; in fact, most likely you will

be fired about five minutes after they find out you've been arrested.

- Even McDonald's does background checks, and 'conviction' isn't going to help you get the job.
- Fighting is not a normal thing and will get you arrested, not yelled at on Monday morning before they ask you if you won.

STEP 12. General knowledge:

- You can really say what you think about the Prime Minister in public.
- Pain is not weakness escaping the body, it's just pain.
- They won't wear anything shiny that tells you they are more important than you are, so be polite.
- And lastly, read the contracts before you sign them. Remember what happened the first time.

34

*Problems are to the mind what exercise is to the muscles,
they toughen and make them strong.*

Norman Vincent Peale

28 June 2004: Day 56

The early-morning sun glints off the terminal building
and rages down through the open roof of the Snatch. I've
been cramped in the back of the vehicle for the past
thirty minutes. It's been the most uncomfortable half an
hour of my life.

The Salamanca Company boys have given me a lift
from the palace to my new accommodation in our
Divisional Headquarters at Basra International Airport.
They're a slick crew, part of an eighty-strong Territorial
Army contingent providing force protection with the
Cheshire Regiment Battle Group. Their principal tasks
are guarding Brigade HQ at Basra Palace and patrolling
the eastern part of the city. These guys aren't just any old

TA unit; they're a highly proficient bunch. They have actions-on for every scenario imaginable, and like the SF they operate in four-man patrols, each containing a medic, a signalman and a machine gunner.

I'm grateful to be alongside them. They know their onions. But sitting inside the back of this Land Rover, hunched up against my kit and inhaling the hot, stale air, makes me feel nauseous and claustrophobic.

As we pull off the highway and on to the long airport approach road, I catch a glimpse of the oil wells burning fiercely on the horizon.

One of the top-cover men glances down at me. His name's Tony. I recognize him from the rocket incident a few weeks ago when the mother and children were killed.

'Checkpoint coming up, boss,' he says.

We pass through a vehicle checkpoint on the outer perimeter of the airfield. The sentries glumly wave us through. Standing against concrete blast walls, they look hot and irritable. So would I be if I had their job.

The moment we're through, the top-cover men drop down on to their seats. We're no longer at threat. Their work is done for now.

'So, what do you do for a living when you're out of uniform?' I ask Tony.

'I'm a doorman at a strip club,' he says with a grin.

For a moment I think he's taking the piss, but it turns out he works for one of the most famous clubs in the UK.

'So you've come over here for a bit of a break?'

'Hasn't really turned out that way. We've had a few dramas, to be honest.'

He tells me that during one incident he was challenged by a masked gunman standing no more than 15 metres away, pointing an AK-47 at him. 'The bastard tried to shoot me but had a dead man's click, so I dropped down on one knee and put two rounds into his chest. The whole place then erupted into a massive firefight. At one point we actually fixed bayonets; we thought we were going to run out of ammo. But on the whole it's been a brilliant tour.' He pauses. 'The trouble is, you just have no idea what's waiting for you round the corner. It can be a bit stressful at times.'

A couple or so miles down the road we pass through another more substantial checkpoint. Despite the fact we're all in British uniforms, carrying British weapons and travelling in a British military vehicle, the sentry still insists on stopping us and checking our ID cards.

It's the rules.

High up in the sangar's fortified watchtower behind him, another soldier watches us, hawk-like, through the sights of his machine gun.

The sentry nods and grunts something inaudible, and

moments later we're heading into the centre of the air station. To our left there are rows and rows of plastic air-conditioned tents like the ones we lived in at the palace, but here they're used as transit accommodation. Further along the road we pass the former airport hotel, now the Divisional Headquarters. Behind it, scores of soldiers are lugging their weapons and Bergens into the huge terminal building. Some are going home, others are heading north.

Finally we reach our accommodation. Waterloo Lines is like a small city. On one side of the road there's a Pizza Hut, a huge, well-stocked NAAFI and several bars; on the other, rows of Portakabin-style huts housing the troops. The ablutions, the cookhouse, a gym, a barber shop, TV rooms, games rooms and more bars stand nearby.

I've never seen anything like it on ops.

The Salamanca boys drop me off at the front gate. I report to the gatehouse, where a young RAF NCO hands me the key to my hut. I find it 20 metres or so along a covered walkway, several rows to my right. The room contains two bunk beds, a locker, a table and chairs, and air-conditioning. It's cold and devoid of character, but that's fine by me: I don't plan on spending much time in it. There are bombers out there, and I'm going to work my tits off to catch them.

I chuck my kit on to the empty bunk and head back to Div HQ. A Land Rover pulls up beside me as I emerge from Waterloo Lines on to the main airport road.

'Hello, stranger, what brings you here?'

Scotty's face is beaming at me. I don't think I've ever seen him looking so happy.

I explain about Behadli and the Sunnis targeting me and how it came to a head with the VBIED outside the hospital. 'So I'm starting this new WIS job today. In fact, in about five minutes . . .'

'Rather you than me, mate.' He's still grinning like an idiot. 'I've handed over. It's endex. I'm outta here.'

He's finally made it to the end of his tour. He's going home to his wife and kids.

'Look, I'd love to stay and catch up,' he says, 'but I'm late for my check-in. I'm going to have to shoot. Stay safe, mate. We'll do it again. Just not out here.'

And with that, he zooms off towards the terminal.

A large sign hanging above the entrance tells me 'Headquarters Multi National Force Divisional Headquarters South East welcomes you'. I go through huge smoked-glass doors and into the marble-floored foyer.

I'm still struggling to come to terms with the fact that I'll be working as a staff officer, with other staff officers. I need to overcome a lifetime of prejudice. As far as the lads at the sharp end are concerned, career staff officers are total tossers. The sort of people who always have to go one better. If you've just bought a garden shed, they already have two. If you've been to Tenerife, they've just come back from Elevenerife. And woe betide you if you stand in their way. If they give you a pat on the back, the chances are it's just a recce.

But hell, I need to get over it. My days at the forefront of bomb disposal are over. This is my life now. I've got a job to do and I promised myself I would give it my best. Whatever it takes to get the bombers off the streets.

I walk through a series of corridors until at last I reach the operations centre. The former hotel dining room is filled with banks of desktop computers. Scores of staff officers of all nationalities are working alongside their British counterparts, tapping away diligently at their keyboards as radio traffic booms out of the speakers and live news feeds play continuously across plasma screens. Everything's being done at a furious pace. People are shouting, the phones are ringing. It's like Brigade HQ, but on a far bigger scale.

A young corporal from the Intelligence Corps sees me standing vacantly at the edge of the room.

'Are you Captain Hunter, sir?' he asks. 'The boss is expecting you next door.'

The room he guides me to is just as large, but deathly silent.

At first glance, the head of J2 (Joint Intelligence) appears slightly older than his forty years, but his marathon-runner's physique belies his prematurely greying hair. I've done my homework on Colonel Peter Austin; Will is a good mate of his, and has given me the guy's life story. I know the colonel will have grilled him for information about me too. Despite his calm and mild-mannered exterior, Austin has spent his entire career on the dark side, working undercover, running sources in Northern Ireland. He's not a man to cross, but then you'd have to go a long way to cross him. He's incredibly charming and laid back beyond belief. This, I suspect, is why he's such a fine handler.

'Chris, I'll cut to the chase,' he says. 'I've worked at length with other ATOs in NI, and I think it's fair to say that you guys are more concerned with making devices safe than the whys and wherefores of who planted them.'

He takes a sip of coffee, then continues.

'But obviously things are different out here. The terrain's different, the people are different and the threat is vastly different to anything we've experienced in the province. We're being forced to change our mindset. We need to start asking the right questions. Lots of them.

That's why you're here. To identify what intelligence we need to focus on to lead us to the bombers.'

He goes on to tell me that he wants me to leave no stone unturned. He needs me to start drilling down through the reports and databases, looking at dismantled devices and interviewing detainees, and he wants me to carry out extensive liaison with our coalition intelligence partners.

'I'm not sure exactly how I would define your job spec. It's technically a staff officer's post, but I see it being very hands-on. You're going to be out on the ground a hell of a lot. And if you come up trumps, I'm pretty certain you'll be going in with the boys and kicking some doors down as well. You're effectively your own boss. I'm just here to give you top cover when you need it.'

This job sounds amazing. He's told me I've got carte blanche to use whatever intelligence assets I need to seek out the bomber networks. He's even sought authority for me to keep my personal weapon in my office, in case I get crashed out in a hurry. The rest of the staff have to keep their weapons in an armoury on the other side of camp.

'Oh, I nearly forgot,' he says. 'I've put you in one of the quieter offices, with three Americans. It'll be a bit of a squeeze, but they're cracking chaps. Last room on the left before the Int Centre.'

As I walk into my new office, I learn something else

about Colonel Austin: he's not prone to exaggeration. The room can't be more than 10 feet wide and 15 feet long – hardly large enough to accommodate a stiff erection, let alone swing a cat. Three desks have been pushed tight up against one end of the room, and there's a fourth at the other, which I take to be mine. A large Stars and Stripes and a Union Jack have been draped above two metal lockers.

'You must be Chris, right?'

The American officer sitting in front of me is the spitting image of Tom Hanks. As it turns out, Eric Casey's story is not dissimilar to that of the Captain Miller character in *Saving Private Ryan*. He is a quietly spoken, hard-working school teacher who, as a part-time intelligence officer in the reserves, was called up for military duty ten months ago. He's been in Iraq ever since. Now all he wants to do is serve out his time and get back home to his wife.

He introduces me to his two senior NCOs. Tex is a Marine from the Deep South. He doesn't say much. He chews tobacco, grunts a bit and taps away at his keyboard. But if that makes him happy, I'm not going to argue. He's built like an ox and is the only man I've ever seen whose neck really is thicker than his head. Sergeant Vasha is a lively, gangly character who's been seconded to the British-led HQ from the 101st

Airborne Division. The two of us hit it off immediately.

'Get a load of this, sir,' he says, demonstrating a fine grasp of squaddie argot.

He's watching a live aerial video feed of an attack on some insurgents. He turns his laptop so that I can see the screen too. Small black and white figures are preparing what looks like a car bomb beside a large concrete building. Four or five of them are wiring up the car while a couple of others pass them artillery shells and other explosives.

'Where is it?' I ask him. The fact that it's live makes it seem completely surreal.

'Ramadi.'

Moments later the picture whites out, then comes sharply back into focus. A huge black cloud billows from the spot where the car once stood.

'They got love from above,' he says with some satisfaction.

'Jesus, what was it?' I say. 'A fucking atom bomb?'

We're both laughing, but out of the corner of my eye I notice Tex and Eric both looking daggers. It suddenly dawns on me that being good God-fearing Southerners, they've taken offence at my using the Good Lord's name in vain. When I apologize, Tex grunts something inaudible and Eric just shakes his head. I can see I'm going to have to make a real effort to stop myself from blaspheming. But after eight weeks on the team I'm swearing like a sailor's parrot.

Vash, still laughing, shows me how to log on to the secure IT system, then guides me through some of the intelligence databases. He opens up Providence, his favourite database.

'Now we're cooking. This little baby can pull up registrations of births, deaths, marriages, political affiliations, business transactions, tax returns, email accounts, telephone numbers, National ID numbers, you name it. If it ain't on here, you ain't gonna find it.'

If I'm going to stand any chance of catching the bad guys, I can see I'm going to have to spend a great deal of the next two months of my life cocooned in here, working my way through these databases.

When Vash has finished briefing me, Eric brings me up to speed on what else has been happening in the country. Until now, I've only really focused on Basra and al-Amarah; now that I'm responsible for the entire divisional area, I'll need to know what's going on across most of southern Iraq. I'll also need to get a handle on terrorist activity elsewhere, in order to predict what we are likely to see next in our own patch.

As Eric continues the rundown on insurgent activity in Baghdad, Fallujah and Najaf, an RMP corporal from the Shack bursts into the office.

'Sir, there's been an IED attack in Basra City. One of our patrols has been hit. We've lost a soldier.'

My heart sinks. The lads from Salamanca Company brought me here as a favour. If one of them has been killed, I'll never forgive myself.

'What's his name?' I ask.

'Fusilier Gordon Gentle, sir. He's nineteen years old.'

Nineteen. Fucking hell. He's just a kid.

'I need all the information you can get me,' I say.

'Roger that, sir. I've just passed the WIS team's quick-look report to ops.'

I rush through to the ops centre. There's a dark mood hanging over the room. I grab a copy of the report.

> The attack took place during rush-hour. A British convoy was being escorted by 2 Snatch Land Rovers, and was travelling towards Shai'ba Log Base. Only limited counter-measures were fitted to the vehicle at the time.

That's the report originator cryptically saying the patrol wasn't carrying the new jammers. It's definitely not the Salamanca boys then.

> The vehicles were moving towards a crossroads when the IED exploded next to the front Snatch vehicle.

The IED was hidden amongst piles of rubbish at the side of the road . . .

It's assessed that this was another keyless entry RCIED . . .

This is outrageous. A nineteen-year-old boy has been killed on the same road we were ambushed on because he didn't have ECM to defeat a keyless car entry system RCIED.

We need to catch these bastards before there's another fatality.

I walk back through to my new office and Eric tells me how sorry he is. On the wall behind him I notice a plaque: 'Fight what is Wrong, Believe what is True, Do what is Right'. I already know that's exactly how he lives his life.

Americans get a lot of grief for the way they conduct themselves in Iraq. There have been some howling errors, but speaking to Eric I can see he, and many like him, really gets it. He's studied Iraqi culture and he empathizes with their strong sense of devotion to tribe, country and religion. And when he speaks about inter-acting with the people, it's obvious he understands not only the concept but also the importance of winning hearts and minds.

General Colin Powell was once asked about US empire building by the Archbishop of Canterbury. He replied, 'Over the years, the United States has sent many of its fine young men and women into great peril to fight for freedom beyond our borders. The only land we have ever asked for in return is enough to bury those that did not return.'

That's how Eric and his guys see it too.

I like these boys. They are the real deal.

This is my first day in the job, but Fusilier Gentle's death has already made me painfully aware that by the time I get to hear about an incident it's probably going to be too late to do anything about it. I'm going to need to drill down into the detail and investigate every aspect of every incident if I'm to stand any chance of preventing such atrocities in the future. If I miss anything, if a single stone remains unturned, then someone else might die.

I immediately begin trawling through reports. I remove four lever-arch box files marked with the abbreviation WPNS INT from my locker. I set the pile of IED intelligence reports down on my desk and begin going through them one by one.

Each of the reports has a date time group, a grid reference showing exactly where the incident took place and a photographic annexe with pictures of the incident as well as mapping and aerial images of the target area.

As I thumb my way through, my eyes scanning the information on every page, my brain is working like a computer to pick up on any similarities in the text or imagery. I'm looking for patterns or clues the bomber may have left. Ultimately, I'm trying to find his signature.

A bomber's 'signature' is a well-documented phenomenon. In the seventies and eighties the notorious Unabomber used to construct pipe bombs in a very particular way, and would sign messages to his victims 'FC' (Freedom Club). A decade later in the UK, the Mardi Gras bomber, responsible for a three-year campaign of blackmail and terror in the London area, made well-machined and perfectly engineered IEDs for his attacks. He always left a calling card containing the incorrectly spelled phrase 'Welcome to the Mardi Gra experience'.

I go through every report, drinking cup after cup of strong coffee and taking copious notes on the similarities between each incident. Several hours later, fighting to stay awake, I've finally finished going through a year's worth of weapons intelligence reports. I feel fucked. Doing this is like reading a really cracking thriller when you're tired.

Just one more chapter . . .

I fire up the computer and begin sifting through the various databases. The reports on the system are more generic and less IED-specific, but they give me a good handle on the individuals we know are operating in Basra, and their associates.

I start by looking for people with electronics or chemistry degrees. There are hundreds of them. As I tap away at the keyboard, inserting new search fields and waiting for the images to download on to the screen, some patterns begin to emerge. Firstly, the keyless entry system IED attacks seem to take place predominantly within two 3-kilometre-square areas of Basra City, one in the north and one in the south. Secondly, many of the components recovered from the Shia devices are made in Iran.

As I mind-map thoughts and ideas on to the pad in front of me, I begin to get a better idea of where we need to focus. If we're going to stand any chance of bringing down the terror groups, we're going to need to start by identifying their support networks. We need to find their facilities, their recruiters, their financiers and their trainers. We need to locate their safe havens, their technical experts, their suppliers and their operators. We'll also need to target their propaganda network, their intelligence capability, their logistics network and their leadership and communications networks. We're going to need strategic national-level intelligence resources for this, so I'm going to have to liaise with some of the spooks already deployed in country – the key players in the intelligence community.

Finally, because my job involves collating and analysing technical intelligence – for every incident past, present and future – I'll need to get right into the nitty-gritty. I'll be looking at the number and type of devices used in each attack; how they were emplaced; what type of explosives were used and where they came from. Most importantly, I'll need to determine exactly how they were constructed.

My notepad is filling up fast.

I've often heard the phrase 'I don't need to be an insurgent to beat an insurgent'. I think that's bollocks. The only way to defeat the network is to think like a terrorist. And if we're to stand any chance of mounting effective tactical operations, I'm going to need to get inside his head.

It's midnight. I've been at my desk for nearly fourteen hours. I'm shagged. It's time to turn in.

I'm expecting Div HQ to be deserted, but people are still tapping away on the keyboards in the ops centre. These men and women are working all the hours of the day and night to ensure that the troops on the ground have the maximum support.

Whatever my preconceptions were about staff officers, they were wrong.

35

I like living. I have sometimes been wildly, despairingly,
acutely miserable, racked with sorrow, but through it all I
still know that just to be alive is a grand thing.

Agatha Christie

1 July 2004: Day 59
The water glimmers in the sunlight. A group of beef-
cakes are strutting their stuff in a game of all-men's
volleyball. Bikini-clad women lie soaking up the rays at
the edge of the pool while some of their mates have
gone for the aerobics or yoga option. But this is no
exotic holiday destination. Even those in beachwear
have assault rifles strapped to their backs, and two
Apache gunships are circling above us in the crimson
haze.

I'm standing just outside the ballroom in the garden of
one of Saddam's palaces at the heart of the Green Zone,
the heavily fortified military and diplomatic nerve centre

of Baghdad. I've been sent up here to attend a meeting with a couple of US government agents.

To say this is a surreal experience would be something of an understatement.

The Green Zone consists of 10 square kilometres of palaces and government buildings linked by wide tree-lined boulevards. In true Saddam fashion, no expense was spared on their interior and exterior decor. The floors and ceilings are marble, and colossal murals adorn the walls. The Ming vases, gold-leaf furniture and Picassos have all gone now, and young GIs can take a piss in the golden urinals once reserved exclusively for the Husseins.

The tantalizing aroma of freshly ground coffee and warmed croissants wafts out of the cafeteria. I'm sorely tempted, but I know that if I succumb I'll end up missing my RV. All I know is that we're meeting by the pool. I have no idea what these guys look like. I just got the standard spook 'we'll find you' instruction on the phone.

As I sit and wait, I spot a journalist using a Thuraya handheld satellite phone. He's obviously *very* important and wants the tooled-up bikini-babes to know it: he's speaking with his editor about his latest news story just that bit louder than necessary. What he hasn't yet realized is that the Thuraya has a moveable antenna which has to be extended from the handset and then rotated upwards so that it points towards the sky. The problem is that if you try to switch hands mid-conversation, the antenna then faces downwards, and the signal is lost. So every twenty seconds or so – each time he moves the phone to the other side of his head – the call cuts off and he has to redial the lengthy number back to London. He still hasn't sussed what he's doing wrong. He's getting more and more irate by the second. At his sixth attempt he completely loses it, goes into meltdown, and launches the phone straight into the pool.

I'm still pissing myself with laughter when I'm approached by two muscle-bound giants dressed in black cargo pants and baggy shirts. They're both sporting beards and wearing *shemaghs* – presumably to blend in with the locals, though I'm not sure they've really got the whole covert merge-with-your-surroundings thing mastered yet. They're both 6 feet plus with blond hair and 'Semper Fidelis' tattoos emblazoned across their 20-inch biceps, and considering they live and work in the Green Zone, the most fortified location in Iraq, they're also carrying an impressive array of weaponry.

Since the ambush I've always carried a rifle, a pistol and a fighting knife when I've gone out on the ground; but these guys have a side-arm in a drop-leg holster, flash-bangs, pistol mags, an asp, handcuffs, a torch and a Gerber multi-tool on their belts, as well as an array of rifles and pistols attached to their various load-carrying systems – and that's when they're inside the wire. Pity the lunatic who tries to take them on outside the wire; I dread to think what they carry when they're on ops.

If we're suddenly overrun by insurgents, these are the boys I want to be standing next to.

We exchange pleasantries, grab some coffee and then get straight down to business.

I explain that our division is keen to take down as many of the terror groups as possible and that we've already got the systems in place to hit lower-level targets such as bomb emplacers and their support teams. But at the high end – the insurgent command and control networks – we need access to national-level intelligence resources.

We spend about an hour chatting through what our requirements are and do a bit of wheeling and dealing. In the intelligence game, everything comes at a price. There's always a quid pro quo. We dance around the handbags for a bit and then right on cue they ask me about one of our specialist technologies.

'Come on guys,' I say, 'that's off limits. You know how it works.'

It always has been. We don't share that stuff with anybody.

And so the rug trading begins. These guys may look like a pair of nightclub bouncers, but they are fiercely intelligent – they wouldn't be working for this particular organization if they weren't – and they're also masters of the Jedi mind trick.

Still, the rules are the rules.

'There is of course a middle way,' I suggest.

I offer to introduce them to one of the technical guys we have permanently stationed in Baghdad, who can put them in touch with some specialist commercial companies, all of whom are based in the US. 'Those guys are selling the best systems money can buy and they're at the top of their game. They'll give you all the information you need.'

We're in business.

We say our goodbyes, and I prepare to move to my next location, CEXC.

'Sexy' – the 'Combined Explosives Exploitation Cell' – is an IED intelligence group consisting of twenty-one American investigators with a couple of Brit liaison officers who spend twenty-four hours a day studying patterns in insurgent bombings and technically and forensically examining IEDs in the US-patrolled sectors of Iraq. They even have their own embedded law-enforcement personnel to carry out onsite forensic work. I'm about to spend four days with them, to get an update on the countrywide threat and to develop a combined targeting strategy to defeat the bomber networks.

I walk back through the palace to the parking area. I can hear sporadic waves of gunfire resonating across the city. A six-man team of British soldiers is waiting for me in two Land Rover Discoverys bristling with antennae. Their sole task is to transport staff officers between Baghdad International Airport and the Green Zone along Route Irish – the most dangerous road in the world. I imagine it's not something they particularly relish. In fact, the job is so dangerous that they only do it for six weeks before being replaced by a new team and returning to their permanent units in Basra.

'Hello, sir,' says one of the corporals cheerily. 'Slight change of plan. We're off tomorrow, so we're going to nip quickly via the Hands of Victory to grab a couple of happy snaps. Perfectly safe, obviously – we'll still be inside the Green Zone.'

For a second I think he's talking about some local pub, but then the penny drops. The Hands of Victory are the enormous sets of crossed swords grasped by giant stone hands that stand at either end of the Victory Parade. Saddam had them built in the late eighties to commemorate his perceived triumph over Iran and insisted that the hands were exact-scale replicas of his own.

I tell them I'm easy, although deep down I'm always a

little concerned when someone feels the need to say 'perfectly safe, obviously'.

There's no such thing as safe in Baghdad.

Several photos and twenty minutes later, the boys are happy and we're pulling on to Route Irish.

The four-lane, 12-kilometre-long boulevard is the only means of getting between the airport and the Green Zone by vehicle, so as far as the insurgents are concerned, Route Irish is a target-rich environment. And we're easy pickings. Military convoys, businessmen and journalists move constantly back and forth along this tree-lined route of muddy brown tower blocks and walled-in flat-roofed houses. A flyover crosses high above us every few hundred metres or so. Their ramparts are perfect for secreting devices, and IEDs have frequently been dropped from them into the traffic below. The risk of being shot at by an AK or an RPG is also very high on this stretch. If the former is the weapon of choice, they'll try to hit us in the head or below the waist. They don't want to risk a bullet bouncing off our combat body armour.

The main danger, though, as always, is from roadside IEDs – hidden behind crash barriers, in sacks, underneath dead dogs, or planted in mounds of earth. They could even be carried by suicide bombers. In Baghdad, the method of delivery is limited only by the insurgent's imagination.

411

We continue west. About a mile into our journey, I notice that all conversation inside the car has ceased. My fellow passengers look as though they're about to shit themselves and the driver is throwing the Discovery around like Colin McRae. As he darts violently in and out of the traffic, weaving past cars and gunning the accelerator, our second escort vehicle falls further and further behind.

We're supposed to be looking out for roadside IEDs, focusing specifically on the rubbish-strewn areas of waste ground that run the length of the highway. But we're going so fast, everything's a blur. I wouldn't mind so much if we were in a Lamborghini, but we're in a 4×4, with a high centre of gravity, that feels like it's going to topple over any second now and kill the lot of us.

I crane my neck around the edge of the driver's seat and clock his speed – 105 mph.

Jesus.

I feel an oblique question coming on.

'Where did you do your advanced driving course?' I ask him.

He looks at me, puzzled, via his rear-view mirror and nearly writes us off in the process. I can see him frowning as he corrects the steering wheel.

Fuck me. That's the last time I distract *him*.

'I've not done one, sir.'

'Well, don't you think you ought to ease off on the gas, just a bit?'

It's a rhetorical question, but my subtlety is lost on him.

'Sorry, sir,' he says, 'no can do. We've been instructed to drive fast and aggressively. And besides, this place is littered with IEDs. The only way to beat them is to drive faster than the explosion.'

This boy's priceless. It's like driving with Baldrick.

'And how fast is that then?' I ask. I can't stop myself.

'About a hundred miles per hour,' he says, clearly plucking the figure out of his arse.

I explain that the velocity of detonation of a military explosive is ten times the speed of sound and that he'd have to be doing thousands of miles an hour if he was to stand even the slightest chance of beating the blast wave.

He just looks at me blankly, so I try a change of tack.

'Please will you slow the fuck down before you get us all killed?'

'Right-ho,' he says, grinning like an idiot.

The boy's in his own world.

I look out of the window. To the side of us, street stalls, pedestrians, unattended goats and rows of shops are interspersed with burnt-out vehicles, abandoned at the edge of the road like broken toys. I try to scan the rooftops for potential firing points, but we're still weaving in and out of the traffic and it's hard to focus.

About four miles into our journey, as the carriageway begins to bend, there's the beginnings of a jam. There must be a roadblock up ahead. The driver slams on the anchors and screeches to a halt.

'The brakes work, then,' one of the lads says, blatantly taking the piss.

I'm just glad I said something when I did. If we'd been doing a ton around that corner we'd have creamed-in big time. The road's virtually gridlocked.

We're in an unarmoured Land Rover and we can't go backwards, forwards or sideways. Right now we're sitting ducks. I'm feeling calm, but my senses are heightened.

I look ahead to the columns of stationary vehicles and spot the cause of the delay. Two cars have collided in the middle of the highway. All the remaining traffic has slowed to go round them. The blockage is about 500 metres ahead of us.

I start to feel uneasy.

We continue to edge forward. Everyone else seems to have gone quiet now. Maybe they've sensed something too.

My heart is soon going like a pneumatic drill, but I don't have a clue why.

Nobody's making a sound.

And then an old Chevrolet saloon pulls out of the line of traffic and begins to accelerate through the dust beside the highway. The driver's ploughing through street stalls and mowing down obstructions with complete disregard. He's insane. People are screaming, diving for cover.

Jesus. He's just hit a woman. He's driven into her square-on. Her lifeless body has just bounced off his car like a crash test dummy. He must have been doing 70 mph.

People are rushing out of their vehicles to try to tend to the wounded. Others are screaming and wailing to Allah.

It's apocalyptic.

Suddenly, up ahead, there's a thunderous explosion. A pulse of bright white light silhouettes the Chevy as a ground-shaking boom and a flaming whirlwind engulfs the street. The car fragments into thousands of tiny pieces of molten metal and dozens of pedestrians are torn to shreds. Rows of cars catch fire. A teenager is thrown up into the air by the force of the explosion. He lands on his stomach on the other side of a roadside ditch, all the skin stripped from his lifeless body.

The streets are filling with screaming, blood-soaked people. The survivors – wounded men, women and children – wander around, dazed and confused. They're all in shock. They all need help. A father is shouting for his son. He's desperate. In the chaos, he's lost sight of the boy. Mangled corpses lie everywhere. Huge pools of blood are starting to form at the edge of the road.

Bile sears the back of my throat. I'm paralysed and utterly helpless. There's nothing I can do for these people from where I am.

Four shots ring out.

People are now banging on their horns, pleading, screaming for the person in front to drive out of the killing area. Some drivers try to bump others off the road.

We cock our weapons and take aim, ready to engage the sniper the moment he appears.

The traffic starts to crawl forwards. We begin to move, slowly at first, but then more confidently.

There are dead bodies everywhere. Bone fragments have peppered the walls of a row of houses. Scorch marks are dotted with chunks of flesh. People have brought out clothing and towels to try to comfort the survivors. A man is carried out and laid on a blanket. He's been stripped naked by the blast. His body is red and blistered. Wherever I look, people are covered in blood.

I see one woman picking up a severed arm from a car roof. It belongs to her father. He's sitting nearby with his back against a wall, screaming in pain.

A group of men are trying to drag smouldering bodies from the mangled wreckage of a car. Others want to help, but are too overcome by emotion and shock to do anything but comfort the dying.

A young mother weeps as she clings to the lifeless body of her baby. Another kneels over her son, trying to shake the life back into him, but his eyes have already died. She lets out a final deafening shriek, knowing that a part of her has just died with him.

Another shot rings out. Now the helpers are screaming and shouting and running for their lives.

Our driver sees an opening and guns the accelerator. The Discovery behind us follows suit. As we break out of the killing area, the nauseating stench of death and burnt flesh fills my nostrils.

We're clear.

'Go as fast as you fucking like,' I tell the driver. 'Just get us the hell out of here.'

We scream along Route Irish, past speeding cars and trucks and out of the mouth of hell. I'm angry, really fucking angry. And feeling guilty that we couldn't do more. But I know, too, that if we'd got out of the vehicles, within five minutes we'd have been hit by every insurgent group in Baghdad.

Within minutes we're approaching the two M111 armoured vehicles that mark the entrance to Camp Victory, Headquarters Multinational Forces Iraq. Two young soldiers from the 1st Cavalry Division step out of them, weapons at the ready.

The guard makes his way over to our vehicle, stuffs

a wad of chewing tobacco into his cheek and examines our IDs.

'Where you boys from?' he asks.

'The UK,' we reply in unison.

'Gentlemen, welcome to Camp Victory.' He spits into an empty water bottle. 'You have a nice day now.'

36

*The truth is the mortal enemy of the lie, and thus, by
extension, the truth is the greatest enemy of the State.*

Joseph Goebbels

5 July 2004: Day 63

I sit back and adjust my safety belt. There are about sixty
of us crammed shoulder to shoulder in the Basra-bound
Hercules. We're in four rows of webbing seats stretching
the length of the aircraft. I can feel the sweat gathering
beneath my helmet and body armour. Some passengers
sleep, others read. I'm typing up notes on my laptop.

It's been a manic week.

During my time at Camp Victory, I've met just about
every key mover and shaker who has anything to do with
the counter-IED fight. Between us we've managed to
get the weapons intelligence post fully integrated into
both the divisional and theatre intelligence communities.
I've also been on a series of heliborne operations,

photographing, evaluating and analysing IED tasks and looking into a significant number of historical incidents for signs of specific MOs and bomb-makers' signatures.

Now I can focus on getting some results.

I crane my neck to look out of the window, but as we spiral down towards Basra Air Station the G force drives my head back against the padded wall. We descend in three precise corkscrew turns, levelling out literally seconds before we hit the runway.

'How was Baghdad, Chris?' Eric Casey asks as I throw my kit into the back of the Land Rover. He's come to meet me straight off the aircraft.

'You should have been there,' I say. 'The Ben and Jerry's was to die for.' Camp Victory was part James Bond set, part Disneyland, and the dining facility is famous for its huge variety of B&J's ice cream.

'So what did you get up to?' he asks.

'I was hosted by the Combined Explosives Exploitation Cell. There's a Brit ATO up there so we spent hours on the edge of the lake, smoking fags and talking about the migration of Jihadist MOs from Afghanistan, Chechnya and the Balkans.'

I know it's terribly childish, but I still can't resist dropping in a comment about 'smoking fags' at every opportunity when I'm talking to Americans. It has a completely different meaning for them, of course, and they bite every time.

'We looked at some of the new devices that have been turning up in Baghdad, and we exploited a few too.'

Eric looks at me enquiringly.

'We got the forensics off them then broke them down, got them on an oscilloscope and determined exactly how they worked.'

I was briefed that 75 per cent of all IEDs in the country are radio-controlled, the most prolific of which are initiated by GSM phones, handheld radios, cell phones and electronic pagers. Vehicle-borne IEDs are used far more frequently in Baghdad than down here, and the insurgents have triggered them by both command and remote initiation.

'Did they give you an update on the counter-measures situation?' Eric asks.

'Not really,' I say. 'We heard the usual common-sense stuff about how jammers work and what their limitations are, but no, there was nothing new.'

As the sun dips below the horizon, we move through the main sangar position and on into camp. The Div HQ building is literally a stone's throw from the airport terminal building, yet because of all the security procedures, we have to do a 6-mile drive to get back to it.

'Are there any new technologies being put into place to counter IEDs?' Eric asks.

I'm starting to wonder if he's a bit of a closet IED spotter.

'Yeah,' I reply, 'there's some cracking kit.'

I tell him about the gizmo that can apparently detect explosive vapours through bomb casings buried underground. It can be used at checkpoints too, to detect the explosive residues left on bomb-makers. If it really is capable of doing what it says on the tin, it will give us a huge advantage over the terrorist. There are also some pretty off-the-wall ideas. One involves a fluorescent spray invisible to the naked eye being deployed over an area deemed likely to be used to emplace IEDs, which is then scanned using an optical detection system.

We pull up at Div HQ and Eric helps me take my bags into the office.

'Pick up any tips from my fellow countrymen?' Eric asks.

I think long and hard. There is a lot to absorb. I'm going to remember that airborne surveillance is a key emerging technology in the fight against the bombers. That ground moving target indicators can reveal a great deal about the terrorists' future intentions. And, crucially, I've learnt that the technology exists to be able to determine insurgents' behaviour when carrying out IED attacks.

'I'm going to use as much of this kit as I can lay my hands on to nail those bastards once and for all.'

Back in the office I start piecing together information relating to the murderers of Fusilier Gentle, killed by a keyless entry RCIED on my first day in the job.

I've spent the last few evenings studying late into the night, learning everything I can about Arab culture, the Muslim faith and the Five Pillars of Islam. I've learnt that Islam is derived from the verb *slm*, which means 'submit' or 'surrender', and that a Muslim is one who has surrendered or submitted to Allah. I've read about the Prophet Muhammad and how at the age of forty he became the prophet of a new religion revealed to him by Allah through the Angel Gabriel.

He encountered much opposition to this new religion, as well as a great deal of persecution. He took flight to Medina, where the first Islamic city-state was established. Over the next ten years they captured the whole of Arabia. The concept of the jihad, or holy war as a religious duty, was born. Muhammad died in AD 632, aged sixty-two. Through military conquest, his successors spread Islam as far north as the Caucasus and in the south to North Africa, reaching Spain and southern France within a hundred years of the Prophet's death.

Eric walks into the office. It's twenty past ten and my eyes are starting to glaze over.

'What are the Five Pillars of Islam?' I ask.

When we were fighting the Russians during the Cold War, British and American forces knew every last detail of every single unit in the Soviet Union. Yet ask a soldier a question today about Muslims or Arabs, especially one about religion, and he'll look at you blankly.

'Ah, the Five Pillars,' Eric says. 'They're basically the code of practice for Muslims. Shahada, the Confession of Faith; Salah, prayer; Sawum, fasting; Zaka, the paying of alms; and Haj, the Pilgrimage to Mecca.'

He knows his stuff.

'I should add,' he says, 'that some, particularly the Salafid Muslims, view jihad as the Sixth Pillar.'

No surprises there really.

'So what about the culture?' I ask him. 'Where do they get off doing the things they do?'

The conversation now centres largely on the treatment of women. To westerners it appears distinctly unjust, but Muslims feel that women are treated with honour, and that all restrictions and censures placed upon them are there to protect their honour and that of their families. The more strictly controlled a woman, the more value she is said to have.

'Which isn't much,' Eric says. 'According to sharia law,

women are worth half the value of men in terms of compensation and testimony. Two female witnesses are equal to one male witness in any legal proceedings, and verdicts are reached by counting the number of witnesses for and against, thus weighting the legal system in favour of men. In Basra, a woman is entitled to half the legal compensation of that of a man, and a woman is entitled to half the share of an inheritance of that of a man.'

My lesson is interrupted by a phone call from Colonel Sanderson. He's in the other side of the building. While I've been away, the entire Brigade HQ, including the IEDD team, has moved out of Basra Palace and into the air station.

He wants to take me in to the brigadier to receive my promotion.

I'd clean forgotten about that.

'Ah, Chris, isn't it?' the brigadier says as I walk into his office. 'Thought you'd be dead by now.'

I admire his sense of humour.

We chat for a while, and then he gets down to business.

'Our bombers are putting themselves about a bit,' he says. 'I want you to track them down and get into their minds, and make sure you debrief us the moment you find anything of interest.'

He hands me a small plastic bag containing a pair of major's rank slides.

'Congratulations. You're either incredibly brave or incredibly fucking stupid. Now, I suggest you get a life and stop pissing around with bombs.'

Both Colonel Sanderson and I are laughing.

'But in the meantime, capture these bomb-makers and get me anything you can on Iran. They're really starting to take the piss.'

37

We think caged birds sing, when indeed they cry.

John Webster

19 July 2004: Day 77

I've spent most of the morning in the Shack with the brigade WIS team, analysing components to link a range of different devices, particularly the keyless car entry RCIEDs, to specific terrorist groups.

I'm now sitting in my office surrounded by scraps of paper upon which I've scribbled names, dates, locations and details of bombings. I stick them on the wall and link them with pencil lines whenever I can find a correlation between one incident and another.

For most of the last fortnight this wall has looked like a giant spider's web.

As I feed the data into the computer, I know we're getting closer. We're building up a much clearer picture of the network. I don't know exactly who the bombers (known in surveillance terms as Bravos) are yet, or precisely what building (Alpha) they're operating from, but I've got a pretty good idea.

I'm going to put in a request for some aerial surveillance assets. It's time to take the game to the next level. Before long we're going to have the bombers under our control, and when we do, we'll be able to fix and strike them on our own terms.

I'm feeling good about this.

As I pour myself another mug of coffee from the percolator, there's a sudden and almighty explosion on the far side of the terminal building – the air side.

'Rocket attack!' somebody shouts.

Everybody's donning body armour and helmets. The sirens begin to wail. Some dive on to the floor, under tables; others, so engrossed in their work that they seem oblivious to what's going on around them, remain seated at their desks, tapping away in their flak vests. We wait like this for around fifteen minutes for the next strike, but the rocket doesn't come. Moments later we hear the sound of fire engines on the runway.

The attack alarms finally go silent.

The huge window in the Int Centre frames the cloud of thick black smoke billowing above the terminal building.

A watch keeper pokes his head around the door and

says, 'You can stand down now. It wasn't a rocket. One of the Pumas has just creamed it on the runway. I'm afraid we've got casualties: the pilot was killed and his two crew have sustained serious burns.'

'What happened?' I ask.

'Too early to say; it may just have been too hot to fly. The bird was apparently hovering at about fifty feet, preparing to land, when it just dropped straight out of the sky. First the rotors and then the nose broke off, and then the whole thing dissolved into a ball of flame. Two of the crew managed to climb out of a side window and crawl to safety, but the pilot was trapped inside. The poor sod was torched alive.'

I feel a sudden pang of guilt about all the times I ground my teeth at the RAF because they couldn't supply top cover. I used to think the 'too hot to fly' thing was just an excuse. It's a sharp reminder of how dangerous the tour is and how quickly our lives can be taken from us. I've been on those Pumas day in, day out. The chances are I probably flew on that one.

Several hours later I'm sitting silently at my desk, examining some aerial imagery of two possible bomb-making locations in Basra. One is a house close to the university in the north of the city. The other is in the south, an imposing building on the Red Route, IED Alley.

As I scan every detail of the photos, Vash lets out a big 'Goddamn!'

I look up.

'My mom just sent me this letter. It's enough to break your heart.' He holds it out to me. 'You want to read it?'

I don't really, but I'm not sure I have a choice. He thrusts it into my hands.

Dear Richie,

I want to share with you a story I was told today by a lady in church. It made me think of you and the girls.

A lady had been in Georgia attending a conference. At the airport, waiting to catch her flight home, she heard people all around her beginning to clap and cheer. She turned right around.

A group of soldiers was moving through the terminal in their fatigues. There were thirty or forty of them, mostly not much more than boys. She said it was wonderful to know she wasn't the only red-blooded American who still loves this country and supports our troops and their families.

She started clapping too, for these young unsung heroes who, like you, my darling boy, are putting their lives on the line for us every single day, so our children can stay in school, and we can work and go home without fear or reprisal.

Just then, a little girl, not more than six or seven years old, ran up to one of the soldiers. He kneeled down and said, 'Hi,' and the little girl asked him if he could give something to her daddy for her.

The soldier said he would surely try, and asked her what it was she wanted to give.

The little girl grabbed him around the neck, gave him the biggest hug she could muster and then kissed him on the cheek.

Her mother stepped forward and told the young soldier that her husband was with the Marine Corps and had been in Iraq for almost a year, and little Courtney missed him real bad. The young soldier began to tear up, and when the temporarily single mom was done explaining her situation, all of the soldiers huddled together. Then one of his companions pulled out a walkie-talkie.

They started talking earnestly into the device, and listening carefully to the replies.

After about thirty seconds of this, the young soldier walked back over to Courtney, bent down and said, 'Honey, I just spoke to your daddy, and he told me to give this to you.' He then gave her the biggest hug you ever did see, and a big kiss on the cheek. 'Your

daddy told me to tell you that he loves you more
than anything in the world, and he's coming home
just as soon as he possibly can.'

The young soldier rose to his feet and snapped a
salute to Courtney and her mom.

As the soldiers began to head towards their gate,
she said, there were very few dry eyes, including her
own.

Before he disappeared, the young soldier turned
around one last time. He blew a kiss to Courtney,
and she swears she saw a tear rolling down his cheek.

Your father and I love you very much, Richie, and
we think of you every single day. You make us proud
to be American.

Stay safe, darling. Our prayers are with you.

All my love

Mom

It's a real choker.

As I hand the letter back to Vash, Colonel Austin walks
into the office.

'Hi, Chris, how's tricks?'

'Very good thanks, Colonel,' I say, trying to swallow the
lump in my throat.

'Listen, I've got something for you. Something that
might be rather useful.'

One of our sources on the ground has just called to say the Iraqi police have captured a team of Sunni bombers and are holding them at the al-Jameat Police Station.

'This is your pigeon, Chris, but if you do decide you're going to go in, a word of warning. During Saddam's reign, the place was known as the Station of Death. The secret police dragged hundreds of people to the al-Jameat compound in the middle of the night and they were never seen or heard of again. Now under Shia control, there are rumours that it's being used for similar activities.'

There have been horrific tales of murder and torture at the hands of the Shia officers – all members of the Mahdi Army – as well as talk of extortion rackets and weapons smuggling from Iran. Apparently they have been working with a local criminal outfit to carry out contract killings, and several of our sources have suggested they're planning roadside attacks against British forces using a sophisticated new type of IED, again probably imported from Iran.

'If there's an ounce of truth in any of this, you're going to need to be extremely careful,' the colonel continues. 'Dozens of Iraqis have reportedly been dragged from their homes, shot in the head and dumped by the al-Jameat gang. Behadli has strong links with them and we're pretty sure he and his stooges are providing protection in return for bomb-making equipment supplied by the Iranians.'

'Hold me back!' I say.

He nods approvingly. 'I've taken the liberty of warning the local RMP SIB commander, and one of the brigade intelligence officers. They'll be going with you. A platoon of RMPs will take you in. Transport leaves in thirty minutes.'

It's not long before we're speeding through the city in Snatch Land Rovers. We need to get a shifty on. I desperately need these bombers to be alive when we get there. The blues and twos are going full pelt but the drivers still have to slam on their horns as they weave through the traffic like men possessed.

We scream into a courtyard and pull up. The Station of Death is a three-storey concrete monster surrounded by a high stone wall. There are IPS running around everywhere, shouting furiously and waving their guns in the air.

I jump down from the back of the Snatch as the huge gate clangs shut behind us. The Iraqi version of the Fat Controller approaches, puffing on a huge Cuban cigar. I can see from his insignia that he's the chief of police.

'Can we help you, Major?' he asks.

'I rather think you can,' I say, shaking him by the hand. 'I'd be extremely grateful if you would allow my colleagues and me to speak with the bombers.'

His eyes narrow. 'What bombers?' he asks. 'We don't have any bombers here. In fact we have no prisoners at all here.'

He's lying like a cheap Japanese watch, and a series of loud screams that ring out from inside the building immediately confirms it.

I nod to the RMPs and head straight past him, through the front door.

Dozens of pairs of eyes stare at me incredulously through a haze of stale body odour and cigarette smoke as I march across the stone-floored reception area. A group of policemen rush out of a door to my left and run hurriedly up the stairs, carrying sticks, wires and a car battery. Subtlety is clearly not these boys' strong suit.

I hear more screams coming from behind the door. I throw it open.

In the corner of the huge, high-ceilinged room, two men are sitting blindfolded, facing the wall. Another is handcuffed and hanging by his arms from a large hook set in the ceiling. His wrists are swollen to twice their normal size. They might even be broken. He has burn marks on his chest and his feet are black and swollen. The interrogators circle around him, hurling abuse.

They have obviously made a bit of an effort to hide the fact they've been torturing this poor bastard, but there are still rubber hoses on the floor and they're so incensed by his refusal to confess they're threatening to make him sit on a bottle. The fact that they feel no need to conceal this means that they obviously think it's quite acceptable.

'Get him down!' I yell. 'Now!'

My new friend the police chief storms in.

'These are our prisoners, Major, and this is no business of yours.'

'This is very much our business,' says a voice behind him. It's Lisa, the Special Investigation Branch RMP captain I met during the petrol tanker incident in Shai'ba. 'We have reason to believe these men are linked to the murder of a British soldier on June twenty-eighth this year. We intend to question them, and if charged, they will be held at the Shai'ba Military Detention Facility. You will of course be able to gain access to them at any time of the day or night.'

He's not at all pleased. He's just been force-fed a shit sandwich and told to get firmly back in his box – by a woman.

As I stare into Osama al-Keshti's dark brown eyes, I still can't quite believe the situation I find myself in. Al-

Keshti is a man with blood on his hands. He's a Sunni, fiercely loyal to Saddam, and one of the city's senior bomb-makers. Yet we've just saved his life, and the lives of his team, by negotiating their handover from the Iraqi Police, who a few minutes earlier were beating them with rubber hoses and threatening to hang them from the ceiling and tear off their skin, strip by strip.

Unlike the Shias, though, we need him alive. He's our key to nailing those responsible for the death of Fusilier Gentle, the nineteen-year-old British soldier killed three weeks ago by a roadside bomb just six weeks after completing his basic training. And now, after weeks of painstaking effort, we're sitting face to face in a dingy office in al-Jameat.

We've finally got the bastard, and the rest of his team. They are one of two Sunni bomber outfits operating in the city. And now that we have the first, we want them to lead us to the second. We've been watching them for so long now, tracking them, wanting to know who they really are, wanting to know more about the sort of people who do these things. To know what motivates them. And now, after ten hours of interrogation – a game of mental chess – he's telling me everything.

He's revealing the attack tactics he and his team have employed, their modus operandi, their various sources of

IED components, the means by which they plan and carry out an attack, how they're taught to construct devices, how long it takes to construct them, where they construct them, who funds them. He's confessed to some of the attacks he's carried out against us, and the lessons he and his team learned as we adapted our tactics, training and procedures. But most chilling of all is his intense hatred – not towards the USA, but towards us, the British. He hates us with a passion. Why? Because of the insults and humiliation he perceives we've inflicted on him and his fellow Iraqis.

I ask him to tell me more.

'Last year I was queuing for gas. I queued for six hours, waiting patiently in line. But I couldn't wait any longer. I had to get back to my family. I walked to the front of the line and filled my can. And then the British soldiers came. They took my can and emptied the gas on to the floor. Then they stamped on my can and then they turned on me. They beat me and kicked me. And I am not alone. My brothers have been beaten too. You come to our country and you beat us, you insult us. You try to take away our honour, you rape our land.'

I do feel some sympathy for him; there must be some truth in what he's saying, even though I don't want to believe it. But that doesn't clear the slate. When I ask him how he feels about killing innocent Iraqis, he responds that it is God's will. What about innocent women and children? Can he justify killing them too? Of course he can, that too is God's will.

I think about his victims. Like bomb victims all around the world, they're the damned, even if they survive. They struggle quietly through the rest of their lives, some without limbs, some with horrendous mental health problems: paranoia, flashbacks, nightmares, panic attacks. Theirs is a world of permanent fear and darkness. We read about them every day, see them on News 24. Our hearts bleed for them momentarily, then we never hear of them again. Another day, another story.

But not for them. For the victims, time stops the moment the bomb explodes.

I think about Bob Cartwright, an old instructor of mine from Kineton, blown up by the IRA in the eighties while rendering a device safe in Crossmaglen. He escaped with the loss of an eye and his hearing. He seems happy with that, but his wife holds an entirely different view. As far as she's concerned, their lives were ruined that day. I'm told she hates the Irish, all of them, with a passion.

The small child maimed, the young man blinded. The faces of every bomb victim I've ever seen come flooding back to me. The once beautiful bride I met in

Colombia, showered in glass confetti on the day of her wedding. The bomb exploded and the shards of glass tore through her flesh. To this day she wonders how her husband can bring himself to love her mutilated and disfigured body.

Sometimes I wonder if the dead victims are actually the lucky ones.

As I look at al-Keshti's arrogant, unrepentant face, I can feel the anger swelling inside me. I'm sitting opposite him, my pistol holstered on my thigh, and he's chatting to me as if we're old friends. The brotherhood of the bomb.

He grins at me. I've seen that grin before. I just don't know where. It's been bothering me all night. A sense of déjà vu.

Then the penny drops. The terrorist from the arms market in Qadimah. Spiderman; the guy who dropped through the skylight. I can see his face clearly now. It was al-Keshti.

Now it's personal.

I'm going to get him to tell me everything. Above all, I want to know who the second team are. And where they are.

But I don't let on that I've recognized him.

'Talk to me,' I say. 'Don't waste your time with the others. They won't understand. They are not educated like you and me. They don't appreciate how difficult it is to make a bomb. They don't realize that building each device is like creating a new masterpiece. They don't appreciate your skills. They don't understand anything. But I do. On our different battlefields you and I have learned many similar lessons.'

It's working. He's actually starting to fall for this crap. He even draws me a circuit diagram of the bombs he used, showing me how he wired them up. We're new best mates. But deep down, all I want to do is pull out my pistol and put a bullet in his head. To administer some summary justice for the horrendous crimes he's perpetrated.

But I don't. Because I'm *not* like him. I can't be. And besides, my work here is not yet done.

As we pull into Basra Air Station the sun is starting to break over the horizon. It's been a long and difficult night, but it's been worth it. I reflect on the huge amount of intelligence al-Keshti and his crew have provided. Having given them the choice of three square meals a day at the detention facility in Shai'ba or unspeakable torture at the hands of the Iraqi Police, they not only admitted to the majority of the attacks (except, shrewdly enough, those that have resulted in fatalities), but also unwittingly given us vital details on the second team, which is operating in the south of the city.

Al-Keshti has told us that the main man is a scrap metal merchant in the Hayy al-Muhandisn area. It's a property I've read about in a number of reports. Now it's time to get it under surveillance.

38

*I hate you – precisely because I have allowed you so much
and even more because I need you so much.*

Fyodor Dostoevsky, *The Gambler*

20 July 2004: Day 78

I haven't slept properly in two days. I've spent a long, emotional night interviewing the bombers and the whole morning tasking surveillance assets and writing up the debriefing reports. I'm worn out, emotionally drained. Hard as I try to dismiss it, my ten-hour performance of Jekyll and Hyde is gnawing away at me. I need to speak to somebody. I need to speak to my wife.

I decide to call home. Even as I dial, I know this is going to be a bad idea.

Lucy picks up the phone and sounds really pleased that I called. For once, I seem to have caught her at a good time. The girls are having a nap and she can

443

actually talk. I hear all her news. She tells me about her art course, the visit to her folks at the weekend and the party she and the girls have been invited to on the patch. 'And Ella said "Dada" for the first time yesterday. You'd have been so proud.'

It melts my heart. I'm more than ever aware of the hollow, echoing space between their world and mine. I wish I could have been there to hear her say it. I've missed so much of her life.

At least Lucy and I seem to be building some kind of bridge here. She's got her sparkle back.

Then she asks me how things are at my end and I hear myself mentioning last night's episode with al-Keshti. It's still so fresh in my mind, I'm still on edge, and I want to talk to someone about it.

I should know better. There's an immediate and uncomfortable silence at the other end of the line. I can feel the wave of her unhappiness building between us again.

And then the floodgates burst.

'Why do you insist on putting us through this, Chris? Are you completely heartless?'

Jesus. Where did that come from? I'm caught completely on the back foot.

'What were you thinking? When we last spoke you told me you were working as a staff officer, that you'd be stuck in an office, tied to a desk. It's just like when you came back from Colombia. You keep offering me these little glimmers of hope, and then snatch them away. I don't know why I keep believing you. It's never going to change, is it?'

As I stand in the hot, cramped phone booth, lost for words, I can almost see the pain in her face and her fiery blue eyes flickering with anger. I instinctively go on the defensive.

'They're good people, Lucy. People like us. People who want to rebuild their lives —'

'Do you honestly believe that?' She's incandescent. 'You're putting your life in danger for people who wouldn't spit on you if you were on fire. Chris Muir was blown up last year doing just that, saving Iraqis, *people like us* . . . How many of *them* do you think are giving his death a second thought? I'll tell you who is, though. His wife and his little boy.'

Chris was an EOD operator who triggered a temperature-sensitive fuse during a disposal operation outside a school here in March last year. They played 'Always Look On The Bright Side Of Life' at his funeral, but I know that for his wife Gill and his four-year-old son that'll be easier said than done.

I can't blame Lucy for feeling this way. I've been oper-ational for such a long time now, and it's placed a massive strain on our marriage. So many op tours: the Balkans, Northern Ireland, Colombia, Iraq. Years serving in counter-terrorism units, getting the call in the middle of the night and being away for days on end, always at ten minutes' notice to move. On the night of Ella's birth I was called out to that raid on an AQ suspect's house in Gloucester.

Just when I think this conversation can't get any worse, there's a loud supersonic crack followed by a thundering shockwave. And then another. The phone booth shakes.

A rocket attack.

'What the hell was that?' Lucy cries.

I pluck out the first pathetic response that comes into my head: 'Oh, nothing. Just a door slamming in the wind.' What am I thinking? You *tit* . . .

There's another shuddering explosion.

'Sweetheart, this really isn't a good time . . .'

Icicles start forming on the earpiece.

'Oh, I'm sorry it's not convenient for you,' she says. 'What do you want me to do? Call you back? Oh, no, I forgot; I can't, can I? Because you're in sodding Iraq.'

'Come on Lucy—'

'*Come on Lucy?*' Now she's really pissed off. 'Come on where? You come on! Jesus! You sod off around the world, putting your head in every passing lion's mouth, while I play the dutiful wife on the patch, bringing up our children alone. I watch you leave for work and wonder whether I'll ever see you again, always with half an ear out for the call that tells me you've been ambushed and shot or blown to bloody bits. I have a heart attack whenever I see a newsflash on the TV. I either have to hush up the kids and turn up the sound, or bury my head in the sand and pretend the real world doesn't exist. And what about the danger you put us in? The enemies you've made. What happens when they follow you home? What happens when they plant a bomb under our car or kidnap our children? Trust me, Chris, this is no kind of life for us. I've had enough.'

As another rocket hits, I wonder how women can be so fantastically articulate at moments like this, while I have no idea what to say. I feel numb, empty.

'Lucy . . . please . . . don't do anything rash . . .'

'This isn't rash, Chris. Rash is what you do without thinking. I've been thinking about this for some time.'

There's another terrible, echoing silence. When she speaks again, there's a momentary flicker of warmth in her tone.

'You're a good man, Chris, and you'll always be special to me. But it's time I was honest with you. I think the love has gone.'

There's a finality in her tone that I've never heard before.

'Please, Lucy, just tell me what I have to do . . .'

I am panicking now, big time.

Before she can answer there's another deafening explosion and the line goes dead.

39

Fast as the wind, quiet as a forest, aggressive as fire, and immovable as a mountain.

Samurai battle banner

12 August 2004: Day 101

As the Puma swoops down low over the desert, its blades beating rhythmically, I can't keep the grin off my face.

Fate, chance, providence? What is it that governs the events of our lives? I am certain there has to be more to it than mere self-determination. How else can my sudden and unanticipated change of fortune be explained?

I hadn't spoken with Lucy in three weeks; in fact we hadn't had any communication at all. Having spent weeks in denial, overcome by an all-consuming melancholy, I'd finally resigned myself to the fact that she was leaving me. We never did finish our

449

conversation, but it was pretty obvious where it was heading. I'd lost everything. My life had fallen through my fingers like sand.

Then, out of the blue, after days of immersing myself in my work, something amazing happened this morning. I was called to the post room in Divisional Headquarters by a furious chief clerk.

'Sir, the next time your wife tries to send you booze disguised as bottles of Ribena, can you ask her to make sure she screws the effing lids on properly?'

A pile of mushy paper sat in front of him. He told me it was today's mail – not just mine, but everybody's – and it was drenched in Pimm's.

Lucy had sent me a food parcel. She never sends me food parcels!

'You've got to give her ten out of ten for effort though.'

He handed me the sopping-wet shoe box. Inside it was a mouldy copy of *Esquire*, some sweets, and two empty Ribena bottles.

I felt desperately guilty that my parcel had trashed so much mail and made the post room smell like a night-club bar on a Sunday morning, but nothing could suppress the overwhelming sense of happiness I felt at that moment.

As I made the short journey along the corridor back to my office, excitedly removing the contents of the

box, there, stuck to the lid, was a greetings card.
I ripped it open.

My Darling C,
I'm not going to give up on you.
Hang in there.
We'll still be here when you get back.
AML
Lxxx

I was gobsmacked. I still am. The card was dated 7
August – five days old. I don't know what celestial powers
made Lucy change her mind, but I'm in shock. I'm the
happiest man alive.

Just a few more weeks to push.

My headset crackles into life: 'Two minutes . . .'

I unclip my seatbelt and stand up as the door-gunner
fastens a safety harness around my waist and clips it to the
ceiling bracket. I take out the Canon Digital SLR from
my pack and drop down next to him on to the floor.
Then I inch forward with my elbows until my head
emerges from the canopy and hot wind from the rotors
scorches my face.

We're hovering about 300 feet above the Hayy
al-Shuhda area of south Basra. I can see the Shia

Flats – the place where we were ambushed.

For the last two or three weeks intelligence reports have warned that the second Sunni bomber team, whom we've had under surveillance, intends to target a logistics convoy en route from Shai'ba. But that's not why we're here. Earlier this morning, as the lead vehicle of a Warrior patrol was approaching Orange 1 – the 90-degree bend in the road – it was hit by a huge, improvised claymore. The colossal explosion engulfed the heavily armoured vehicle in flames and peppered it with hundreds of steel ball-bearings. Amazingly, the commander survived; by sheer chance he'd dropped down into the turret moments before. But the driver never stood a chance. Marc Ferns was killed instantly, torn to pieces by marble-sized fragments travelling at three times the speed of sound.

'Chris, we need to get out of here,' the pilot says. 'I'm really not happy about those *dushkas* . . .'

During the pre-flight intelligence briefing we were warned that the Mahdi Army had mounted Russian-made DShK heavy anti-aircraft machine guns on the roofs of some of the more prominent buildings. With its armour-piercing warhead, the *dushka* is capable of bringing down a heli from a mile away, so the thought of getting brassed up by one while we hover above the most dangerous part of the city isn't a prospect the pilot particularly relishes.

It's a fair one.

'I'm almost done,' I say. 'Just thirty seconds more . . .'

I zoom in on the area immediately below us and snap away furiously. Because the situation in the city is so fraught, the WIS team haven't been able to stay on the ground for long, so I've come up to take some images from the air, trying desperately to build up a picture of the terrorists' tactical design.

I can see everything: the choke point where the bomber knew Private Ferns would have to slow down, the pool of blood on the road, and the mound of earth where the off-route mine had been secreted. The WIS team recovered nothing. Not a single component. There was just a big hole in the ground.

There's something very familiar about this attack. I've seen this MO somewhere before. Not in Iraq; there's never been an attack like this in Iraq. Certainly not something this advanced, where the claymore is specifically designed to vaporize all the firing circuit's components and so destroy the forensics. No . . . this MO has only ever been seen in southern Lebanon.

It's a classic Hezbollah anti-armour, off-route mine. Which means Lebanese Hezbollah are almost certainly in Basra. And if they're in Basra, they've been sent here by Iran to train the Mahdi Army. The insurgency has just been taken to the next level.

'OK, Jules, I'm done.'

He pulls on the collective and gently nudges the cyclic. The engine whines and we begin a sudden and rapid ascent. Within seconds we're at 10,000 feet, high above the desert, travelling west towards Basra Air Station.

I pack away the camera and return to my seat. If Hezbollah and the Iranians are providing the Mahdi Army with improvised claymores, it's just a matter of time before they start using their other signature dish, the explosively formed projectile. The EFP – once famously used by the Red Army Faction in the assassination of Alfred Herrhausen, the former head of Deutsche Bank – is a cylindrical, dish-shaped charge designed to penetrate armoured vehicles. A particularly lethal version is used by Lebanese Hezbollah: when detonated, it projects the dish forwards, causing it to form an armour-piercing slug travelling at well over 1,000 metres a second. Worse still, they are armed remotely and initiated when a vehicle passes a passive infrared trigger, which makes them extremely difficult to detect or defeat.

This is serious. There have been mutterings about LH and the Iranians in Basra for some time now. If they are here, and they've brought their technology with them, we're royally fucked.

As the heli thunders across the brilliant blue sky, Jules's voice crackles over my headset.

'Chris, there's been a change of plan. Looks like you're in for a busy day. We've just been tasked by Div to take you to the palace. Apparently you're going on an op.'

It's news to me.

'Did they tell you anything else?'

'Sorry, mate, that's all I know. ETA three mikes.'

The airframe judders violently as Jules rolls us hard right. Within minutes we're flying low and fast along the Shatt al-Arab. A fisherman waves from his dhow as the Puma soars overhead, banking right at the last possible minute and swooping down into Saddam's garden. Clouds of dust are churned up by its downdraught as the deafening beat of its blades reverberates around the palace walls.

I step out and drop down on to one knee, closing my eyes tightly to avoid the inevitable sand-blasting as the bird lifts off again.

The palace is virtually dead. Now that Brigade HQ has relocated to Basra Air Station there are only a few specialist troops and some British government representatives living here. But there's no visible sign of them.

Moments later there's a deafening roar. A dozen

Warriors come screaming through the gates and the lead vehicle pulls up level with me. The vehicle commander is a sergeant in the Black Watch. I jump aboard, but I've still no idea where we're going or what we're doing.

We're soon on the other side of the compound. A tall, hardy-looking major steps out of the Med Centre and introduces himself as Alex McGill.

'Come on in,' he says. 'We'll grab a brew and I'll fill you in on why we're here.'

The concrete building is buzzing with activity. Weary soldiers lug packs into a room at the end of a long, drab corridor while others set up camp-beds or clean their weapons. The ops room is closest to the front door. Signallers man a bank of radios that stretches the entire length of one wall, busy scribbling into their log-books as live feeds transmit the battle group and company radio traffic. Riots have broken out across the city and troops have become embroiled in a series of crowd disturbances.

Nothing new there.

Alex asks me how I take my coffee, but I'm momentarily distracted by the distinctive voice procedure of one of the brigade's surveillance and reconnaissance teams blaring out of a nearby speaker. 'Zero, this is Kilo One. Bravo One complete in Charlie One.' Then, a few seconds later, 'Kilo One, that's Bravo One mike to Purple

Three.' The SR callsign is on a stake-out, telling control that the insurgent – their quarry – has just climbed into a vehicle and is travelling towards one of the sectors in the northern part of the city.

I suddenly remember my manners. 'Sorry, Alex, white none please.'

He smiles. 'You recognize the chat then? Thought you might. One of my spies tells me you've just finished commanding Alpha Troop.'

I nod.

'I was airborne forces myself for a while.'

It doesn't surprise me. He's intelligent without being arrogant, and exudes the infectious optimism and resilience so typical of the infantry officers who serve with the Parachute Regiment. He reminds me of Jason Bourne. He even looks like Matt Damon.

On an adjacent table, the CSM and Alex's second-in-command are poring over maps and aerial photographs of the southern part of the city. They've been having a face to face with one of their sources.

'Right, time to explain why you're here,' Alex says. 'Let's go next door where it's a bit quieter.'

He tells me that following my pattern analysis work, the brigade SR teams were tasked to keep an eye on a number of buildings around Red 3. 'We gave them the report on your little soirée with the northern bomber team. You suggested the main man in the south is a scrap metal merchant, so they shifted their focus on to the *only* scrap metal merchant in the Hayy al-Muhandisn area, and surprise surprise, he turned out to be Bravo One.'

After several days of staking him out it very quickly became apparent that he was normally the trigger-man, while his son, Bravo Two, was the bomb emplacer. Over the last couple of days Bravo One and Bravo Two had been seen carrying out reconnaissance on a number of military bases, focusing principally on the routes taken to and from the camps. They'd been doing dummy runs – rehearsing the choreography of moving into the killing area, emplacing the device, firing it and then driving off in the opposite direction. We try to change our patterns as often as possible, but the fact is there are only so many routes we can take, and by the law of averages, if the bombers sit on one long enough, a target's eventually going to present itself.

This morning the bombers were followed from their house, Alpha One, to the thieves' market where they bought bomb-making components, including detonators and PE4-A plastic explosive. They then collected high-explosive artillery shells from a couple of other addresses.

'Where are they now?' I ask.

'Purple Three, the last I heard. The radio traffic next door was our man and his son doing the rounds.'

I ask him where I fit in.

'They're planning on hitting a convoy tomorrow morning. We're going to leave the SR boys on the ground for the rest of the day and then we're going to go noisy and do a company assault on Alpha One. We'll need you to confirm the IED componentry and, if necessary, make it safe.'

This is brilliant news. If we succeed in taking them down, we'll have effectively removed the entire Sunni bomber capability in Basra. There'll be no more keyless car entry RCIED attacks and after a couple of days of fun and games with the joint force interrogation team they'll be singing like canaries. Then we can take down the entire network: recruiters, financiers, training camps – the whole shebang.

Several hours later, around a hundred of us are sitting in a large briefing room, waiting to receive orders for tonight's arrest operation. The majority of the audience is made up from Alex's company, the brigade's dedicated operations company, but tonight it's supported by a Royal Engineers search team, some RMP SIB investigators, and me. Everybody knows why we're here. We've all been given a warning order – a heads up

– but now Alex is going to put some meat on the bones.

'Gentlemen,' he begins in his cut-glass accent, 'tonight we're going to a party. A Molotov cocktail party.' He explains how the insurgents have gone completely nuts and that there's gunfire and sporadic RPG attacks taking place all over the city. 'In order to reach our objective, we're going to need to drive straight through the middle of it.' He doesn't even blink.

He flashes up PowerPoint slides of the target area, showing maps, high-definition aerial photography, 3D fly-throughs of the approaches, and pictures and detailed descriptions of the suspects. Kafeel Haneef is the father and Sabeel Haneef is the son. The SR teams will be maintaining eyes on Bravos One and Two throughout the rest of the evening and at 2345 hours they will complete a final drive-by of Alpha One. At that point Alex will make the call as to whether it's a go or a no go.

'It will only be a no go if the two Bravos are physically not inside the target building,' he says. 'Your mission is to conduct a deliberate cordon and search of Alpha One in order to seize bomb-making equipment, gather evidence of illegal and terrorist activity and capture Bravos One and Two.'

He repeats the mission twice, verbatim, then goes through the choreography of the raid. It's a four-phase operation, phase one being the insertion.

At exactly 2355 hours the company's fourteen Warrior infantry fighting vehicles will leave the palace and weave their way through the labyrinth of streets that lead on to the Red Route. We'll then rocket straight through the centre of the city, heading south until we're about 200 metres short of the target. At that point, the four platoons that make up the assault force will split. Two will break off left and skirt around the eastern side of the target area. One of the platoons will take up positions there and the other will go firm when they're south of the target area. The remaining two Warrior platoons will take up positions to the west and north, completing the ring of steel.

Phase two is the assault.

Once the area is secure, the dismounts will hit five houses, not just Alpha One, so that we can make it look as though we've chosen them at random. To do otherwise could result in some of our intelligence sources being compromised; and in the case of human source intelligence, 'compromise' usually means torture and a bullet in the head. 'There's a set of steel double doors protecting the entrance to Alpha One. Chris, I need you to make up some explosive breaching charges so that we can get through them. If you see Sergeant Macintosh, our assault pioneer, after orders, he'll give you everything you need.'

Phase three is the search phase.

The sappers will go through each of the buildings with a fine-tooth comb, but will focus principally on Alpha One. 'I want you to take that fucking place apart – give it the full treatment.' If any bomb-making materials are found, I am to ensure they are in a safe condition before handing them over to the RMP SIB to be logged as forensic exhibits.

Phase four is the extraction.

A Chinook will land on the waste ground immediately to the south of Alpha One and the Warrior crews there will secure the HLS while the house assaulters escort the bombers onboard. The rest of us will then move direct to Basra Air Station in the Warriors while Bravos One and Two are escorted to the detention facility at Shai'ba.

'In short, gentlemen,' Alex concludes, 'we need to catch these bastards. They are almost certainly responsible for the death of Fusilier Gentle.'

The second-in-command then briefs the company on what radio channels, frequencies and code words we'll be using. I make a mental note of 'Red Sunrise' – it means Bravo One and Bravo Two are on target and it's a go. The sergeant major throws in some words of inspiration too. He goes through some of the actions-on and checks everyone's carrying their morphine in their chest pocket. Then he goes through the Rules of

Engagement, a compulsory briefing reminding everyone of when they can and cannot open fire.

Finally, the six-foot-four giant quotes Malcolm X: 'Be peaceful, be courteous, obey the law, respect everyone; but if someone puts his hand on you, send him to the cemetery.'

40

Some places are too evil to be allowed to exist.

Dan Simmons, *Song of Kal*

Day 101

2330 hours and I'm just making up the final breaching charge. I select two packets of PE4 plastic explosive and remove the putty-like substance from its wax-paper wrapping. I mould the two 6-inch sticks of explosive into a ball and place it on my work table.

I can hear mayhem on the battle group and company nets. It's been like that pretty much constantly for the past three hours. I can hear harried voices screaming 'Contact small-arms fire!' or 'Contact RPG!' then, seconds later, I feel the boom of the explosion outside the wire. The place is in chaos. The city reverberates to the sound of automatic gunfire. Every few minutes there's another explosion. The jet-black sky is alight with tracer and RPG fire. It's *Apocalypse Now*.

I take about a metre of detonating cord and cut it with a sharp knife. The cord looks not dissimilar to electric cable but is packed with powdered PETN high explosive. I place a sliver of tape over each of the sliced ends to stop the powder from falling out, then tie a knot in one end and push it into the soft PE4, folding the plastic explosive around the det cord as if I were kneading bread.

Next I mould the charge into a rectangular block the shape and size of a small paperback novel, and cover it in black gaffer tape. I slide my hand along the tail of det cord that leads from it and when I get to the end I fold and tape the final couple of inches back on itself. That's where I'll attach my detonator, but not yet. I'll do that on the ground, if and when I need to. The last thing we want is the det to function accidentally when we're in the back of a Warrior.

Alex walks in with a couple of coffees. I show him the four strip charges I've made, used for explosively breaching locked doors inside buildings. When the charge detonates, it literally cuts the door in half. Lying on the table next to the strip charges are two frame charges. We'll use those for blowing out the windows should we need to hit Alpha One through multiple entry points. Finally, I show him the charges I've just completed, the book-shaped *brisance* charges. These are the ones I'll use on the steel doors, if necessary. When they're placed flat against the surface, the detonation literally shatters the metal.

2340 hours.

This is the worst part, sitting and waiting. You can cut the tension with a knife. People are doing whatever they can to occupy themselves. As usual, some run around like lunatics doing their last-minute checks and tests. Others replace the batteries in their night vision goggles or squeeze spare magazines and stun-grenades into their assault vests.

Circling high above us, American satellites and one of our own high-flying Nimrod spy planes provide us with a stand-off surveillance capability. Live images of the target are being beamed straight on to the plasma screens in our makeshift ops room. The grainy black and white thermal pictures show tiny figures on the roof of the building. There's no way of telling whether they're our Bravos; the definition isn't good enough to show the detail of their faces in the darkness. We need physical eyes on – the man in the link – to confirm.

We're all waiting.

There's no movement now. Just rigid silence. You'd be able to hear a pin drop were it not for the urgent voices blasting out of the speakers on the net. The city is still like Beirut on a bad night.

The SR radio suddenly sparks up.

'Zero, this is Kilo Four, That's two Echoes, three Echo minors and two Bravo minors on lower-level Alpha One.'

I listen in, fixated. The team's just confirmed there are two women and five children – three girls and two boys – on the ground floor of the target building.

'Zero, this is Kilo Two. That's Bravo One and Bravo Two complete on top-level Alpha One. Red Sunrise. I say again, Red Sunrise.'

There's a loud cheer. The second SR team has just confirmed the two men are on the roof. We're in business.

We grab our kit and hurry outside to the Warriors. Most are shrugging on their CBA and Kevlar helmets in the dusty glare of the headlights. Some fit magazines to their weapons, check radios, test their ECM and fit their goggles.

The Warriors' powerful Rolls-Royce engines roar into life.

Everyone runs through their last-minute mental lists, triple-checking weapons, confirming actions-on. We pack ourselves and our kit into the wagons, adrenalin pumping, bombed up and ready to go.

At 2355 hours on the dot the Warriors' steel blast-doors clank shut and we roll out of the gates into the warren of narrow, darkened streets. We dog-leg our way into the centre of the city, along streets barely wide enough to get the Warriors through, past rows of parked cars and tall residential buildings. I can feel my stomach performing somersaults. Here I am again, stuck in the back of an iron coffin, trundling out into the unknown. This time I'm in Alex's Warrior. I'm just thankful he's allowed us to open the rear crew compartment hatches: at least we can return fire if we're bumped, which is pretty likely considering the night sky is still filled with tracer and automatic gunfire.

Five minutes later we pull on to the Red Route. I can hear the unmistakable sound of bullets pinging off the vehicle. We're taking incoming, but as we race down the 6-mile stretch of dual carriageway, it's impossible to see where the enemy fire's coming from.

'Get down!' Alex shouts, before traversing the turret right and ordering his gunner to fire off a long burst from the chain gun into a building about 100 metres away.

We do as he says. The noise from the chain gun is deafening when the crew hatches are open.

'Two minutes!' Alex yells.

Thank fuck for that. We're almost at the objective.

We continue to scream along this stretch of road and the firing seems to stop. Against us, anyway.

Alex gets on the net: 'Hello all stations, this is Zero

Alpha, stand by, stand by . . . five, four, three, two, one –
go, go, go!'

The Warriors veer off the road and bounce across the
waste ground. We're thundering past shops and houses.
People rush to their windows in disbelief.

We screech to a halt.

Alex does a radio check with the other vehicle
commanders to ensure everyone else is in position.

The ring of steel is in place.

41

After the game, the king and the pawn go into the same box.

Italian proverb

Day 101

As we debus from the Warriors and stack up in front of a shuttered house, the sound of barking dogs ripples around us. We're supposed to be in one of the more upmarket parts of town, but the place is a complete hovel. There's shit and rubbish everywhere.

Directly ahead of me I can see the scrapyard in front of Alpha One. It's silhouetted against the main road about 20 metres away from our position. There are large mounds of rusting scrap around three sides of the property. Each of them contains old bits of pipe, useless automobile parts and broken engines. It's going to limit our access to one face of the building, but on the plus side that means there's only one exit point for the terrorists should they try to escape.

'Prepare to move,' Alex says.

Our weapons are covering every arc, fingers on the triggers. I'm the second man in the team, so I'm covering the front right arc. The guy in front of me covers front left.

'Move.'

My heart is pounding against the inside of my ribcage as we lurch forwards at breakneck speed. My breathing is rapid and shallow. Any second now we're going to be face to face with these boys. And if they're still on the roof they'll know we're here. Speed, aggression and surprise are going to be crucial now.

We move low and fast, hugging the walls as we run towards Alpha One. Elsewhere other platoons are making their way towards the other four Alphas.

The haphazard streets are lined with potholes and large, iridescent puddles. As we push on through them, I notice the house opposite Alpha One has a bedroom light on. There are two little children looking out of the window. The brother and sister are no more than 20 feet away from the double steel gate – our primary entry point.

'Sir,' the sergeant major barks, 'you're on.'

They want me to breach the steel doors.

They're secured by a chain – and it's not a standard

padlock chain, it's more like a fucking anchor chain. Bollocks. I'll need the *brisance* charge for this, but that will smash every window within a 50-metre radius, which means those kids are going to get fragged.

The assaulters aren't best pleased. A minor argument sparks up. Somebody says, 'Come on, sir, it's only a bit of collateral,' but it's not going to happen. Not for them. Not for anybody. I'm not going to frag a child.

'Look,' I say, 'can't we just climb over the bloody thing?'

Almost before I've finished the question one of the infantrymen has scaled the 7-foot-high doors and is over the other side. 'Open Sesame,' he says cheerfully as he slides back a couple of bolts and we all pile in.

The assault is back on.

Seconds later two stun-grenades are tossed into the ground-floor kitchen. There are two loud bangs and bright flashes of light. We burst in, each man covering a different firing lane, and make our way through the smoke and into the crowded living area. The women and children are lying on the floor, terrified. Everybody's screaming. The children are all crying. One of the little girls is sitting in a puddle of her own urine.

We burst up the stairs to the second floor and another two grenades are tossed on to the landing. The hallway fills with smoke. If the Bravos are on this floor they'll be momentarily disorientated by the intense noise and light. And unless they're superhuman, they'll almost certainly be lying on the floor. We move fast.

At the end of the corridor an overweight man in his fifties, wearing a *dish-dasha*, stumbles across the hallway. It's Kafeel Haneef – Bravo One. He's got mad, staring eyes, and is mumbling gibberish. I suddenly realize he's quoting Saddam's rhetoric at us: 'We are ready to sacrifice our souls, our children and our families . . . Allah is on our side . . . we will beat the aggressor . . .'

'Oh fucking really?' one of the infantry shouts before giving him a solid jab to the face, grabbing his wrist and kicking the man's legs out from under him. Two more lads wade in, roll him over, force his arms tightly up behind his back, and cuff him.

'Where's Sabeel?' one of them asks.

The man just flashes them a gap-toothed smile.

'I said, where the fuck's Sabeel?'

The young NCOs are getting angry now.

'Fellas, the flash-bangs . . . he can't hear you,' Alex says. 'Cool it.'

Another section of dismounts runs past us up the final flight of stairs and out on to the roof. There are two more ear-piercing explosions. Bravo Two is on the roof, cornered and desperate. His face is racked with pain. He looks around wildly, praying for a miracle. He's weighing up the options in his mind. The soldiers are shouting commands at him, but he can't hear properly either. He turns, pauses, then vaults the wall, leaping off the roof and landing on one of the rusty engine blocks so hard it drives the breath from his body and concusses him. Moments later, when he opens his eyes, he's surrounded by British soldiers.

'You try a stunt like that again and I'll fucking snatch the life right out of you,' warns the sergeant major as he pulls him up by his hair. Then a pair of soldiers cuff and hood him.

Now it's time for the Royal Engineers to work their magic – phase three.

These boys are quite simply the best searchers in the world. Searching for weapons and IEDs in a scrapyard is going to take them an age, but if they're hidden here, they will find them.

It's no spectator sport, so I decide to move over to one of the other houses and leave the sappers to do their thing. They're not going to need my services for a little while yet.

I walk back through the house and across a stretch of waste ground to the back of Alpha Two, another two-storey flat-roofed block. I make my way around to the front, and as I step inside I'm greeted by the owner.

'*Salaam alaikum*,' he says, smiling.

Behind him, soldiers are turning his house upside down.

'*Wa alaikum salaam*,' I reply, shaking his hand and touching my chest.

His wife is standing beside him, wearing a black *burqa*, jigging a crying baby on her hip. Her face is partly exposed, revealing piercing blue eyes. She looks distressed and upset. She's been crying.

I think instantly of Lucy, and how I would react if soldiers came blundering into my home for no good reason.

'Do you have any weapons?' one of the Int Corps translators asks him.

'Yes,' he replies. There's a tremor in his voice. 'We have one gun, for protection.'

'Where is it?'

'In the bedroom.' The man breaks into English. 'I will get it for you.'

'That's all right,' the NCO says. 'We'll take care of it.'

'Please, sir,' the Iraqi says. 'Not our bedroom. Please don't go into our bedroom. We have nothing to hide.'

We have no choice. The teams have to search the place, and they'll have to turn it upside down. Failure to do so would result in his compromise as soon as he and the neighbours hold the inevitable post-raid discussion.

This is a part of my job that I'm not proud of. I know it is a necessary evil, but seeing the fear etched on the faces of these innocent people; the crying women and children; the humiliated men. It grieves me. In this part of the world women are not supposed to be seen by foreign men, yet here we are, hoofing them out of their bedrooms, waking their sleeping babies and emptying out their underwear drawers as their husbands stand by, humiliated and helpless.

I go upstairs to witness the scene for myself. There are about twenty soldiers going through drawers, cupboards, shelves and cabinets, emptying out the contents of each on to the floor. The place looks completely trashed.

I have to remind myself that we're doing this to safeguard the lives of our sources, but I can't help wondering what effect this is going to have on the hearts and minds of those whose lives we've invaded tonight.

As I walk sheepishly back downstairs, I'm not prepared for what happens next. The husband is carrying a tray of sweet *chai* and a plate of *baklava*. His wife has just baked them for the soldiers who are ransacking their home. He pours the hot sweet liquid into one of the little glasses and offers it to me, along with the plate of cakes.

I touch my heart. I'm about to say, 'I'm sorry, I couldn't,' but I think better of it. To do so would only add insult to injury.

'*Shukran*,' I say, unable to look him in the eye.

I've never witnessed anything like it. I'm struck once more by the strength and generosity of spirit of the Iraqi people.

As I walk out into the warm evening air, I feel morally bankrupt. Thank Christ I don't have to do this sort of thing more often.

I walk around the other side of the house and make my way along the unlit track towards Alpha One, trying to shake the image of the woman's tear-stained face out of my mind. A huge, snarling dog leaps out of a gate and lunges at me. It's a beast; it looks like a Rottweiler; it's stretching its chain to the limit as it tries to take chunks out of me.

Back at Alpha One, the father and son sit outside, cross-legged, handcuffed and hooded, while the searchers continue to tear apart their home. The boys have only been at it for an hour and already they've found explosives, detonators and at least a dozen illegal firearms.

As I look down at the two terrorists, I think about the hundreds of innocent people they have maimed or murdered with their IEDs. We've had to disturb some good people tonight; we've probably made enemies of them; but looking at these two evil men, I know deep down that this time the means definitely justify the end.

Two hours later the thud of the approaching Chinook reverberates through our bodies. As the giant bird descends on to the HLS, Kafeel and Sabeel Haneef are bundled through the dust storm towards it. Still hooded and blindfolded, they're led up the tailgate, and almost immediately the heli climbs rapidly into the black, lifeless sky.

Their killing spree is over.

42

I wanted a perfect ending. Now I've learned, the hard way, that some poems don't rhyme, and some stories don't have a clear beginning, middle and end. Life is about not knowing, having to change, taking the moment and making the best of it, without knowing what's going to happen next.

Gilda Radner

6 December 2004

I'm losing the will to live.

I'm sitting in a cold lecture hall with 240 thrusting majors, listening to an AGC officer banging on about resource management and accounting. The lieutenant colonel has been talking at us for three hours now, and he's sapping the life from us all. Even the alpha personalities are struggling.

I've been here at Staff College for three months now, training to become a fully fledged chair-borne warrior before I take up my new post with the Defence Intelligence Staff next year. It's a far cry from the life I've been forced to leave behind.

'So, ladies and gentlemen,' the colonel says in a particularly grating voice, 'let's talk about financial statement analysis . . .'

Let's not, I think to myself. Instead I allow my mind to drift back over everything that's happened since I left Iraq.

I left Basra at a time of complete chaos. We'd managed to capture both Sunni bomber teams, and by doing so ensured that there were no more keyless entry system attacks there. Unfortunately the same could not be said for the Mahdi Army's Shia bombers. They just went from strength to strength. The bastards seemed to be completely untouchable, not least because they had penetrated the highest echelons of the national infrastructure, including the police and the Army.

On 21 August, two weeks before I left theatre, a search team operating in the west of the city found an improvised claymore mine, hard-wired to an explosively formed projectile. The claymore, like the one used in the murder of Private Ferns, contained 10,000 ball-bearings and over 20kg of high explosive. As we'd realized, the Shias had begun using identical devices to those used by Hezbollah against the Israelis in southern Lebanon.

It seems the Iranian Islamic Revolutionary Guard Corps and their LH bomb-makers have been providing the hardware, encouraging the Mahdi Army to up the ante and kill as many British soldiers as possible. The presence of these new charges marked the beginning of what's become an unprecedented campaign of IED terror.

When I left the city, it was with a mixture of elation and trepidation, but also with a certain amount of disappointment. Though I was missing my family terribly, I felt frustrated that my work still wasn't finished. Then, at the airport, I saw the station padre walking up to anybody who'd make eye contact and chatting to them, handing them a piece of paper. He was getting the cold shoulder from most people, but when he saw me he came straight over.

'I just want to say thank you for everything you've done,' he said.

Then he handed me my slip of paper:

For everything there is a season,
And a time for every matter under heaven:
A time to be born, and a time to die;
A time to plant, and a time to pluck up what is planted;
A time to kill, and a time to heal;
A time to break down, and a time to build up;

A *time to weep, and a time to laugh;*
A *time to mourn, and a time to dance;*
A *time to throw away stones, and a time to gather stones together;*
A *time to embrace, and a time to refrain from embracing;*
A *time to seek, and a time to lose;*
A *time to keep, and a time to throw away;*
A *time to tear, and a time to sew;*
A *time to keep silence, and a time to speak;*
A *time to love, and a time to hate;*
A *time for war, and a time for peace.*

Ecclesiastes 3:1–8

He waited until I'd read it, looked me in the eye and said, 'Now it's your time.'

He was right. It was time to move on.

I arrived back in the UK with a mixture of excitement, impatience and anxiety. I'd spent hours during the flight reflecting on the surreal experiences I'd had in Iraq, wondering how I was ever going to adapt to life back home. I was also very conscious that after living with the blokes day in and day out for two months, I'd developed an advanced form of Tourette's. It was something I was going to have to cure myself of quickly. Still, because we were flying 'Crab Air' I had all the time in the world:

only they could turn a six-hour flight into a thirty-six-hour epic. When we finally touched down, the two hundred or so passengers let out a loud cheer. Others closed their eyes and said a quiet prayer.

My Iraq tour was finally over.

I walked through the terminal building and felt a wave of emotion wash over me when I spotted Lucy and the girls in the arrivals hall. She looked more beautiful than ever, and the girls seemed to have grown up more than I could possibly have imagined.

But so much had changed. Ella didn't recognize me, and Sophie, who'd always been a daddy's girl, hid behind her mother when I appeared. They all looked so nervous.

Given the sentiments she'd aired in her card, I hadn't expected Lucy to be this distant, or for our reunion to be so uncomfortable. I don't know what I'd expected, but there was a terrible awkwardness about the whole affair – no loving embrace, no tears of joy. It was as though Lucy was there out of a sense of duty, because she was being nice rather than because she loved or missed me. Don't get me wrong, it was good to be back and an enormous weight had been lifted from my shoulders; but it was dangerously clear there was still work to be done.

Several hours later we were sitting in our new home in Shrivenham, where I was about to start at Staff College.

The house is surrounded by fields, woodland, lakes and streams. It's beautiful – a far cry from the Didcot cooling towers. Lucy had packed up and organized the move here entirely, knowing that I would be too busy to do it when I started at Staff College the very next week.

She smiled. 'I wanted it to be a surprise.'

First the cold shoulder treatment, then this. I wasn't sure where I stood with her. I had to keep reminding myself that however hard I was finding it, it must have been ten times harder for her.

'Thank you, my love,' I said. 'I really, really appreciate it.'

I hesitated, then plunged right in at the deep end. I needed to know.

'Lucy, are you going to leave me?'

She paused.

'I told you I'm not going to give up on you.'

The smile had disappeared, but I knew she meant it. And I knew it wasn't going to be easy. While I'd been fuelled by adrenalin for the last four months, she'd been up on a different kind of high wire, and had worked hard to create a few safety nets for herself and the girls. She'd become used to her own routines; she'd developed her own way of doing things. Whatever else needed to be healed, it was going to take time for us simply to adjust to being a two-parent family again.

Over the last few weeks there have been lots of

arguments and plenty more tears. But she hasn't given up.

It's been tough on the girls too. Iraq was the longest I'd ever been away, and I'd been warned by some of the other dads that reunion following a long separation can be a very stressful experience for your kids. It makes sense. When you're little, every day seems to last for ever, and every shadow holds a monster.

I've learned to welcome rather than demand their affection. The girls have grown up so much, but how can they even begin to understand the world in which I've been immersed? Not too long ago, Sophie asked, 'Daddy, why couldn't the naughty men have shot you with a water pistol?' That's not a question any three-year-old should be asking her father.

It hasn't been easy, but things are definitely starting to improve. After weeks of treading on eggshells the kids are finally sticking to me like limpets and Lucy has begun to warm to me again.

At least she talks to me now.

'And that, ladies and gentlemen, is your introduction to RMA.'

'That was fucking shite,' says one of the Royal Marines next to me.

Good job I didn't waste precious time listening to it then.

As we make our way back to the college building, along the tree-lined promenade that leads to the tall, red-bricked halls of study, our breath clouds in the cold winter air. Simon, one of the infantry majors in my syndicate, taps me on the shoulder. He's tall and thin and has just come off SAS selection with a bad injury. He wants to be here about as much as I do.

'Good to hear your man is out of his coma,' he says.

For a moment I wonder if Simon's mistaken me for somebody else. I don't have a frigging clue what he's talking about.

'The signaller, Corporal Brennan. You know, the guy who was blown up when that suicide bomber hit the EOD team at Camp Dogwood last month. It was on the news this morning.'

43

In war, there are no unwounded soldiers.

José Narosky

My stomach turns to liquid.

How on earth did I manage to miss that? I know I've been living in an information vortex for the last few weeks, but I can't believe I didn't know Mick had been hit. What the fuck was he doing out there anyway? His tour should have finished months ago. And what about his family? What are they going to do now?

I race towards the college building and throw open two sets of double doors, frantically making my way to the nearest military phone. I punch in the number for the Joint Services EOD Operations Centre at Didcot. The call is taken by Steve Holmes, the 11 EOD Ops warrant officer.

'Three of your old team were sent back out to Iraq about six weeks ago,' he says. 'We had nobody spare, so they were redeployed to Camp Dogwood with the Black Watch battle group, as part of the IEDD team.'

He tells me the cordon appears to have been collapsed before the ATO and his team had finished the task. At that point a suicide bomber drove up and detonated his car bomb right next to the Warrior. Mick Brennan and Neil Heritage have both lost their legs. By some complete miracle, Dan was largely uninjured, but God knows how he's going to come to terms with the whole episode.

I'm devastated. These boys are more than just members of my old team, they're my friends. And I've been so submerged in this stupid fucking course that I wasn't aware they'd been hit. Jesus, I didn't even know they'd redeployed.

I stand at the end of the phone in stunned silence.

'Where are they now, Steve? Do you know?'

'Mick and Neil are at Selly Oaks,' he says. 'Dan is on leave, but nobody knows where.'

As soon as I'm off the phone I ask Gareth, one of the instructors on the staff course, if I can take compassionate leave and go to Birmingham tomorrow.

'Are you related to either of the casualties?' he says, stony-faced.

I let out a snort of laughter before I realize he's serious.

'Of course I'm not related to either of them, Gareth. I was their commander.'

'Well I'm sorry, Chris, but if they're not relatives or spouses, I'm afraid I can't authorize your compassionate leave request.'

My teeth clench. Fuck him. If I can't go and see them tomorrow, I'll go and see them now.

Three hours later, having bombed up the M5 like a man possessed, I make the long walk across the car park and into the hospital reception. I spoke to Mick on the phone en route.

'Text me when you find a space and I'll meet you in the foyer,' he said.

As I step into the reception area, I'm bombarded by the pungent odour of stale, recycled air and old disinfectant. There's no sign of Mick, so I make my way towards the elevator. I know he's on the third floor.

The door pings open.

Mick is sat in a wheelchair, with two bandaged stumps where his legs had once been.

'All right, boss?' he says, smiling.

I shake him by the hand, not knowing what the fuck to say. I can see he's just as uncomfortable as I am. He's trying to put a brave face on it, but when he speaks, his voice gives him away. His broad Yorkshire accent is laced with sadness.

'Neil's upstairs. He can't wait to see you too.'

'Come on, mate,' I say, grabbing the handles of his wheelchair. 'Let's do it.'

We make our way into the military ward. Neil's busy fleecing some of the other soldiers at cards.

'We've got a visitor, mate,' Mick says.

Neil wheels himself over and we shake hands warmly. He also has stumps for legs. I try not to stare, but it's so hard not to when the last time I saw them they were both brilliant runners and as fit as ten men.

We sit around Mick's bed, and the boys fill me in. Mick tells me he doesn't remember much about it, so Neil does the talking.

It was Sunday, 7 November and the lads had been working since 0530 clearing IEDs. They'd just completed the task and were loading their kit into the back of the Warrior when the cordon was collapsed and the car accelerated towards them. The fearsome blast slammed the door of the Warrior shut and threw Neil inside. The fireball consumed everything, including Neil. At this stage he didn't actually realize he'd been injured; he just wanted to get the hell out of the vehicle and put himself out. He pushed the door open and fell flat on his face. There was nothing there to hold him up.

His legs had been severed by the blast. Mick had also been standing at the back of the Warrior, but instead of blowing him inside, the shockwave that passed underneath the armoured door amputated both his legs and blew him across the road.

'But the hardest thing,' Mick says, 'is that it's affected my brain. It's like having Tourette's. I swore at a young kid the other day; poor little bugger only cut me up on the pavement. I called him a little black bastard. I couldn't believe the words came out of my mouth. You know how I feel about racism, Chris. I'm just really fucking struggling to control my temper. I hate it. And so does my wife.'

I feel desperately sorry for them both. I'm still grappling with how this was ever allowed to happen.

'And what about Dan?' I ask.

'He's doing OK,' Mick says. 'He was closer to the VBIED than any of us, yet despite getting blown over the front of the Warrior and into a field the lucky bastard came away with nothing more than cuts and bruises. He definitely had a guardian angel watching over him that day.'

'Fucking hell, that reminds me, I meant to tell you about Vince. Have you heard?'

Mick tells me he was made to go back to his battalion and absolutely hated it. He kept asking to go back to an

IEDD team but was just messed around endlessly by his battalion, so he decided enough was enough.

'He's gone AWOL,' Mick says. 'But on the plus side, being the consummate professional he was, he laid all his bullets down, slipped out of camp, took a taxi to Kuwait and booked a flight home. As far as I know, he's still on the run.'

Only Vince could pull off such a ballsy plan. The boy's got style, I'll definitely give him that.

I step outside into the crystal clear night. It's freezing cold. All around me car roofs and windows are glimmering in the moonlight. The pavement sparkles with frost.

I've spent several hours with Mick and Neil. As I pull out of the car park and head back towards the M5, the image of the boys, wheelchair-bound and waving, plays over and over in my mind. I know their haunted and exhausted expressions will stay with me for a long time yet.

I gun my VW Golf along the motorway.

I spent a total of four months with the boys in Iraq, two as a high-threat counter-terrorist bomb disposal operator and two as a weapons intelligence officer charged with identifying and targeting the bomber networks. My team and I attended forty-five IED incidents during the first two months of their tour. When I left, the boys presented me with a signed Basra spot map – it's now a Det tradition. I read mine recently and noticed what Mick had written: 'Normally a man of many words but the time has come when I am lost for things to say. Wish I had more of a chance to work with you. Not only have you been a good boss but a great friend as well. Thanks for saving my career. I will not forget that. All the best, Mick.'

I feel a deep sense of guilt. Mick thanked me for saving his career, but perhaps my failure to punish him twice was down to a lack of courage. And if I had binned him, he'd not be where he is today.

I turn off the main drag and into the picturesque Oxfordshire village of Shrivenham. Soon I'm pulling into our driveway. It's a quarter to midnight. I'm physically and emotionally drained.

I slowly turn the door key and let myself in.

I first look in on the girls, our pair of sleeping beauties. I watch them breathing silently and think about the months we've lost. I lean over their beds and kiss each of them on the forehead.

Then I go through to my wife, asleep in our bed. She looks so beautiful and at peace. As I pull back the duvet to climb in next to her, she puts out her arm and pulls me tightly towards her. I look at her for a moment. She could have chosen any man; why on earth did she choose me? I draw her close and kiss her goodnight.

She opens her beautiful faraway eyes and flashes me a look of absolute love.

'I missed you,' she says.

Afterword

Once you've got Baghdad, it's not clear what you do with it . . . I think to have American military forces engaged in a civil war inside Iraq would fit the definition of quagmire, and we have absolutely no desire to get bogged down in that fashion.

US Secretary of Defense Dick Cheney, 1991

30 June 2007

I returned from Iraq three years ago. Looking back, there's been nothing else like it. I've never taken drugs, but I don't believe there's anything that will ever equal the exhilaration of that tour. It was one of the most powerful and defining periods of my life.

It was also a deeply harrowing experience. Some of the things I witnessed still haunt me. I saw damaged lives and destruction on an unprecedented scale. I experienced an intense and extreme range of emotions on a day-to-day basis. Harder still, I came within a whisker of losing my family.

But in spite of everything that happened, I don't believe I was overly traumatized by the experience. I was a soldier for over seventeen years. I knew then, just as I know now, that conflict is the way of the world. Conflict is inevitable, and innocent people will continue to die. As much as we try to kid ourselves, violence is the planet's common language. But I still believe that love is too.

Iraq taught me that the world can be a dark place; and that those who criticize our presence there, while curled up safely in their beds at night, are quicker to denounce a soldier's existence than to stop to think of the lives he saves and the fears he allays. The burdens placed on the men and women sent out to preserve our way of life are greater than most people could ever imagine. Yet the good they do, the lives they touch, the scale of damage they prevent – those successes are rarely documented.

There *are* evil people in Iraq – terrorists who bomb innocent civilians, husbands who beat their wives, and fathers who cut their daughters' throats. But they're the tiny minority. Iraqis are good people. People like us. People who want nothing more than to rebuild their country and live their lives in peace. They deserve that chance. Whatever the rights and wrongs of the war, it would be a tragedy to fail them now, simply because we all grew tired of trying.

When I watch the news, read the papers or speak with friends who've recently returned from Iraq, I realize that little has changed. The country continues to be dangerous and unpredictable, and for the bomb disposal teams operating there, the switch continues to flick rapidly and repeatedly from full-off to full-on.

But they love what they do. It's a vocation, a way of life. I've yet to meet a member of a bomb disposal team who isn't completely, intellectually and spiritually, absorbed by what he does. Operators desire only two things: to try to save the lives of the innocents, and to make it back home to their families. We're not men of the system. We're not even particularly interested in the cause. We're here to do a job – nothing more, nothing less.

That job was something I'd spent years training for. But being the victim of a violent ambush and having to kill a man in the process was an intense experience for me. It changes a man's life for ever; how could it not? It was the first time I'd seen the head of another human being in my rifle sight, and squeezed the trigger.

Shortly after I returned from Iraq I said to Lucy, 'I don't mean to sound like some sort of weirdo, but I've been thinking a lot about death, recently.'

'Do you mean death,' she said, 'or do you mean your own mortality?'

She was right, of course. She usually is.

Since that tour I've become more chilled out; I've also become far more aware of the power of the human spirit. I value my life more, and what I have: Lucy, the girls, my friends. Given the choice, we choose life. Every time.

And if I felt any anger, it was really just towards Behadli. I'd hoped to meet him again one day, in a quiet back street. But the last I heard, he ended up getting murdered by his own side. Maybe he did, maybe he didn't; either way, it's time to move on. Anger is only one letter short of danger. And life's just too fucking short.

The same goes for Piers Morgan. Even though he stirred up the hornets' nest which resulted in numerous British casualties that night, I just think, with hindsight, he made a foolish error of judgement and his over-inflated ego got the better of him.

As for Mick and Neil, I still feel guilty about that terrible day. Once you've served with someone in a place like Iraq, been down in the dirt with him, tasted victory and defeat, he becomes far more than just a soldier under your command. The feeling of brotherhood is immense, the like of which you rarely experience elsewhere. I didn't drive the car bomb into their Warrior on that fateful day, but I still can't help feeling a sense of responsibility.

The back-to-back tours and constant loneliness had a

terrible effect on all our lives too. What's exciting and gratifying for a single lieutenant in his early twenties more often than not becomes a terrible strain for the family of a married major in his thirties. There is a limit to how much any of us can cope with before things reach critical mass. We came dangerously close. We were in a bad place, and I don't want us to be there ever again.

Was it all for the greater good? I hope so. 'Fight what is Wrong, Believe what is True, Do what is Right'. It's a difficult path to tread, but I keep trying. I also try to be a better husband and father. There's one sentence muttered more than any other by soldiers dying on the battlefield: 'Tell my wife I love her.'

By the time I found my way home, I'd used up eight of my nine lives. I had two wonderful daughters and a beautiful, loving wife, and I'd spent too much of my life focused on my career instead of them. What happens in the future, only time will tell. But I'm eight lives down, so I'm not going to waste my last.

Glossary

Types of improvised explosive device (IED)

CWIED
Command wire improvised explosive device. An IED utilizing an electrical firing cable which affords the terrorist complete control over the device right up until the moment of initiation.

RCIED
The trigger for this IED is controlled by a radio link. The device is constructed so that the receiver is connected to an electrical firing circuit and the transmitter operated by the perpetrator at a distance. A signal from the transmitter causes the receiver to trigger a firing pulse which operates a switch. Usually the switch fires an initiator; however, the output may also be used to remotely arm an explosive circuit. Often the transmitter and receiver operate on a matched coding

system which prevents the RCIED from being initiated by spurious radio frequency signals.

Cell phone RCIED A radio-controlled IED incorporating a cell phone which is modified and connected to an electrical firing circuit. Cell phones operate in the UHF band in line of sight with base transceiver station (BTS) antennae sites. Commonly, receipt of a paging signal by the phone is sufficient to initiate the IED firing circuit.

Petrol bomb A hand-thrown device containing a flammable composition (not necessarily petrol) that functions on impact. It is not considered an incendiary.

Pipe bomb A crude IED containing either high or low explosive confined within a metal tube sealed at each end. The device is usually initiated by a crude timer such as a hand-lit fuse and delivered by throwing. In effect it is a crude hand-propelled time IED.

Secondary device   The underlying purpose of a secondary is to attack those involved in responding to an initial IED incident. Usually secondary IEDs are deliberately placed to target EOD teams, possible ICP locations, or predicted first-responders' cordon or monitoring positions. Successful secondary-device attacks are undertaken by terrorists who are able to correctly predict first-responders' response procedures to a primary IED incident.

Suicide IED   Explosive devices that are delivered to a target and initiated by a human being with the deliberate loss of life of the bomber. The logic behind such attacks is the belief that an IED delivered by a human has a greater chance of achieving success than any other method of attack. In addition, there is the psychological impact of terrorists prepared to deliberately sacrifice or martyr themselves for their cause. Commonly, suicide IEDs are worn by the bomber or carried in personal

503

luggage. In addition, suicide devices have been incorporated into vehicles, bicycles and powerboats.

VBIED

An IED which incorporates a vehicle as an integral element of its construction. The vehicle provides concealment for IED components, and contributes to the fragmentation hazard of an explosion. Vehicles are usually cars or SUVs but can be anything from a bicycle or handcart to a lorry. VBIEDs are mobile, and thus afford the terrorist a degree of tactical flexibility. The quantity of explosive within a VBIED may vary depending on the type of damage the perpetrator wishes to achieve and the availability of explosive. VBIEDs may be activated by timer, remotely by command initiation systems or by suicide. In addition, incidents have been recorded where VBIEDs have been driven to target areas by victims of coercion, or in ignorance (proxy).

VOIED	These are designed to function upon contact with a victim; also known as booby traps. Victim-operated IED switches are often well hidden from the victim or disguised as innocuous everyday objects. They are operated by means of movement. Switching methods include: tripwire, pressure mats, spring-loaded release, push, pull or tilt. Common forms of VOIED include the under-vehicle IED (UVIED) and improvised landmines.

Types of explosive

ANFO	Ammonium nitrate fuel oil
C4	Composition 4 – military plastic explosive (US)
HMTD	Hexamethylenetriperoxidediamine
HMX	High-melt explosive
NG	Nitroglycerine
PE4	British plastic explosive
PE4-A	Portuguese plastic explosive (used in massive quantities by Iraqi insurgents)
PETN	Pentaerythritol tetranitrate

RDX	Research developed explosive – cyclotro-methylenetrinitramine
TNT	Trinitrotoluene (standard military high explosive)
TATP	Triacetone triperoxide

General

5.56	5.56 × 45mm round fired from SA80 A2 assault rifle
7.62 short	7.62 × 39mm round fired from AK-47, RPD and SKS
9 milly	9mm pistol
AC 130	'Spectre' aerial gun platform based on a Hercules C130 airframe
Actions-on	The term used to describe SOPs for a given scenario
AGC	Adjutant General's Corps
AK-47	Soviet Kalashnikov assault rifle; fires 7.62mm short ammunition
AOR	Area of Responsibility
Apache	US and UK twin-engine attack helicopter (aka AH-64)
APC	Armoured personnel carrier
AQ	Al-Qaeda
Asp	A telescopic truncheon

AT	Anti-tank (usually landmine)
ATO	Ammunition technical officer (the Army's counter-terrorist bomb disposal operators, all members of the Royal Logistic Corps)
AV	Anti-vehicle (usually landmine)
Bergen	Pack carried by British forces
BDO	Bomb disposal officer (specialists in de-mining and World War Two aircraft bombs; all members of the Royal Engineers)
Bleep	Royal Signals ECM expert
Blue	Friendlies/friendly forces
Bravo	A known or suspected terrorist
CAM	Chemical agent monitor
Casevac	Casualty evacuation
CBA	Combat Body Armour
CBRN	Chemical, Biological, Radiological, Nuclear
CEXC	Combined Explosive Exploitation Cell
CF	US-led coalition forces
CID	Criminal Investigation Department
CO	Commanding officer (usually a lieutenant colonel)
Come-on	A technique used by terrorists to draw a victim or target into the vicinity of an unanticipated IED or other type of ambush. Successful come-on scenarios are usually executed by terrorists who are able to

	accurately predict the victim's reaction to a particular event or set of circumstances.
COP	Close observation platoon
CPA	Coalition Provisional Authority
CSM	Company sergeant major
CTR	Close target recce
the Det	The EOD detachment
dish-dasha	An ankle-length shirt, usually with long sleeves, similar to a robe
Div	Divisional HQ
DS	Directing staff
Duro	Bucher Duro high-mobility off-road EOD truck
ECM	Electronic counter-measures
Endex	End of Exercise
EOD	Explosive ordnance disposal
ERV	Emergency rendezvous
FARC	Revolutionary Armed Forces of Colombia
GPS	Global positioning system
Green Zone	The international zone in Baghdad
Gympie	GPMG (general-purpose machine gun)
HE	High explosive
Head-shed	A person in authority
Hesco	Sand-filled protective blast wall made by Hesco Bastion
HLS	Helicopter Landing Site

Hotrod	Water-filled IED disruptor
HQ	Headquarters
ICP	Incident control point
IEDD	Improvised explosive device disposal
Int	Intelligence
IPS	Iraqi Police Service
IR	Infrared
ISO	International Organization for Standardization shipping container
JAM	Jaiysh al-Mahdi (Mahdi Army)
KES	Keyless entry system – radio-controlled automobile locking/unlocking system
LCD	Liquid crystal display
Mike	A minute (when used in the context of radio voice procedure)
Minimi	Light machine gun firing 5.56mm ammunition
MO	Modus Operandi
MWR	Morale, welfare and recreation
NAAFI	Navy, Army and Air Force Institute
NCO	Non-commissioned officer
Net	Communications network
NVG	Night vision goggles
OC	Officer commanding
OP	Observation post
PATO	Principal ammunition technical officer

Pig stick	An IED disrupter used to disrupt thin-cased Improvised Explosive Devices
PIRA	Provisional Irish Republican Army
PRR	Personal role radio
PWRR	Princess of Wales's Royal Regiment
QBO	Quick Battle Orders
QRF	Quick Reaction Force
RAF Regt	Royal Air Force Regiment (the RAF's infantry)
RAMC	Royal Army Medical Corps
RE	Royal Engineers
REME	Royal Electrical and Mechanical Engineers
RIB	Rigid Inflatable Boat
RF	Radio frequency
RLC	Royal Logistic Corps
RMP	Royal Military Police
RPG	Rocket-propelled grenade
RSM	Regimental sergeant major
RSP	Render safe procedure
RV	Rendezvous
SA80	SA80-A2 5.56mm Assault Rifle
SAM	Surface-to-air missile
Sangar	Fortified bunker/sentry position
SF	Security forces, or Special Forces
the Shack	The home of the WIS at Divisional HQ
shemagh	An Arab headscarf

Shrike	A hand-held 'exploder' device used to initiate IED disruptor weapons
SIB	Special Investigation Branch
Sig	Sig Sauer 226 pistol
Sitrep	Situation report
SKS	Russian semi-automatic rifle
Snatch	British Armoured Land Rover
SO2	Staff Officer Grade II (usually a major or equivalent rank)
SOP	Standard operating procedure
Spectre	*see AC 130*
SR / S&R	Surveillance and reconnaissance
STT	Special-to-Theatre (training course)
TA	Territorial Army
Thuraya	Satellite phone
Tiffy	Artificer
TPU	Timing and power unit
UAV	Un-manned aerial vehicle
WIS	Weapons Intelligence Section
WPNS	Weapons

OUT OF IRAQ
by Lewis Alsamari

Aged seventeen, Lewis Alsamari was conscripted into the Iraqi army. Once his superiors discovered his ability to speak English, things went from bad to worse. Lewis was selected for Saddam's elite, top-secret intelligence service, an offer he literally could not refuse. He was left with only one option – to flee from his native land, leaving his family behind . . .

Going under the wire of the army compound where he was posted, Lewis was shot in the leg making his escape – it was to be a gruelling journey in disguise across the desert at night with a group of Bedouin, at the mercy of ravenous wolves. Against the odds, Lewis made it across the border into Jordan, and eventually sought asylum in the UK, where he had spent his childhood.

Now he had to work out how to rescue his mother, brother and sister, who had been apprehended and thrown into jail in Iraq once Lewis's escape became known. The only thing which could help was money and lots of it. At which point Lewis hatched the most audacious plan of his life . . .

9780552155397

CORGI BOOKS